DEMOCRACY AND TOTALITARIANISM

DEMOCRACY AND TOTALITARIANISM

A Theory of Political Systems

Raymond Aron

Edited and with an Introduction by Roy Pierce

Ann Arbor Paperbacks
The University of Michigan Press

First Edition as an Ann Arbor Paperback 1990
Editor's Introduction copyright © 1990 by
The University of Michigan
All Rights Reserved

© 1965 by Editions Gallimard
English translation by Valence Ionescu
© 1968 by George Weidenfeld and Nicolson Ltd
First published in French in 1965 under the title
Démocratie et Totalitarisme by Editions Gallimard

Published in the United States of America by
The University of Michigan Press
Manufactured in the United States of America

1993   1992   1991   1990   4   3   2   1

Library of Congress Cataloging-in Publication Data

Aron, Raymond, 1905–
    [Sociologie des sociétés industrielles. English]
    Democracy and totalitarianism: a theory of political systems /
Raymond Aron; edited and with an introduction by Roy Pierce. — 1st
ed. as an Ann Arbor pbk.
        p.   cm. — (Ann Arbor paperbacks ; 203)
    Translation of Démocratie et totalitarisme which was first
published under title: Sociologie des sociétés industrielles.
    Reprint. Originally published: London : Weidenfeld and Nicolson,
1968.
    ISBN 0-472-09451-3 (alk. paper). — ISBN 0-472-06451-7 (pbk. :
alk. paper)
    1. Political sociology. 2. Democracy. 3. Totalitarianism.
4. Comparative government. I. Pierce, Roy. II. Title.
JA76.A7513 1990
306.2—dc20   90-33727
                                                    CIP

CONTENTS

DEMOCRACY AND TOTALITARIANISM

CONCLUSION

AUTHOR'S INTRODUCTION

This book, which was first published by the Centre de Documentation Universitaire under the longer but more accurate title *Sociologie des societés industrielles, esquisse d'une théorie des régimes politiques,* is the third in a series, of which the first two are *Dix-huit leçons sur la societé industrielle* and *La lutte des classes* (published by the CDU as *Le développement de la societé industrielle* and *La stratification sociale*. Although each of the three books is complete in itself and can be read separately, it is only through reading the series that the real meaning of the investigation can be grasped.

The nineteen lectures which go to make this book were given at the Sorbonne during the academic year 1957-8. I must therefore repeat the warning which I gave in the preface to *Dix-huit leçons sur la societé industrielle.*

This course of lectures, which represents a period in my research and which was meant to be useful to students, although it suggests a method, outlines conceptual notions, puts forward facts and ideas, bears the inevitable traces of the lecture room and of improvisation. The lectures have not been edited; the style is therefore that of the spoken word, with the unavoidable flaws that later correction can smooth over, but cannot eliminate.

The reader should not forget the date on which these lectures were given – 1957-8 – if he would find the right interpretation for them, especially for the eleventh, 'The corruption of the French system', and even more particularly for the last, the nineteenth, which was delivered during the second half of May, after the events of 13 May and before General de Gaulle came to power. The result is, naturally enough, that the reflections on the French regime, that is to say on the Fourth Republic, are no longer of contemporary interest. They are retrospective in character just as are those on the Weimar republic. Yet they have not lost all their significance. They may possibly even have gained in historical scope what they have lost on the political or journalistic plane. The transition from the Fourth to the Fifth Republic is already in its way as classic an example of the end of a degenerated democracy as was the transition from the Weimar Republic to the Third Reich. In some ways it is as reassuring an example as that of the Weimar Republic was terrifying.

In both cases, a legal or semi-legal *coup d'état* took place – Hitler was appointed chancellor by President Hindenburg just as General de Gaulle, appointed by René Coty, was legally invested by the French National Assembly. But the vote only seemed to be free. Sedition had preceded seduction. Historians are still arguing about the part played by General de Gaulle himself in events in Algeria. He was not alone in desiring or encouraging the revolt of the French and of the army in Algeria but, after the declaration to the press of 15 May, at the moment when those who were on the brink of revolt in Algeria seemed to hesitate to cross the Rubicon, it was he who directly or through intermediaries took the lead, keeping a great enough distance between himself and the men of Algiers to enable him to appear as an arbitrator, if not a saviour, to political circles in the Fourth Republic. The politicians were aware that they would lose power when the lone wolf from Colombey assumed it once more, but if the operation which was known as Resurrection had been carried out, they would have lost more than power. The French again showed themselves to be expert in the art of *legal coups d'état,* to use once more a phrase from the nineteenth chapter. The vote of June 1958 in the National Assembly was taken under pressure and can be compared in this respect to the vote in the National Assembly in Vichy in June 1940. The shadow of the pretorian guards loomed over the 'windowless house' of the Palais Bourbon, just as eighteen years earlier it had fallen on the Casino in Vichy. The Republic of deputies in the twentieth century had no martyrs whose names can be remembered by historians in the way that Baudin, the victim of the overt *coup d'état* of Louis Napoleon has been remembered.

Whatever judgment one makes of the transition from one republic to the other in May–June 1958, it cannot be denied – and these lectures bear witness to it – that both actors and onlookers in the Fourth Republic in 1957–8 had a sense of the crisis of the regime. The crisis arose from the superimposition of the difficult problem of the destiny of Algeria – French as one said at the time – on weak and discredited institutions. To historians of today, with the objectivity of hindsight, the balance sheet of the Fourth Republic does not seem to be as disastrous as it appeared to be at the time, eight years ago. Adaptation to the world situation, the reconciliation with the German Federal Republic, the Coal and Steel Community were realities; the treaty of Rome had been signed. Before the Fourth Republic could marry its century, only two obstacles remained to be surmounted: to put an end to the merry-go-round of governments which, even if its consequences were not as tragic as the eternal anti-parliamentarianism of the French claimed, made *le pays légal* (the establishment) ridiculous abroad; to bring the Algerian conflict to an end and to accept the decolonization demanded by the spirit of the times, the anti-colonialism of the two Great Powers and France's own weakness after the Second World War.

These two obstacles were probably insurmountable. General de Gaulle would never have given his sanction to decolonization unless he himself were given both the responsibility and the credit for it. He was not an elder statesman, anxious to enlighten the nation, but a politician, impatient to reach the only office which he thought worthy of him, the highest, 'the embodiment of the law'. In any case, it would have been difficult for the Republic of deputies to reform itself. The historical and social circumstances which lay behind the experience of the Fourth Republic are many and varied. Since 1789, France has never had a government which was accepted by the whole nation; it has never had a few organized political parties, unwritten and respected parliamentary ethics or cabinet stability within a parliamentary system. Nor for two centuries has there been any example of a French regime which knew how to reform itself.

The few opportunities which the Fourth Republic might have had to overcome these obstacles vanished, largely because of the composition of the Fourth Republic's last National Assembly and of the action within it of the Gaullists. General de Gaulle shut himself away in a mysterious silence; every visitor returned with the feeling that de Gaulle agreed with him. The liberals were even more convinced of this than were the 'ultras', but what the ultras counted on was that power should bring the former leader of the Free French back to the principle which had been his during the war: to preserve every inch of French territory over which the French flag flew. While waiting, the Gaullist ultras were full of hope and denounced their compatriots who advocated a policy which they themselves were to carry out some years later.

Thus, the man whom eight years ago I called the lawful saviour became the heir of the 'degenerated Republic' (a degeneration which he had done his utmost to bring about). He assumed in turn, as I outlined in the nineteenth chapter, the offices of *dictator* (in the classic meaning of the word) and of *legislator*. The end which he brought to the Algerian war seems to confirm the theory which I suggested in that chapter: The French are wrong when they blame their regime for the loss of empire, or 'the decolonization' which were the result of irresistible world forces. In fact, it can truly be said that the Fourth Republic was unable not to keep, but to give up Algeria. France had need of a strong government if it was to rise to the heroic heights of renunciation. The shadow of General de Gaulle and of his henchmen prevented every government in the Fourth Republic from doing what most of them thought was inevitable and desirable. Only a few tragic personalities, such as Georges Bidault, for example, remained true to themselves right to the very end, in exile or in prison, or perhaps true to their idea of General de Gaulle who never gives up anything. I cannot help feeling some sympathy with those who, in contrast to the wholly dedicated Gaullists, put loyalty to their ideas above loyalty to a person.

If de Gaulle's record as *dictator* seems to confirm the analyses in these chapters, is the same true of his record as *legislator*? The conclusions of the second lecture were based on the premises of the political situation in the Fourth Republic. They did not take into account the eventuality of a revolution, even a peaceful and semi-legal one. But the regime of the Fifth Republic does not fit into any of the types which political scientists distinguish classically; it is not an example either of parliamentary government (of which Britain is usually taken as the purest example) nor of presidential government (of which the most frequently quoted example is always America); it represents a return to a parliamentary type of empire in which the emperor, elected for seven years by universal suffrage, exercises the authority of the head of the executive and freely uses referenda and plebiscites.

The regime since 1958 has been essentially Gaullist, by which I mean that it is more influenced by the personality of the head of state than by the text of the constitution. No one can be in any doubt about how authority is divided between the President of France and the Prime Minister, as long as General de Gaulle occupies the Elysée. It is also thanks to the General that in 1962 a parliamentary majority composed of UNR deputies and of independents drawn to the coalition with the UNR was elected. In different circumstances rivalry between the two heads of the executive and opposition between the parliamentary majority and the president is conceivable. It would then be rash to state that the 1958 constitution, which is treated somewhat cavalierly by the man who framed it, is designed to bring to an end the politico-constitutional trials and tribulations of France.

Any return to the games, to the pleasures and delights of the Third and Fourth Republics seems to me to be out of the question. The constitution of the Fifth Republic, no matter what changes may be made in it after General de Gaulle has disappeared from the scene, gives the executive powers that make the revival of a *république des députés* for some time at any rate unlikely. It is fashionable today to hold that the decline of parliament and the strengthening at the same time of the government and of the administration answer to the needs of an industrial society. The cunning of reason, to borrow Hegel's expression, made use of the emotions of the defenders of *Algérie française* to bring about a revolution which the 'historic hero' in turn used to give to France institutions which answered to the needs of modern civilization.

This interpretation does not rule out a second one which is also drawn from history and which I shall call the swing of the pendulum. The *république des députés* in which the head of state, often almost unknown to the people, is thrown up by the obscure rivalry of parties and the ambitions of a few leading personalities has once more been replaced by a consular republic of one man. The spotlight is directed on a single man, whose fate absorbs the fate of the whole nation and who is more powerful than any rightful king of France ever was. But his legitimacy is derived from the popular will, as expressed in referenda rather than in elections. The historical parallel for the Fifth Republic is clearly the Third

Empire, liberal and parliamentary at first but increasingly less parliamentary after eight years (perhaps even less parliamentary in 1965 than it was in 1959).

These two interpretations – in order to simplify let us call one sociological and the other historical – illuminate two aspects of the political situation in France. One can say that the present regime is repeating the experiences of the past in a special style, inseparable from the personality of a particular individual: one can say, too, that he has introduced a new phase. The present constitution permits practices which alter according to the state of relations between the two heads of the executive, the parliamentary majority and the prime minister or president. Present practice will inevitably change when General de Gaulle retires: possibly the text of the constitution may even be modified in the direction of presidential or parliamentary government; in either case this will restrict the presidential powers.

I am well aware how uncertain the future is, but I am not too downcast. Observers, when assessing political regimes, are inclined to leave out of account the tasks which confront them. The Fourth and even the Third Republic had heavy tasks. After 1945, France had to rebuild its ruins, had to find its place in a diplomatic situation without precedent, had to agree to a united Europe, modernize her economy and transform fundamentally, and finally give up, her empire. The incessant conflict between General de Gaulle and the political parties from 1946 to 1958 weighed upon the Fourth Republic and was a paralysing factor as the Gaullists never stopped criticizing the work of European unification and decolonization – a work which today is the Fourth Republic's best claim to the gratitude of the French.

The Gaullist Republic will leave behind no such rich legacy. The main problems facing France after 1945 have now been solved. Unless something unforeseen happens, no such difficulties are likely to arise. Perhaps the most difficult problem will be the erasing of some Gaullist features of authoritarianism and arbitrariness which the President's style has passed down to the petty taskmasters, a foreign policy which prefers to dazzle, putting theatrical success above lasting results, and which fails to distinguish between tactics and strategy, the game and the goal, in other words which seems to have no objective other than to take part in a game which is continually renewed.

I have taken the Fourth Republic as a model for the degeneration of a constitutional-pluralistic regime in the first part of this course of lectures. I have taken the Soviet regime as a model for the monopolistic party regime in the second part. I must therefore say a few words about the evolution of the Soviet regime between 1958 and 1965.

The changes are, clearly, more limited than those which have taken place in France. Generally speaking the Soviet regime has remained the same as it was when I gave these lectures denouncing Stalin and the personality cult. The change has been in the direction which seemed to me at that time most probable and which it is convenient to call liberalizing. I am even inclined to think that the contradictions in the monopolistic party regime which I analysed in the sixteenth, seventeenth and eighteenth lectures have since come into the open.

The main contradiction is summed up in the following formulation: when the intelligentsia is given the right to discuss nearly every question, how can it be denied the right to discuss the monopoly of the party – that is the identification of the proletariat and the party – and thus the very foundation of the regime's legitimacy? This may seem to be a purely theoretical contradiction and thus of little danger to authority, but the opposite is true. The calling in question of legitimacy means that the regime itself is called in question. When, simultaneously, terror is reduced to a minimum, if not completely eliminated, Montesquieu's two principles, fear and enthusiasm, are no longer valid. What is there to fear, if socialist legality is respected – in other words, if only the guilty need fear the rigour of the law? And, on the other hand, what will whip up enthusiasm if the main preoccupations are those of economic rationalization and if this, in turn, demands economic calculations, interest rates, prices which take account of the relative scarcity of goods; in short, most of the ideas and mechanisms of capitalism or, more accurately, of the market economy?

I do not mean to draw the conclusion that the Soviet regime is already doomed, unless in the sense that all political regimes are doomed to perish from the moment that they come into being. The Russians are proud of their country, of the power which it has won and to a great extent they identify their regime with their country. Custom has taken the place of fervour or fear. The standard of living is improving. The return to daily life (*die*

Veralltäglichung, in Max Weber's phrase) dispels both the illusions of the idealists and the nightmares of the Cassandras.

But it still remains true that the monopolistic party regime as we see it in the Soviet Union today is both too despotic for the liberties it wants to allow and too liberal for the despotic features it wants to retain. Abroad, it runs the risk of losing the monopoly of revolutionary ideas to the Chinese communists, who are at once poorer, more fervid and more tyrannical. At home, it is now led by men of the third generation, who took no part in the seizure of power or in the civil war and who are the products of the regime itself and not of the revolt against the former regime. These men can no longer ignore the unsuitability of Stalinist methods of planning to the needs of a complex economy. They admit that agriculture, after the progress it made between 1953-9, has not progressed in the last five years. Can they simultaneously rationalize the economy, satisfy the consumers and restore to the Soviet Union the prestige of the revolutionary idea? It was during the great purge that the great lie that the Soviet Union was the most humane system in the world was spread. History has its own strange logic. The Soviet regime has need of Stalinist madness and terror if it is to fascinate. The more the Soviet planners recognize market necessities, the less do they impress the West with rates of growth (which in any case are decreasing). The more the Soviet leaders give freedom to the intellectuals and security to the ordinary citizens, the less can they boast of fictitious accomplishments. Normality at home paralyses propaganda abroad. Here and there, the truth breaks through. Will the builders of the future resign themselves to being what they are, leaders of a hierarchic and administrative society, who are eager to imitate the West and not merely to overtake it?

1965

EDITOR'S INTRODUCTION

When a book that has been out of print for any length of time is brought back into print, three questions must be answered:

1. What is of particular importance about the book that warrants readers' attention at this time?

2. Why did the book go out of print in the first place?

3. Regardless of the book's particular qualities, is it so dated in other respects that it is now too difficult for or confusing to readers?

I will try to answer these three questions, first in brief terms, and then in more detailed fashion.

The book's current importance is twofold. In the first place, it presents a theoretically founded, logically constructed framework for comparative political analysis. At the same time, the framework it creates is admirably suited to understanding and analyzing the dramatic political transformations that have been occurring in the Soviet Union. The political upheaval that the Soviet Union is experiencing is not a series of random events, but rather the working out of an almost inexorable repatterning of institutions and practices that has its own inner logic.

The book no doubt went out of print because it had only limited appeal, and this was almost surely because of a combination of factors. The most important of these, and the only one I will mention here in short form, is that it appeared at a time when fashions in U.S. political science were moving in directions different from those taken in the book. It would not be correct to say that fashions have changed direction and Aron's approach to political analysis is now the new orthodoxy in political analysis. But the appropriateness of Raymond

Aron's approach for making the recent changes in the Soviet Union intelligible gives his analytical method a fresh and strong claim to attention.

The dating problem is real and requires some patience and effort on the part of readers, but it is far from insuperable. Close students of France and the Soviet Union will be troubled the least, as the sometimes veiled references to developments in those countries will be more transparent to those readers than to others. But if one sticks to the main arguments and does not become excessively concerned about points of particular historic detail that are irrelevant to those basic arguments (and to which I will refer later), reading this book should be a stimulating and rewarding experience.

I will now spell out these answers in fuller form and more detail. In doing so, I will try to keep in mind the special needs of students. That is particularly appropriate, as this book was originally the lectures that Aron gave in a course that he taught at the Sorbonne (the University of Paris) and, as Stanley Hoffmann (1983) reminded us shortly after Aron's death, Aron was above all a teacher.

I

Aron's approach to the comparative study of political systems rests on the notion that political systems are intelligible systems. Political systems, in his view, are not simply collections of institutions, assembled helter-skelter, but rather sets of institutions and practices that are logically interrelated. A political system is coherent, in the sense that its parts mesh with one another to form an intelligible whole that can be understood by the attentive observer and whose consequences can be predicted, at least within reasonable limits.

Aron's application of this notion to modern political systems compatible with industrialization is parsimonious in the extreme. He argues (in chaps. 4 and 5) that for such systems, there is one main variable from which the essential characteristics of a political system can be deduced. This variable is simply the number of parties that are legally entitled to participate in the exercise of power. Aron distinguishes sharply, at the outset, between political systems in which two or more parties legally participate and those in which a single party holds a monopoly of political power.

Starting from that basic distinction in his main variable, Aron proceeds to spell out the implications that flow from one kind of party system or the other, and sketches the main characteristics of two different types of political system.

Where there is pluralism in the party system, there is competition for the exercise of power, opposition to the rulers is legal, the competition is settled by elections, and the entire political process is governed by constitutional rules. Those implications are all procedural. Aron adds still another that is substantive; in such a system, where legality prevails, the exercise of authority is likely to be moderate.

Where one party has a legal monopoly of power, the implications are different. In this kind of system the privileged single party becomes identified with the state, tends to proclaim an ideology both to legitimize its rule and to serve as a guide for action, imposes intellectual orthodoxy, and dispenses with rules that might limit its authority. There is no inherent necessity that such a system be violently repressive. Here, much depends on the nature of the ruling party's ideology and ambitions. All single-party systems, however, carry a risk of violence.

In that fashion, Aron sketches out the main characteristics of two radically different types of political system, which he calls the constitutional-pluralistic system, on the one hand, and the monopolistic party system, on the other hand. These types correspond, of course, to the "democracy" and "totalitarianism" of the book's title, although Aron generally avoids using those terms in the book except in very specific circumstances. Aron's intention in building the two different types of system on the basis of the number of parties was, in part, to avoid using some variable that would imply a philosophical choice or assign a prejudicial character to one type of system or the other. He preferred to use an inherently neutral variable that proponents of both real-world plural-party systems and single-party systems would not reject out of hand. Similarly, he deliberately coined the terms "constitutional-pluralistic" and "monopolistic party" (which he later admitted were "a bit barbaric") in order to avoid using ideologically loaded language. As Aron writes in his introduction to this book, when the lectures on which the book is based were first published (and directed at a student audience), they carried a different title, which Aron describes as being "more accurate" than the title under which the commercial versions of the book appeared.

The deceptively simple way in which Aron constructs his two basic types of political system is rich in implications. Two are particularly important. First, Aron's typology provides a powerful, theoretically based framework for comparing political systems at different times and places, within each basic type. Second, his analysis makes it possible to understand, better than any other analytical scheme I know, the logic of the dramatic political transformations that have been taking place in the Soviet Union and Eastern Europe since the late 1980s.

With respect to an agenda for comparing political systems, Aron is clearer and more systematic concerning monopolistic party systems than constitutional-pluralistic ones. He tells us specifically that on the basis of his model "one can distinguish between the different kinds of monopolistic party regimes according to the nature of their doctrine, the scope of their projects, the violence of their methods and the ideal image of the society which they want to create." When he discusses constitutional-pluralistic systems, however, he seems to despair of finding useful dimensions of comparison because of their startling diversity.

It does not seem to be enough for him to designate the successive implications of a plurality of parties as dimensions for the comparison of constitutional-pluralistic systems, as he does in the case of monopolistic party systems. He could have logically concluded that constitutional-pluralistic systems can be compared according to the character of their party systems, the electoral systems they employ for determining who wins in the partisan competition, their constitutional arrangements, and the degree of moderation of the policies that they adopt. Instead, Aron passes in review, in chapter 6, not only several of those theoretically deduced variables, but some half a dozen others as well, including pressure groups, the political elites, the social infrastructure, the bureaucracy, and the social environment. Those are all legitimate objects of comparison, but they appear to be selected on an ad hoc basis rather than derived from the logical underpinnings of Aron's basic typology.

However, there is no need to follow Aron literally; it is enough simply to take one's cues from his method. Since *Democracy and Totalitarianism* was first published, many scholars have done important research of a kind that fits the terms of Aron's own system that he himself ignored. The work on parties is most voluminous and need not be cited here. There is important work on electoral systems (Rae 1971, Dummet 1985, Grofman and Lijphart 1986) and on constitutional arrangements (Lijphart 1984, Powell, 1982, 1989). Policy moderation is not directly studied so often, but there are cross-national studies of civil strife (Zimmerman 1983) as well as the annual reports of Amnesty International.

Ideal Types and Real-World Systems

One possible source of difficulty in following Aron's arguments, particularly for beginning students, lies in the way in which Aron moves back and forth between discussions of the particular properties of real-world political systems and of the theoretically deduced characteristics of his two main types of political system. Real systems are highly diverse; we have already commented on Aron's quick review of the large number of forms that the institutions and arrangements which together constitute any particular political system can take. Those individual characteristics cannot all be deduced from the key variable of the number of legal parties. Only the essential, defining features of basic types of systems can be logically deduced from the key variable. The characteristic features of each of Aron's two basic types of political system mesh together to constitute two abstract, ideal types. They economically capture the essence of two radically different political systems. They do not exhaust the descriptive detail with which any real-world political system can be portrayed, but they express those qualities that make a system one type rather than another. In biological terms, an ideal type is the genus, while the real-world systems of that type are the species. Sometimes Aron discusses one or another of his genera, at other times he discusses their more numerous species. In doing the latter, he sometimes treats variations of the elements that define the type, but sometimes he also discusses system properties that are not essential (as in his summary comparative panorama of constitutional-pluralistic systems).

Philosophical Origins. Aron was steeped in the classic works of political and sociological theory, whose central ideas were constant sources of inspiration for him. He tells us in this book that his basic distinction between monopoly party and plural-party systems is a deliberate application to modern political systems of the classic political philosophers' distinction among rule by one, by few, and by many. His favorite authors were Marx and de Tocqueville. From Marx he acquired the conviction that the distinctive characteristic of modern societies is their enormous productive power. From de Tocqueville he derived the distinctly non-Marxian conviction of the autonomy of politics, and his consequent belief—expressed in the sketches of the two types of political system presented in this book—that more than one type of political system is compatible with modern industrial society.

It was from Montesquieu and the German sociologist Max Weber that Aron derived his reliance on ideal types. Montesquieu wrote well before Weber coined the term "ideal type" and his method of political analysis was not identical to Weber's, but there are close similarities in their approaches. In a general sense, ideal types are models of social reality that express both the structure of the social unit and the logic of the connections among its constituent elements. They are analytical representations of a social unit that include the unit's constituent elements without describing it in detail and without references to the many variations that the unit may display in reality. One can even say that the ideal type represents the "pure" form of the unit being analyzed, even though departures in one particular or another from that form do not mean that there is a change to another basic type. To move from one basic type to another would require major changes in the *essential* elements that define the type in the first place.

Applications. Much of the analysis in this book consists of the confrontation of the ideal constitutional-pluralistic and monopolistic party systems with actual, real-world systems. In chapter 5, for example, Aron writes: "Let us now take the possible and real kinds of multiparty regimes. In the ideal type, which I have constructed, there were many parties, authority was exercised according to constitutional rules, and all the citizens shared in the electoral competition which was observed with all fairness. We do not need much imagination, only a little observation, to realize that these different characteristics do not always occur together." Similarly, in chapters 7 and 8, Aron discusses the tension in the real world between the electoral component and the constitutional component of the constitutional-pluralistic system. Chapters 9 through 11 continue the discussion of the problems of actual constitutional-pluralistic systems, although now in terms that are rather more distant from those used to define the type. Chapters 9 and 10 apply the classical writers' concern with the corruption of political regimes to the problems of modern constitutional-pluralist systems, and chapter 11 deals with the specific problems of the French Fourth Republic (1947–58).

Chapter 12 is a discursive transitional chapter between part 2, which deals with constitutional-pluralistic systems, and part 3, which discusses the monopolistic party system. The chapter briefly discusses the contemporary French situation, acknowledges the variety of real-world political systems, compares the Nazi and Soviet systems, and explains why Aron will discuss only the Soviet system in detail, as the representative of the monopolistic party system.

Within part 3, the device of the ideal type plays the most central role in chapter 15 on totalitarianism. In both chapter 5, where the ideal-type monopolistic party system is discussed briefly, and in chapter 15, which is entitled "On Totalitarianism," Aron makes it clear that a totalitarian political regime is the most complete and extreme expression of the monopolistic party system, but that not all real-life monopolistic party systems are totalitarian. Totalitarianism results when a monopoly party system governed by a party driven by vast ambitions imposes ideological orthodoxy, harnesses virtually all economic and professional activity for its purposes, and employs violence in order to achieve its ends. Not all monopolistic party systems have displayed all of those characteristics simultaneously. There have been periods in the history of the Soviet Union, Aron argues, when it was totalitarian, in the sense just described, but there have been other times—including the period when Aron was giving the lectures out of which this book emerged—when it was not. Aron, however, was skeptical about the likelihood that monopolistic party systems in industrial societies would avoid totalitarianism. In his view, although it was by no means inevitable that monopolistic party systems become totalitarian, that type of system carried the risk of becoming totalitarian.

We can see now in what ways the commercial title of this book is misleading. Within the framework of the interplay between ideal types and real-world political systems, the term "democracy" would not be seriously inappropriate. Aron is not prevented by the logic of his argument from labeling his constitutional-pluralistic system "democratic." He refrained from using the term because proponents of the Soviet Union considered their system to be democratic, and he did not want to bias his analysis in advance by applying to one type of system a label that supporters of the other type also claimed. But monopolistic party systems are not necessarily totalitarian systems, even if some such systems, in the real world, have been totalitarian at one time or another.

Implications for System Change in the
Soviet Union and Eastern Europe

Raymond Aron did not predict that the Soviet Union and Eastern
Europe would undergo the kind of startling political transformations
that began to occur during the late 1980s and continued into the
1990s. No one else did either. But Aron, in this book (and in some
later comments on it), comes closer to making those transformations
intelligible than does any other political analyst of my acquaintance.

Aron discusses both the future of the western democracies (mainly
in chap. 10) and the future of the Soviet Union (mainly in chap.
17). Insofar as Aron has a common method for considering the
probable evolution of the political systems representative of his two
basic types, it is a latter-day application of Montesquieu's concept
of the principle of a political system. Montesquieu believed that each
basic type of political regime (of which he designated four: monarchy,
despotism, aristocracy, and democracy) was characterized by a particular
structure and a particular principle. The structure of a regime consisted
of the number of rulers (one, few, or many) and the mode of rule
(by law or by caprice). The principle of a regime consisted of the
human passions that activated the structure. What Montesquieu calls
the principle of a regime was what one might today call the climate
of opinion or prevailing set of attitudes or political culture that governs
people's behavior as citizens. For Montesquieu, the characteristic principle of despotism was fear and that of democracy (rule by the many
under law) was what he called virtue, by which he seems to have
meant a combination of love of the republic, respect for equality
(but not extreme equality), and personal frugality.

The concept of principle is important to Montesquieu because he
believed that when a political system became corrupted, thereby
entering a phase of transformation from one type of regime to another,
the process began with the corruption of the regime's principle. When
people no longer held the beliefs appropriate to the particular type
of system under which they lived, the system would no longer
operate in its characteristic fashion. The motivating force necessary
to run the system's institutions consistently would become diluted
or disappear, and fundamental political change would begin to occur.

Aron borrows both Montesquieu's concept of principle and his
concern for corruption, and applies them to his own basic types of
political system. Aron's equivalent of Montesquieu's principle for con-

stitutional-pluralist systems consists of respect for legality and respect for and the sense of compromise; for monopolistic party systems it is faith and fear.

Aron's discussion of the corruption of constitutional-pluralistic systems by dilution of their principles is heavily influenced by the foreign policy failures of France and Great Britain during the 1930s and the tendency toward paralysis in decision-making during the Fourth French Republic (excessive compromise) as well as the specific circumstances of France in the winter and spring of 1958, when he perceived the possibility of France departing from respect for legality (the "silken thread" of chap. 12). But we are more concerned here with his analysis of faith and fear as the principles of the monopolistic party system. In such a system, faith in the ruling party as the vehicle to accomplish its goals is essential, at least among party members, if the system is to maintain the kind of enthusiasm that revolutionary parties, in particular, require. Among the opponents, unbelievers, or skeptics, Aron continues, the kind of attitude that maintains stability in the system is fear, or—as he alternately puts it—awareness of their impotence.

What happens when dilution of the appropriate principles of Aron's two basic types of system sets in and, for this or other reasons, the systems become corrupted? Aron is clear enough about the constitutional-pluralistic systems. At the end of chapter 10, he says there may be a coup d'état or the legal or semilegal accession to power of a revolutionary group that will eventually produce a revolutionary upheaval. The result may be one or another different species of system, or even a monopolistic party system, which would mean the establishment of a wholly different type of system.

Aron is less categorical in his parallel discussion of the Soviet Union, which is his main illustration of the monopolistic party system. In part, this is because he has no historical precedents on which to rely. The Weimar Republic, which gave way to the Nazi regime in 1933, is his main (but not sole) case of the transformation of a constitutional-pluralistic system into a monopolistic party system, but the evolution of the Nazi regime provides no guidance for estimating the probable evolution of the Soviet Union. With the passage of time, the Nazi regime revealed its essential characteristics increasingly clearly (and despicably). In Aron's terminology, the Nazi regime, far from becoming corrupted in Montesquieu's sense, became increasingly perfect. When Aron wrote *Democracy and Totalitarianism*, however, the

Soviet Union was already in a state of considerable flux. Stalin had been dead for several years, Nikita Khrushchev had emerged as the principal Soviet leader, and he had undertaken a campaign of de-Stalinization as well as a variety of measures designed to liberalize the Soviet system.

Aron, like other scholars, considered the implications of those and related developments—most notably the economic development of the Soviet Union—for the future evolution of the Soviet regime. It would have taken extraordinary prescience and courage for anyone to have suggested in 1957 or 1958 that in about thirty years a Soviet leader would emerge who would urge the abandonment of the monopoly of power of the Communist party. Aron certainly made no such assertion. Like other scholars of the period, he held that while there had been changes *in* the system, there had not been changes *of* the system. But more clearly than most, Aron understood that the margin for reform within the Soviet system was narrow, and that major changes would require the abandonment of the system's central features: the single-party monopoly, ideological orthodoxy, and bureaucratic absolutism in economic and social affairs. He did not rule out the possibility of liberalizing developments, but anything approaching the advent of a system similar to those of the Western democracies would represent a fundamental transformation of the political foundations of the Soviet Union.

In effect, Aron argued that the Soviet Union was constrained by the logic of the monopolistic party system to restrict intellectual freedom, retain the capacity to use violence against the citizenry, and confer political and social privileges on the party elites. Within those limits, reform was possible. But genuine political freedom, legal restraints on the use of violence, and diffusion of power would require nothing short of fundamental change, in the form of a massive shift from the monopolistic party system to the constitutional-pluralistic system. Aron never predicted that such a revolutionary change would occur. He would, I believe, have been better prepared intellectually for the moment when that change actually began to take place than virtually anyone else.

Direct analysis of the specific issue of large-scale transformation of the Soviet political system appears briefly in this book, reappears in the introduction to the book that Aron wrote seven years after he had given the lectures it comprises, and appears still a third time in reflections upon the book that he sets out in his memoirs, which were first published, in French, in 1983. Each time he falls short of saying that the Soviet Union will become a constitutional-pluralistic system, but on each occasion his logic points to the conclusion that if the Soviet Union is to accommodate the forces making for change it will have to abandon its *essential* characteristics, which means to become another system, with different institutions, different principles (in Montesquieu's sense), and a different unifying logic.

Aron touches briefly on this big question at three different places in *Democracy and Totalitarianism*. In chapter 15 he writes that many subjects may be debated freely in the Soviet Union except the question why there are no parties other than the ruling party. The implication is that liberalization stops when basic constituent principles might be challenged. Still, in chapter 17, he writes that the "introduction into the Soviet Union of multiple parties and liberal institutions such as there are in the west," while improbable, is possible. Grappling with the problem from another vantage point, he revives the classical political philosophers' notion of a political cycle, including the transition from a single-party system to a competitive plural-party system. For the moment, he tells us, there is "no proof" that such a stage of development will ever be reached.

In the introduction that he wrote for the first French edition of *Democracy and Totalitarianism*, which appeared in 1965 and a translation of which is reprinted in this volume, Aron returned briefly to the same theme. If people in the Soviet Union are allowed to discuss almost every question, why should they not be allowed to question the monopoly of power of the Communist party? Without appearing to answer the question, he in fact does answer it: because to challenge the monopoly of the party is to undermine the whole regime, whose structure and behavioral characteristics derive from the very party monopoly itself.

Moreover, in the introduction, Aron both refers to the inadequacy of the Soviet economic system and returns to the concept of the principles of a regime. In the book itself, he discussed the damaging consequences for constitutional-pluralistic regimes of the dilution of their principles, but he did not make an extensive parallel analysis of the effects on a monopolistic party system of the degradation of its principles. In chapter 17, however, he does write that the corruption of the Soviet system would amount to the "desovietization of the regime," that is, the abandonment of at least some of its characteristic features. In the introduction to the book, the references to changes in the principles of the system are fleeting, but Aron asks what will happen if there is nothing beyond economic growth for party members to put their faith in and if there is nothing for skeptics and dissidents to fear as long as they do not break the law. Again, he draws no firm conclusions. Instead, he expresses a paradox of a kind of which he was fond: the monopolistic party system in the Soviet Union is both too despotic to be consistent with such liberalization as it wants to allow, and too liberal for the despotic features it wants to retain. The implication of this argument is that the Soviet Union has a political structure that is unsupported by the kind of animating attitudes that it requires. What happens in such a case? Aron does not draw the conclusion to which the argument points.

Finally, Aron returns to the same question in his memoirs, in passages where he looks back on the book he had written a quarter of a century earlier (and which he tells us he could reread "without shame" [Aron 1983, 403]). He now thinks that he may have been too optimistic about the Soviet Union in the original book. He tells us that he underestimated the implications for the Soviet Union's standard of living of heavy military burdens and the inefficiency of the economic system. He would not now write, as he had done in the book, that the establishment of a plural-party system and liberal institutions in the Soviet Union is "possible," but neither would he say that it is impossible. "I would say that such liberalization would bring about the collapse, peaceful or otherwise, of the regime itself" (Aron 1983, 407).

Aron is not simply saying here, in 1983, that if the Soviet Union had a plural-party system and liberal institutions, it would be different from what it actually was, a single-party system without liberal institutions. That would be an inane truism. What he is saying is that the main features of the Soviet Union—the single party, the intellectual orthodoxy, the centralized planning system, and the bureaucratically organized state hierarchy—are so interrelated and mutually dependent that a change in any one of them would produce changes in the others and, in particular, that the abandonment of the single-party monopoly would mean the collapse of the entire system. Whether it would also mean transformation into a constitutional-pluralistic system would depend on how quickly and how well the characteristic institutions of that type of system—parties, elections, appropriate constitutional rules—could be put into place and how soon and how wholeheartedly the principles appropriate for such a system—respect for legality and respect for, and the sense of, compromise—were accepted. Early in 1990 the Soviet Union, under the leadership of Mikhail S. Gorbachev, started to dismantle the monopoly of power of the Communist party. As I write these words, the Soviet Union's political system is, in part, collapsing and, in part, being transformed in the direction of a constitutional-pluralistic system.

II

There are four main reasons why the original English-language editions of Aron's book did not enjoy more success and a longer shelf life. Two of these have to do with the book's presentation: the title and the quality of the translation (Colquhoun 1986, 2:155–61). The other two are more substantive in nature: the book appeared in English at a time when both the prevailing conceptual frameworks for comparative politics and the methods of conducting political research were moving away from those employed by Aron.

The book's title, *Democracy and Totalitarianism*, was doubly unfortunate. On the one hand, as we have already indicated in this introduction, neither term is actually employed by Aron in a general sense in the book. On the other hand, the English translation appeared under its misleading title at more or less the same time that English-speaking scholars were abandoning the concept of totalitarianism as a device for analyzing the political system of the Soviet Union. This is the more important aspect of the problem. The fact that the title was misleading would in itself not necessarily have adversely affected the book's reception; indeed, a jazzy but not wholly appropriate title may well increase a book's sales. But when totalitarianism was rapidly falling out of favor as a useful analytical concept, Aron's book could appear from the title alone to be merely a variant of obsolete Cold War literature. (Such a fate would not necessarily befall the book, under the same title, in France, where totalitarianism as an analytical concept was employed long after it was more or less abandoned in the English-speaking scholarly world [Grawitz and Leca 1985, vol. 2, chaps. 2–4].) There is considerable irony in a situation in which Aron's book may have suffered because it carried a title that included a concept that English-speaking scholars were abandoning for reasons that Aron himself, some seven years earlier, had been among the first to suggest. The present Ann Arbor Paperbacks edition preserves the original title of the book, but it also gives equal weight to the book's subtitle, *A Theory of Political Systems*, which was part of the title of the course in which Aron gave the lectures that constitute the book.

The second aspect of the book's original presentation that may have weakened its impact is that it was not served as well by the translation from the French as it might have been. Financial limitations have ruled out extensive revisions of the original edition, but I have made the necessary corrections and tried to make the text read more smoothly.

The substantive, and more important, reasons why the earlier edition of this book did not enjoy a longer life are also two in number. These relate to method and to theory. I will deal with the issue of method first and briefly. Then I will discuss the central theoretical issues at greater length.

The relationship between Aron's method of analysis and the reception his book received is simply that Aron was not an empirical political scientist (or sociologist) and by the middle and late 1960s, empirical investigation and, in several particular domains, quantitative analysis were the orthodox canons of social science research. Although Aron came closer than most scholars to expressing a happy medium between the two extremes of what C. Wright Mills (1959) called "grand theory" and "abstracted empiricism," he must certainly have looked much more like a political philosopher than a data-grubber to most U.S. (and at least the younger British) political scientists. After all, Aron took Aristotle, Montesquieu, de Tocqueville, and Marx as serious guides for contemporary political analysis, and the only counting that he did distinguished among one, the few, and the many. Aron almost surely suffered a certain amount of neglect because he was an idea man and a synthesizer at a time when specialization and analytical reduction were the hallmarks of social science in the United States.

Even among political scientists with broad perspectives, intellectual currents were starkly different from those that Aron represented. Aron deliberately limited his range of application to industrial societies, because he thought that such a common base made political comparisons possible and fruitful. In the United States, the urge was to create systems of classification that would be universally applicable, to all kinds of political systems at any time, place, or level of economic development. Aron's principal arguments point to the existence of two radically different types of political system, whose differences are more interesting theoretically than their similarities. American political science was, in contrast, emphasizing not what was different about political systems but what was common to them, in the belief that the theoretically important aspect of political science is the search for regularities. Aron's main variables for analyzing political systems were institutional; his decisive variable is the party system. In the United States at the time, the main variables being singled out for investigation were functional. Finally, Aron argued that political systems are not random but coherent, and that it is the task of the theorist to discover the logic that gives them their coherence. The conceptual frameworks that circulated widely in the United States at more or less the same time sometimes gave lip service to the notion of coherence but never, to my knowledge, either revealed its existence in a real-world political system or demonstrated theoretically in what it would consist. Instead of emphasizing coherence, the analytical formulations of the period display an almost uncontrolled eclecticism.

Structural-functionalism, which had been launched by Almond and Coleman (1960), was rapidly becoming the dominant framework for analyzing political systems, at least on an elementary level. The structural-functional approach treats certain political functions (such as political socialization, political recruitment, and rule making), which are deemed to be performed by all political systems at all times and places, as the main variables for comparative analysis. According to this scheme, one compares political systems by investigating the institutions by which and the manner in which identical functions are performed in different systems.

Aron also understood that all political systems perform certain identical functions. He discusses these, in general terms, in chapter 3: the maintenance of domestic order, the formulation of rules governing the behavior of persons and groups within the community, and the conduct of foreign relations. But he does not pursue those common factors further; he mentions them only to establish that all political systems do indeed belong to a common genus, not because he has any interest in investigating them separately and in detail. For Aron, the common functions are necessary and real, but they are not his principal objects of investigation. It is institutional arrangements (plural-party systems or single-party systems) that command his attention. For the structural-functionalist, it is almost the other way around: functions are the fundamental concepts, while the institutions that perform those functions, although they are not incidental, are so variable in real-world systems that they cannot be employed as the basis for identifying intelligible types of political systems.

The structural-functional approach gained and retained popularity mainly because it provides a framework within which the most diverse political systems can be described. One *can* ask how one or another function is performed in one country or another. It is comforting to know that if one asks certain questions one will be sure to find the answers. The scheme, however, is essentially atheoretical. It contains no deductive syllogisms, it produces no coherent patterns, it leads to no generalizations, and it contains no dynamic for explaining political change.

Aron's formulations have all of those properties. The analysis in *Democracy and Totalitarianism* deduces the leading characteristics of two distinct types of political system from a single variable, attempts to show in what ways those characteristics are interconnected, leaves ample scope for generalizations about the effects of variations in those characteristics, and (perhaps less persuasively) revives an old concept (the principle—read political culture—of a system) that can at least be employed to understand the meaning of political change.

At the present time, Aron's analytical method, or some variant of it, is the only viable alternative to structural-functionalism as a framework for comparative political analysis. Structural-functionalism is well known; Aron's scheme has been much less accessible. But Aron's analysis has one towering advantage over its hitherto dominant rival: it makes the great upheaval in the Soviet Union (and its Eastern European neighbors) intelligible in ways that structural-functionalism does not. The latter simply furnishes the observer with categories for describing a succession of institutions. Aron's method highlights the dynamic implications for the whole pattern of institutional relationships when the critical feature of a political system—the number of parties legally permitted to participate in the system—is decisively changed. One may, indeed, derive an analogy from the biological sciences. Structural-functionalism is the equivalent of old-fashioned biology, preoccupied with the classification of species, while Aron's outlook comes closer to resembling the molecular genetics that is uncovering the processes of life itself.

III

It is the mark of a classic work that however relevant its contents may be for understanding events that occur long after it was written, it inevitably contains references to people, places, and situations that attracted the attention of the author at the time of writing but which, in the long run, are not essential to the main arguments of the book. In the cases of the great classic works of political theory, written long ago, we are familiar with that problem, and we manage to extract what we think are the permanent kernels of wisdom they offer without becoming distracted by the great welter of detail concerning long-gone political systems they also contain.

The problem of sorting the substantive wheat from the ephemeral chaff can be more difficult when we are dealing with works of such recent vintage that they are almost, but not quite, contemporary. Some of the detail that appears in recent works is sufficiently familiar to us that we puzzle over it, wondering how it may fit in the larger picture the author is trying to present, while points of detail that are obscure to us also nag at us because we feel that we may be missing something here that is central to the argument.

This book poses some problems of the kind I have mentioned, but they are not great and they are wholly manageable. The main point the reader must keep in mind is that the lectures which constitute the book were given during the academic year 1957–58. This has three orders of implications: for the larger, diffuse political environment of the period, for the situation in the Soviet Union, and for the situation in France.

With regard to the broad political environment, it is obvious that changes of all sorts are constantly occurring, with the result that any book (and especially one directed at students, who are naturally drawn to current events) will inevitably include references that sooner or later become inexact. Readers of this book will, therefore, not be surprised at and should easily take in stride the references to Mr. Gomulka as the general secretary of the Polish Communist party, to the "recent revolution" in Egypt, to Portugal and Spain as authoritarian states, and to obsolete French political parties, including the Poujadists, among other references of similar ilk.

With regard to the relationship of the period to developments within the Soviet Union, we have already pointed out that Stalin had died only a few years earlier, that Nikita Khrushchev was emerging as the central figure in the Soviet leadership, and that he had recently launched the de-Stalinization campaign and undertaken a number of other initiatives that had the effect of liberalizing the Soviet system. These developments are discussed tentatively, somewhat skeptically, but in the final analysis optimistically. In relation to what readers may know of what was to follow in the Soviet Union, the discussion of the early Khrushchev period inevitably appears to be limited and incomplete.

By the same token, the discussion of various aspects of the Stalinist period in the history of the Soviet Union, particularly the treatment of ideology and terror in chapter 14, may seem to be giving excessive attention to what may have been an important (and repugnant) phase of the development of the Soviet Union but which is by now part of a comparatively distant past. Before adopting such a perspective, readers would do well to keep in mind that Aron, in 1957, was closer to the beginning of the Stalinist period (in 1928) than readers in 1990 are to Aron when he wrote the book. Quite apart from the intrinsic importance of Stalinism as an expression of the monopolistic party system, the Stalinist past loomed far larger on Aron's horizon than the early Khrushchev years do on that of readers today.

Finally, with respect to the political situation in France, readers would do well to remember that while Aron was giving the lectures that became this book, France was unsuccessfully waging a colonial war in Algeria in circumstances that increasingly revealed the political bankruptcy of the French Fourth Republic. The last chapter of the book was delivered as a lecture on May 19, 1958, less than a week after French colonists in Algeria revolted against the government of the republic and the French military authorities in Algeria urged the return to power of Charles de Gaulle, who had been out of office since 1946. Within two weeks after that lecture, the National Assembly voted de Gaulle back into power, under conditions that led to the foundation of the Fifth French Republic, which survives to this day. Throughout much if not all of the period during which this book was written the future of democratic government in France was seriously in question. In these circumstances, it is not particularly surprising that Aron should appear preoccupied with the French case generally or that the text should seem to have a disproportionately large number of references to Algeria and de Gaulle in particular.

In fact, the wonder is, to the contrary, that Aron was not really diverted from his central themes by the ominous events going on about him. If any proof were needed that this is not a book that was written to fit the circumstances of 1957–58, it is precisely that the inability of the French Fourth Republic to deal successfully with the nationalist revolution in Algeria plays as small and uncontrolling a role in the analysis as it does. This is not a book that we can understand and interpret only in the light of the declining days of the French Fourth Republic. It is, rather, a book whose basic theoretical structure can conveniently accommodate political phenomena from many places and times, including the then current events in France, which are given supplemental attention because they are understandably of more than normal interest to Aron's student audience.

Nevertheless, readers should be warned that Aron devotes a large portion of his introduction to the book to discussing events surrounding the end of the Fourth Republic, including an obscure reference to a press declaration of May 15 that will be comprehensible only to specialists. (Rumors were circulating in Algiers and Paris that the French military forces in Algeria were on the point of mounting an invasion of metropolitan France when de Gaulle announced, on May 15, that he was in the process of forming a new government. He had no legal authority to form a government at the time, but his announcement was interpreted by his sympathizers as designed to prevent a military invasion and by his opponents as a gambit to force the pace toward his return to power.) Chapter 11 discusses the French Fourth Republic, which is no more. The first five pages of chapter 12 refer to the "present" crisis over Algeria. The final pages of the book return to that crisis, which is now even more acute, because the old regime has already fallen but a new regime is not yet in place. In this way, Aron linked a powerful book with an enduring message to a specific set of local circumstances. I have tried to show in this introduction how the same book may be linked to far more momentous developments in the Soviet Union. This wide-ranging applicability, in time and place, testifies to the permanent importance of this book.

Roy Pierce
February, 1990

References

Almond, Gabriel A., and James S. Coleman, eds. 1960. *The Politics of the Developing Areas*. Princeton, N.J.: Princeton University Press.

Aron, Raymond. 1983. *Mémoires*. Paris: Julliard.

Colquhoun, Robert. 1986. *Raymond Aron*. Vol. 2, *The Sociologist in Society, 1955–1983*. Beverly Hills, Calif.: Sage Publications.

Dummet, Michael. 1985. *Voting Procedures*. New York: Oxford University Press.

Grawitz, Madeleine, and Jean Leca. 1985. *Traité de Science Politique*. Vol. 2, *Les Régimes Politiques Contemporaines*. Paris: Presses Universitaires de France.

Grofman, Bernard, and Arend Lijphart. 1986. *Electoral Laws and Their Political Consequences*. New York: Agathon Press.

Hoffmann, Stanley. 1983. "Raymond Aron (1905–1983)." *New York Review of Books*. December 8.

Lijphart, Arend. 1984. *Democracies: Patterns of Majoritarian and Consensus Government in Twenty-One Countries*. New Haven: Yale University Press.

Mills, C. Wright. 1959. *The Sociological Imagination*. New York: Oxford University Press.

Powell, G. Bingham, Jr. 1982. *Contemporary Democracies: Participation, Stability, and Violence*. Cambridge, Mass.: Harvard University Press.

———. 1989. "Constitutional Design and Citizen Electoral Control." *Journal of Theoretical Politics* 1, no. 2:107–30.

Rae, Douglas. 1971. *The Political Consequences of Electoral Laws*. New Haven: Yale University Press.

Zimmerman, Ekkart. 1983. *Political Violence, Crises, and Revolutions: Theories and Research*. Cambridge, Mass.: Schenkman Publishing Co.

PART ONE

CONCEPTS AND VARIABLES

CHAPTER ONE

ON POLICY AND POLITICS

The word 'politique' in French has a variety of meanings. We speak of domestic policy, of foreign policy, of Richelieu's policy and of the policy on alcohol or beets; and sometimes it seems impossible to find the connecting link between these different usages. Bertrand de Jouvenel in a recent book has said that the word is used to convey such different meanings that we had better simply decide for ourselves the meaning which we want to give it. Perhaps he is right, but it seems to me that we can bring some order into the chaos if we concentrate on the three basic ambiguities which, when we analyse them, appear to be well-founded. Auguste Comte liked to compare the different meanings of the same word and to unravel the deep common denominator in the apparent diversity.

The first ambiguity arises from the fact that the French word 'politique' is used to translate two English words, both with an exact meaning. 'La politique' is a translation of both policy and politics.

Policy is a conception, a programme of action or the action itself of an individual, a group or a government. When we speak of the policy on alcohol, we think of the whole programme on a given problem, the problem of production surpluses or deficits. When we speak of Richelieu's policy, we think of his conception of the country's interests, of the goals he wanted to reach and of his methods. In the first sense the word 'politique' means a programme, a method of action or the action itself of an individual or group on one or all the problems of a society.

The other meaning of the word 'la politique' is the one used when it is applied to the realm in which different policies challenge

3

or oppose each other. The realm of politics is the arena in which individuals or groups, each having their own policy, aims, interests, and sometimes philosophy, come to grips.

These two meanings of the word 'politique', although they are separate, are connected. Policies, in the sense of programmes, always run the risk of coming up against other policies. Programmes of action do not necessarily agree; in this sense, the realm of policies carries with it an element of conflict, as well as an element of consensus. If the policies, that is the objectives of individuals or groups within a community, are absolutely contradictory, then there is conflict without any cooperation and the community ceases to exist. A political community is defined by the way in which partly contradictory and partly compatible purposes come to terms.

Those who govern have programmes which cannot be implemented without the consent of the governed. But the governed seldom give unanimous approval to those whom they ought to obey.

Many well-meaning people imagine that the policy *qua* programme of action is noble and that political conflict is base. The idea that it is possible to have a policy without conflict is, as we shall see later, a false one.

The second ambiguity lies in the fact that the same word is used in French for both the reality and our awareness of this reality. 'La politique' is used both to describe the party struggle and our awareness of this struggle. The same ambiguity is to be found in the word 'history'. The same word 'history' describes the way in which societies or epochs succeed each other and our awareness of this succession. The word 'politique' describes both the realm and our awareness of it and I think that in both cases the root of the ambiguity is the same. *Consciousness of reality is part of reality itself.* History, in the full meaning of the word, is the extent to which men are conscious of their past, of the distinction between past and present, and are aware of the differences between various historical periods. In the same way, the realm of policy presupposes a minimal consciousness of this realm. In each community, individuals should know approximately who the men in command are, how they are chosen and how they wield power. Every political system presupposes that those who are part of it are aware of the regime itself. We cannot live in a democracy, such

4

as we have in France, if the citizens do not have a minimal awareness of the rules by which the regime functions. Political awareness is the realization of this spontaneous consciousness of politics. Also all political awareness acknowledges the discrepancy which can exist between the policies which are actually being carried out and other possible policies. But when it goes beyond the defence and interpretation of the existing regime, it tends either to suppress judgment values (we do things in a certain way, others do them differently, and I refrain from judging the relative value of our methods and those of others) or to try to find a criterion of the best regime. The fusion between political consciousness and political reality sets the problem of the relation between judgments of fact and judgments of value. It is a different matter when the question is one of natural realities in which consciousness is not part of reality itself.

The third, most important, ambiguity arises when we use the same word to describe, on the one hand, a particular sector of the social scene and, on the other, the social scene itself, seen from a particular point of view.

Political sociology deals with institutions in modern societies such as parties, parliaments or administrations. These institutions may possibly form a system, but it is a partial one when set against the family, religion or work. This particular sector of the social scene has a peculiarity in that it determines the choice of those who govern and the way in which they exercise authority. In other words, it deals with a partial sector, the repercussions of which on the whole are immediately apparent. Against this it can be said that the economic sector, too, influences the other sectors of the social reality and this is true; but those who govern society do not rule the parties or the parliaments: they direct the economy and they have the right to take decisions which relate to all sectors of the social scene.

The link between the partial sector and the social community can be presented again in the following way: all cooperation between men implies authority; now the method by which authority is exercised and the choice of those who govern is the essence of politics. Politics is the major feature of the entire community because it conditions any cooperation between men.

These three ambiguities are both intelligible and well founded. The politics *qua* programme of action and the politics *qua* realm

5

are linked together because the realm is where politics comes to grips with programmes; politics *qua* reality and politics *qua* awareness are linked, because awareness is an integral part of reality itself; lastly, politics *qua* partial system leads to politics *qua* aspect, encompassing the whole existing community, in which the partial system exerts a dominant influence on the whole of the community.

Let us go further. 'Politics' is a translation of the Greek word *politeia*. Politics is essentially what the Greeks called the way in which the city is run, that is the method of establishing command, taken as characteristic of the method by which the entire community is run.

If politics is essentially the regime of the whole community, or of the method by which it is run, we see the ambiguity between its limited and its overall meaning. In fact, the limited meaning applies to the particular system which decides who will govern and the method by which authority is exercised, but at the same time the word can be applied to the way in which individuals cooperate within each community.

The second ambiguity arises out of the first. Each society has a regime and cannot be aware of itself without being aware of the different kinds of regime and the problems posed by this variety.

Thus in the end, the ambiguity between the use of the same word for programmes of action and the realm itself at last becomes intelligible. 'Politics' in the sense of programmes of action carries various shades of meaning; the policy of those who have authority and how they use it; the policy of individuals or of groups which have their own objectives and want to use certain methods; and also the policy of those who want to modify the regime itself. All these policies represent programmes, either partial or all-embracing, according to whether it is a question of objectives within the regime or of objectives concerning the regime itself.

I have explained that the word 'politics' does not mean only a partial sector of the whole community, but also an aspect embracing the whole society. If this is so, it would seem that we give a kind of primacy to politics. Now this course on politics follows one course on economics and another on social classes: does not this suggested primacy contradict the method followed hitherto?

I started with the contrast between the thinking of de Tocqueville and that of Marx. Tocqueville held that the democratic movement was leading all modern societies towards the elimination of differences in status and condition between individuals. According to him, this irresistible trend could lead to two types of society, an egalitarian and despotic society or an egalitarian and liberal one. Tocqueville has given us a starting point; I will confine myself simply to saying that we shall see, after having studied the development of industrial society, to what extent one or other of the two kinds of society is the more probable.

Marx, on the other hand, looked to transformations in the economy for the explanation of social and political changes. He thought that capitalist societies, being the victims of fundamental contradictions, would as a result run into a revolutionary explosion and that after this revolutionary explosion a socialist regime in a classless society would arise. The political framework would tend to disappear, because the state, which in Marx's eyes was the instrument by which one class was exploited by another, would tend to disappear together with class distinctions.

I have never thought that these changes in the economy would necessarily *determine* the social structure or the political constitution, but wanted to submit the hypothesis of this unilateral determination to a critical examination. This is a methodological, and not a doctrinal, question. Yet the conclusions to which I have come tend to refute the theory which can be drawn from the classification which I adopted.

I began with the economy, in order to define a certain type of society, the industrial one, and I left open the question as to whether a certain type of economic development *determines* the relation between classes, the political framework. Now the result of an examination of the question during the two past years has tended to reveal the paramouncy of political phenomena over economic ones.

As a matter of fact, at the very root of the Soviet-type industrial society, one finds an event, a fact: a revolution. The 1917 revolution was caused by many different things, some of which were economic, but it had as its direct ancestor a political fact, and we are right to stress the adjective 'political' because, according to those who actually made the revolution, the conditions of economic ripeness had not been fulfilled.

7

Furthermore, the main features of the Soviet economy derive, at least in part, from the party and its ideology. We can understand neither the method of planning nor the allocation of collective resources nor the rhythm of growth of the Soviet economy, if we do not remember that all these phenomena are influenced by the picture which the communists have of what an economy should be and the goals they set themselves; these are decisions of a political order, in the fullest meaning of the word, because they are questions not only of the communist leaders' plan of action, but of a plan of action embracing the entire set-up of the community.

In fact, Soviet economic planning is the direct outcome of decisions taken by the party leaders; decisions taken within the particular social system which we call policy. The Soviet economy is to the highest degree dependent at the same time on the political regime of the Soviet Union and on the day-to-day programmes of action of the party leaders.

This politization of the Soviet economy, this subordination of the structure and the functioning of the Soviet economy to political considerations, proves that the economic system is no less influenced by the political system than is the political by the economic.

In the West, the politization of the economy appears curiously enough to be less insisted upon. I say curiously because the ideology which the Soviet regime proclaims presupposes the paramouncy of the economy, while the ideology which western regimes claim for themselves presupposes the paramouncy of politics. According to the picture which western Europeans have of the good society, many of the decisions which are important for the economy are taken outside the political sector in the strict sense of the term. For example, the allocation of collective resources between investment and consumer goods, which in the Soviet regime is decided by the planners, is, in the West, the outcome, more often than not involuntary, of a great many decisions taken by the consumers themselves. If the Soviet economy is the outcome of a given policy, western economy is the outcome of a political system which accepts its own limitations.

As far as social classes are concerned, the politization seems even greater. We are agreed that all societies, Soviet as well as western, are heterogeneous – a heterogeneity of individuals and of groups. There exists a hierarchy of authority, a hierarchy of incomes. There is a difference between the way of life of those at the foot and those at the top of the social scale. More or less well-defined groups are formed by individuals who have the same income, the same outlook and somewhat similar ways of life.

But when we come to the fundamental question of the extent to which distinct classes do or do not exist, i.e. groups aware that they belong to a distinct class, which the mass of the people cannot enter, we come to a fundamental difficulty: on the one hand, the groups have the right to organize themselves; the workers, the right to set up trade unions, to elect the secretaries of these unions; all the pressure groups, in a democratic western-type society, are permitted to form organizations and to press their case. On the other, in a Soviet-type society, no pressure group has the right to exist. This is a major difference which struck me when comparing a Soviet-type society with a western-type society. On the one hand, the social mass is heterogeneous in many respects; it does not split off into groups which are organized and aware of themselves; on the other, the social mass splinters into pressure groups or a number of ideological groups, all authorized to choose their representatives, to defend their ideas and to compete with each other.

This fundamental difference between the right to sectional organization and the denial of this right is politics. How can we understand that in one type of society classes assert themselves as they are and in the other appear not to exist, if we do not remember that, on one side, the political regime allows groups to organize and on the other forbids them to do so?

The problem of social classes cannot be treated in the abstract as an abstract reality of the political regime. It is the political regime, that is the constitution of power and the idea that those who govern have of their authority, which decides the existence or nonexistence of classes and above all their self-awareness.

In the same way as we have found the political will at the root of the economic system, we find a method of exercising power, a particular political regime, is at the origin of social classes, of the degree of class consciousness, and of the degree of social mobility between groups in the whole society.

In what sense are we to understand this primacy of politics? I want at this point to avoid any ambiguity.

It is not a question of exchanging the doctrine of the unilateral economic determination of society for the doctrine of the political determination of society which would be just as arbitrary. It is not true that technique, the degree of development of the economic forces or the allocation of collective resources *determine* the whole of society; nor is it true that one can deduce all the characteristics of the society from the constitution of the public powers.

We can go further. It can be shown quite easily that every theory of the unilateral determinism of the community by a part of the collective reality as a whole is false. This can be shown in various ways:

Sociologically. It is not true that given one type of economy, one determined political regime, and one only, will ensue. If one presupposes a certain stage of development of the productive forces, different modalities of the organization of public powers within it are possible; in the same way, if one imagines a constitution of public powers, for example, a certain type of parliamentary regime, one cannot foresee what kind of system or functioning of the economy might result.

Historically. Historically, starting from any given event, we can retrace the causes, without ever arriving at the very first. The after effects of an event can never be stopped in advance. In other words the formulation 'in *the last analysis* everything is explained either by the economy, by technique or by politics' is meaningless. If you start from the state of Soviet society today, you go back to the Soviet revolution of 1917, beyond that to the tsarist regime and so on indefinitely, observing at each stage sometimes political and sometimes economic factors.

Even the notion: *one particular order of things is more important than any other order,* is an equivocal idea. Let us suppose that we believe that economic causes are more important than political ones. What do we understand by this? Let us take a Soviet-type society. Individual freedom is feebly guaranteed; on the other hand, the worker usually finds work and the absence of unemployment gives a rapid rate of growth. The proposition according to which the economy is essential can be related to the rapid rate of growth. In this case, the importance of the economic factor is decided by the importance we attach to the disappearance of unemployment or to the rate of growth. But if our main preoccupation is with freedom, and not with the relative merits of planned or unplanned economies, then the political regime is more important than the rate of growth. In other words, the notion of 'importance' can relate to the value which the observer attaches to the phenomena. In this case, the importance varies with the observers' interest.

What then does the primacy of politics which I have suggested mean? It has two meanings.

1. In our time, anyone who compares the different types of industrial society finds that the characteristic of each type of industrial society is dependent on politics. I come back thus to an idea put forward by Alexis de Tocqueville: all modern societies are democratic, in that they lead to the gradual disappearance of differences in condition or in personal status, but they can be of a despotic or tyrannical or liberal kind. Personally I would say that modern industrial societies, which have many features in common (distribution of man-power, growth of collective resources, etc.) are differentiated above all by the way public powers are organized, this organization influencing many features of the economic system and its relations with other groups. In our century everything happens as if, within the kind of society called industrial, it is politics which determines the different variations. The whole way of life in common is modified by differences in politics taken here in the sense of the party system.

2. The second meaning which I give to the primacy of politics is a human one. It is true that others might consider the volume of overall production or the allocation of resources as the fundamental phenomenon. In relation to man, politics is more important than economics, by definition, because politics is concerned more directly with the very meaning of existence. The philosophers have always thought that human life is made up of human relationships. To live as a human being is to live with other men. The relationship between men is the fundamental feature of every community. But, then, the constitution of authority affects more directly ways of life than any other aspect of society.

Let us be quite clear. Politics in a restricted sense, that is the particular sector in which the governors are chosen and act, does not determine all the interactions of men in the community. There are relations between individuals in the family, in the churches, at work, which are not determined by the constitution of authority in the particular sector which we call politics. However, even if we do not agree with the Greek philosophers who held that human life is essentially politics, it remains true that the way in which authority is exercised, the method by which leaders are selected, contributes more than any other institution to mould personal relations. And, in the measure in which the style of these relations is the very definition of human existence, politics is nearer to what should engage above all the interest of the philosopher or of the sociologist than any other sector to the community.

The primacy of which I have spoken is then a strictly limited one. It is not in any degree a question of causal primacy. Many economic phenomena can influence the form taken by the constitution of public powers in a given society. I do not claim that the public powers determine the economy without being determined themselves. Any notion of unilateral determinism, I repeat, is meaningless. I do not mean to say that we should be more interested in the party struggle or parliamentary life than we are in family life or in the churches. Various aspects of social life are more or less interesting according to whether the observer is more or less interested in them. It is doubtful whether even philosophy is able to establish a scale between the aspects of social reality.

But it remains true that the social sector which, in a restricted meaning, is called political is the sector in which those who rule and the procedures by which they rule are chosen. It follows that this sector of social life reveals to us the human or inhuman character of the whole community.

We thus come back to the proposition which is at the root of all political philosophies. The philosophers of the past, when they thought about politics, were actually convinced that the constitution of authority was identical with the essence of the community. This conviction is itself based on two propositions: there is no society without a constituted authority; this can be judged by whether or not the conduct of social relations is humane or not. Men are only human if they obey and rule humanely. When Rousseau elaborated the theory of the *Social Contract*, he discovered simultaneously the theoretical genesis of the community and the legitimate source of power. The link between the legitimacy of authority and the basis of the community is a feature of the greater part of the political philosophies of the past. The idea is still relevant today.

The aim of these lectures will not be to develop a theory of legitimate authority or the conditions in which the exercise of authority is humane, but to study the particular sector of the community known as political in the strict meaning of the term. We shall try to understand simultaneously the influence of politics on the whole community, the dialectic of the limited and of the overall meaning of politics on the plane of causal relations and on the plane of essential features of collective life. My aim will not only be to describe the differences between multi-party regimes and the one-party regime, but to trace the consequences of the fundamental choices implied by the essence of each regime. In other words, I shall try to study the particular system which is called politics to see to what extent the philosophers of the past were right to state that the fundamental characteristic of communities is the constitution of power.

CHAPTER TWO

FROM PHILOSOPHY TO POLITICAL SOCIOLOGY

What does the sociological as distinct from the philosophical or juridical study of political systems mean? The usual answer runs something like this: philosophy studies political systems in order to assess their individual merits; it tries to determine either the best regime, or the legitimacy of each regime or of all regimes; in any case, it aims at setting up norms, while sociology is essentially a factual study, which lays no claim to value judgments. Juridical study concentrates its attention and interest on the constitution itself; for example, the jurist seeks to find out how under the British, French or American constitutions, governments are elected, laws enacted, decisions taken. The jurist concentrates upon the problem of the correlation of any given event to constitutional laws; was the law declaring a State of Emergency of March 1933 in conformity with the Constitution of the Weimar republic? Was the vote in the French parliament in June 1940 giving full powers to Marshal Pétain in conformity with the French constitution or not? To be sure, juridical study does not confine itself to the formal analysis of texts but also examines the way in which constitutional rules are or are not applied at a given moment in a given country. Nevertheless, its main interest remains the rules of the constitutional game, as they are laid down by the documents. On the other hand, sociology takes the rules of the game as one element among many; it is equally interested in the parties and the pressure groups, in the recruitment of politicians and in the way in which parliament works. The sociologist analyses the rules of the political game without giving more weight to the constitutional rules than to the unwritten ones which govern behaviour inside the parties and between the parties, while the lawyer begins by specifying what is laid down by the constitution and goes on to observe the way in which the constitution, in its strict meaning, is observed.

These two answers which try to differentiate political sociology from philosophy and from law are not false, but they are superficial. I should like, in the course of this lecture, to go into the specificity of what sociology really is.

This piece of research can be justified by two observations. Sociologists are hardly ever neutral; most of them are not content to study the way in which political systems work. They presuppose that we are unable to decide which is the best regime and what principle is in the end valid. They nearly always have a philosophy, either sociological dogmatism or historical relativism.

There are no examples of a political philosophy which does not carry with it the sociological element; all the great political philosophers have based their choice of the best regime on an analysis either of human nature, or of the way the different systems which they can see function. What remains therefore is to know how the actual study, as it is practised by the philosophers, differs from the actual study as it is practised by the sociologists, if indeed there is a difference between the two.

Let us start from Aristotle and his *Politics*, the author and the book which has played the most momentous role and has had the most pervasive influence on the history of western thought. Aristotle's *Politics* has for centuries been at the same time both political philosophy and political sociology. This august book, which still today is worth studying profoundly, does not only deal with simple value judgments but is also a bold analysis of facts. Aristotle collected extensive evidence on the constitutions of the Greek city states: he tried to describe these constitutions (not in the contemporary meaning of the word constitution, which is a written document, but using the word to mean regime) and to analyse the way in which the regime of the Greek cities worked. Once this comparative study was done, he established the well-known categories of the three basic systems of government: monarchy, in which the sovereign power is vested in one person, oligarchy in which it is vested in more than one person and democracy in which the sovereign power is vested in all the people. He added to this classification the antithesis of healthy and corrupted forms, and finally he studied mixed forms.

Such an inquiry is, in the exact meaning of the term, sociological. In particular, the chapter on revolutions is still today a model of sociological analysis. Nothing interested Aristotle more than the two questions: how does a regime maintain itself in power? and how does a regime change or how is it overthrown? The scholar's duty is to advise the statesman. Aristotle's *Politics* gives the leaders of every regime advice on how best to preserve the existing regime. In the chapter in which Aristotle shows tyrants the way in which tyranny can be safeguarded, is to be found the anticipation of Machiavelli's famous book *The Prince*. As a tyrannical regime is an evil, the methods necessary to its preservation will resemble the regime, that is they too will be evil and immoral.

Aristotle's *Politics* is not purely and simply sociology, it is also a philosophy. The study of different regimes, of the way they function, of the methods they use to maintain themselves in power and of the way in which they are overthrown is centred round a fundamental question which is in itself a philosophical one: which is the best system? Now the search for the best system is *essentially* philosophical, because it amounts to discarding in advance the arguments according to which all regimes, however different, would be interchangeable, and could not be ranged in order of values. According to Aristotle, the quest for the best system of government is legitimate because there exists a purpose in human nature. The word *nature* does not mean simply the way in which men behave individually or collectively, but also the end to which men are destined. If one subscribes to a finalistic conception of human nature and admits that human life has a purpose, it is legitimate to ask the question as to what the best system of government is.

Furthermore, according to the current interpretation of Aristotle's *Politics*, the distinction between the three fundamental regimes has a suprahistorical value and is applicable to all systems at all times; the distinction between the three regimes not only holds good for the Greek city states in a given social framework, but is universally valid and presupposes that the principle behind every category is the number of those who hold the sovereign power.

These three ideas in Aristotle's political philosophy have in the course of history been abandoned one after the other. Nothing remains of them today when we who are sociologists, too, are examining anew the problem of political regimes.

Let us take first the third proposition, that of determining the universal value of the categories of political systems according to the numbers of sovereign power-holders.

The classic question of 'Who is in command?' having thus been put at the centre, it receives by the same token three replies and three replies only. It is with *L'Esprit des Lois* that one sees most clearly when the universal validity of the categories of regimes according to numbers – one, many, all – was abandoned. Montesquieu, too, lays down categories of political regimes: republicanism, monarchy and despotism; but at once a fundamental difference appears. Each of these regimes, according to Montesquieu, is characterized by a *social type*. Montesquieu held to Aristotle's idea that the nature of a regime depends on those who hold sovereign power. A republic is the regime in which all the people or some of the people hold sovereign power; monarchy is the system in which a single individual governs, according to established laws; lastly, despotism is the regime in which a single individual governs, but arbitrarily without any laws and rules. The result of this is that the three kinds of government are not definitely and exclusively defined by the number of power-holders. There is no difference between monarchy and despotism concerning the number of those who hold sovereign power; sovereignty is vested in a single individual both in a monarchy and in a despotism. Here the categories presuppose a second criterion: Is sovereign power exercised according to established laws or without any rules and laws? The regime is based either on honour or on fear, according to whether it is legal or illegal.

Montesquieu goes further and says clearly that he took as the model for his republic the city states of antiquity, for his monarchy, the modern kingdoms of Europe and for his model despotisms the Asiatic empires: he adds that every one of these regimes appeared in conditions which were economically, socially and, as we would say today, demographically determined. A republic is only possible in small cities; a monarchy based on honour is the regime characteristic of medium sized states. When states become too big despotism becomes almost inevitable. Montesquieu's category of regimes carries with it a twofold contrast. First, the contrast between moderate and despotic systems, or, again, between regimes in which the law is respected and arbitrary systems: on the one hand, republics and monarchies and, on the other, despotism. Then, opposition between the republic on one hand, and monarchy and despotism on the other. But in the end these two contrasting forms are resolved by a dialectic which runs more or less as follows: the first kind of regime, which can be democratic or aristocratic, is that in which the people as a whole possess sovereign power. Its essence is equality of the citizens, its principle, virtue. Then there comes a regime, the monarchy, which is the negation of republican equality; monarchy is based on the inequality of classes and persons; it is in the measure in which each individual is linked to his order and does all that honour demands of him that the monarchy is stable and prospers. We pass from republican equality to the inequality of aristocracies within the European monarchies. As for despotism, in one way it brings us back to equality. In a despotic regime, a single person governs; as he possesses absolute power and is above the law, only he alone is secure. All men live in fear and at the same time all men from the top to the foot of the ladder are brought back to equality, but instead of this being the equality of free men it is the equality of men who live in fear. Let us take an example which will offend no one; let us say that during the last months of Hitler's regime no one was protected by the fact that he was near the top man; to a certain extent the danger grew as one rose in the hierarchy.

Such categories preserve part of Aristotle's conception: the key question is to know how many men possess sovereign power. But this question is no longer exclusive because, to use sociological language, a second variable is added, that of the way in which power is exercised and whether it conforms to the law or is arbitrary. Furthermore, the method of government cannot be considered as an abstraction made up of economic and social organizations. The categories of political regimes entail, at the same time the categories of societies, but a method of government is linked to an economic and social framework and cannot be separated from it.

From the example of Montesquieu we draw, if not a conclusion, then at least a question: if we try to establish categories of political regimes, will they be valid only in connection with a certain economic and social framework or for all ages? In fact, I shall be cautious here and confine myself to outlining a classification of political regimes and limit its application to modern industrial societies.

Montesquieu does not ask, at least not explicitly, what the best system is, as does Aristotle. He observes two kinds of moderate regimes, republic and monarchy, and he states that the principle, that is the attitude which maintained and gave life to both regimes, was in the first case virtue, the feeling of equality and obedience to the laws, and in the second honour, that is to say, that every one respected what his social position demanded of him. We cannot assert at first sight that one of these two principles is more valuable than the other, for aristocratic honour has its own merits.

In the most general terms, from the moment when the political regime is linked with a social framework, the diversity of social frameworks, both possible and real, seems to discourage in advance the abstract search for the best regime. The recognition of the multiplicity of social systems and principles seems to sweep aside the search for the best regime, by the simple fact that it rejects the finalist conception of human nature. This in the past was indispensable, if the question of which was the best regime was to have any meaning.

Why did the question about the best regime disappear simultaneously with the finalist interpretation of human nature?

We shall find the answer by referring to another of the great political authors. Hobbes had a strictly mechanistic conception of the universe: man is defined by desire, the will to save his life and to enjoy it; his behaviour is governed by interest.

Such a conception excludes the question of what is the best regime, unless one begins by deciding what is the supreme goal towards which the strictly mechanistic man is striving.

According to Hobbes, such a simple, prosaic goal exists; it is survival. Men, being the playthings of their passions, are enemies if they do not obey a common law. From this springs Hobbes' central problem: what should be the kind of regime which would ensure peace between men? Instead of the question: which is the best regime given the finality of human nature? his theory puts the question: man's behaviour being what it is what should the state be in order to ensure security and to free men from the danger of violent death?

In such a philosophy, the question of the extension of sovereignty arises. With what should power be endowed to enable it to prevent civil war? In the finalist conception, the question was of the kind of sovereign which should be found so that men could live virtuously.

A mechanistic view of human nature does not imply a doctrine of absolute and unlimited sovereignty.

Another philosopher, who lived a generation before Hobbes, chose the same starting point, but arrived at a different conclusion. Men, according to Spinoza, are torn by their passions; left to themselves they are enemies because they are not reasonable and each one wishes to triumph over the other. Therefore, a sovereign power must be created which will impose peace among the citizens by promulgating laws. But whereas Hobbes, who feared that without unlimited authority there would be civil war, concentrated almost exclusively on allotting to the sovereign sufficient power to enforce peace in any circumstances, Spinoza wanted to limit the power of the sovereign so that the peace could be the peace of free men and the philosophers would be respected.

A last phase in the dissolution of the traditional political philosophy is marked by what is called indiscriminately historical philosophy or sociological philosophy.

Philosophies of history or sociology such as those of Marx or of Auguste Comte, for example, have in common the subordination of the political problem to the socio-economic one. Sociology, one can say, was founded in the nineteenth century by reversing the traditional primacy of the political regime over the economic and social structure. Marx was aware of this reversal and of its import.

For him, the fundamental questions were: How is production organized? What are the relations between classes? As for the political system, an analysis of the economic structure would explain it also.

This conception, which subordinates political regimes to economic and social structures, is threatened by the swing of the pendulum between integral relativism and dogmatism, which justifies fanaticism. The proof of this swing is to be found in the use of the word historicism (or historism). These words are used sometimes to express different meanings and sometimes identical ones, and they are common to German as well as English and French. They describe, accordingly, doctrines which are apparently antithetic.

When Professor Popper of the London School of Economics wrote his book *The Poverty of Historicism* he put forward an interpretation of history according to which one could, by using deterministic methods, foresee the regime of the future (and this inevitable regime of the future represented for some an end of history). But historicism is sometimes used for an apparently opposed conception according to which, throughout the ages, economic, social and political systems succeed one another, each one being unique and irreplaceable. Professor Meinecke's book, which is now out of print, *The Formation of Historicism*,[1] puts forward a way of defining historicism which differs from that of Professor Popper. According to Meinecke, historicism is defined by the recognition of the plurality of economic, political and social regimes and by the affirmation of the equal value of these regimes: according to the well-known phrase of a German historian 'every age belongs directly to God'.

It is not difficult to reconcile these two apparently opposed meanings. In Marx's philosophy, we see the transition from integral relativism to historical dogmatism. Let us take the usual interpretation of the Marxist theory of politics and of political regimes. Every society hitherto has been characterized by the class struggle; in all societies there has been a class which governed and a class which is governed, a dominating and dominated class, an exploiting and an exploited class. In all societies, the State has been the instrument which has helped the dominant class to exploit the dominated one. The state therefore is simply the tool by which one class exploits another. If all societies fit into this pattern, we slide towards integral relativism because there is no reason why one regime should be preferable to another. If, at one particular date or in a given foreseeable economic or social regime, opposition between the exploiting and the exploited class is to disappear, there will no longer be rival classes, and together with social homogeneity, a completely sound regime will appear.

It is enough to say that all systems, *with one exception*, justify a pessimistic conception of the social organization; they only have to be on the verge of relativism to fall back into dogmatism. But this dogmatism is easy to avoid: it is only needful for the so-called socialist system to present the same characteristics as those of its predecessors, that in the socialist system there should

[1] *Die Entstehung des Historismus.*

be an exploiting and an exploited class and that the State should be the instrument with the help of which the ruling class maintains its domination over the exploited classes. Thus one emerges from dogmatism and returns to relativism.

This dialogue which I am reconstructing is not imaginary. One can even say that it was Pareto's reply to Marx. Pareto was content to reply: Marx was right, in everything with one exception. He was absolutely right about the past and present systems, but he cherished illusions about the systems of the future. He imagined that the class struggle, the exploitation of some classes by other classes which he so sharply perceived, would disappear with the coming of socialism. But the class struggle, far from disappearing at a given stage in the evolution, will continue for as long as we can foresee. Marx held that exploitation would disappear at the same time as the State disappeared, stating in principle that the State only existed in order to maintain the domination of one class over another. Pareto confined his reply to going back again to regimes of the past.

The main problem is not that of knowing how wealth is distributed among the members of a community: this distribution is much the same in all known societies. The real question is one of knowing who governs, and it is a question which will be asked in the future as well as in the past and present. Pareto introduced simple categories of political regimes, not according to the number of power-holders, but based on the psycho-social character of the power-holders and the way in which they exercise power. Some of those who govern resemble lions, others foxes (especially those who use cunning, that is, in word and speculation). This contrast between lions and foxes is drawn from the past; it is drawn from Machiavelli (Pareto draws freely on Machiavelli). Such categories do not eliminate differences between regimes according to the character of the men who wield power and the kind of methods used by both kinds. But all regimes have in common certain features which in the end make them more or less the same or at least make nonsense of the question of which is the best regime.

All regimes are essentially defined by the struggle for power and by the fact that a small number of men exercise power. What is politics? The struggle for power and the benefits which power brings with it. The struggle is permanent. Pareto would agree, following Hobbes and Spinoza, that the struggle is permanent because each man wishes to be the first and it is impossible for all men to reach this goal. Or, again, he would have said that men wish to obtain for themselves the benefits which go with authority: but it is impossible for them all to possess authority and its attendant benefits. What remains of the ideas and the philosophies is no more than a construction of arguments which are at bottom interchangeable. When this is so actual politics is reduced to a struggle between men for power and profits, and the science of politics becomes, in the words of an American sociologist, Who gets What, When, How. We have come to what today is called Machiavellian philosophy, the last stage in the dissolution of classical philosophy or of the moral conception of politics.

Within such a philosophy, ideas and justifications remain, but they are at the mercy of the will to power. The merits of a political *formula* do not lie in its worth or in its truth, but in its usefulness. Ideas are merely weapons, methods of combat used by men engaged in the battle; but in battle the only goal is to win.

Such an interpretation of politics would seem to be the basis of completely objective sociology, because it begins by eliminating any reference to universal values. In reality this sociology, sometimes called objective, implies a philosophy which is just as open to discussion as the finalist philosophy of human nature with which we began. This cynical philosophy of politics, under the pretext of not being a philosophy, puts forward a certain philosophy. Instead of a philosophy of sense it puts forward a philosophy of nonsense according to which the meaning of politics is the struggle and not the search for a justified authority. But the denial of meaning is no more objective or scientifically demonstrable than the affirmation. To decree that man is a futile plaything of his passions is no less philosophical than to give a meaning to human existence.

Political sociology, as I would practise it, is not linked to a finalist conception of human nature which implies the choice of the best regime to suit men's purpose, but neither is it linked to Machiavellian or historical philosophy. Machiavellianism which sees the essence of politics in the simple struggle for power is a biased philosophy, which tends to contradict itself as do all sceptical philosophies.

To sum up, here are some presuppositions of the method which I shall adopt:

1. I shall try to define political regimes as we can observe them

in modern industrial societies, without stating that the categories of these regimes are valid for societies of a different type. I do not exclude the possibility that universally valid categories can be found; certain concepts can be applied to political regimes which are the superstructures of extremely diverse societies, but as a starting point I shall confine myself to drawing up categories of the political regimes of industrial societies.

2. The political problem appears to me to be defined by one question. The fact is that today we have different objectives; we seek for values which are not necessarily contradictory, but nor are they necessarily in agreement. For example, we are anxious to establish a *legitimate* regime, that is, one which conforms to the idea which we have of what authority should be, but at the same time we ask how the system can be organized *effectively*. It did not seem to me to be proved before, and it does not appear to me proved after, having studied the question, that a regime can be the best from both points of view. A political regime can be better from one point of view and worse from another. All regimes are not equivalent, but our terms of reference are numerous. Nothing goes to prove that we can come to an unequivocal conclusion when we compare regimes.

3. The sociologist does not appear to me to be doomed either to cynicism or to dogmatism. He does not necessarily become a cynic because the political or moral ideas which he calls upon in judging political regimes are part of reality itself. The great illusion of cynical thought, obsessed by the struggle for power, consists in neglecting another aspect of reality; the search for *legitimate* power, for recognized authority, for the *best* regime. Men have never thought of politics as exclusively defined by the struggle for power. Anyone who does not see that there is a 'struggle for power' element is naive; anyone who sees nothing but this aspect is a false realist. The reality which we study is a human one. Part of this human reality is the question relating to the legitimacy of authority.

The result of this rebuttal of Machiavellian cynicism is not that we are capable of defining, once and for all, the best regime. It may be that the question is in itself meaningless. What is necessary for political sociology, as I try to practise it, is that the *plurality* of regimes, of values and of political institutions should not be *incoherent*. To this end, it suffices that different political institutions should appear as the answers to a permanent problem. The problem which is always set, as a political one, is how can *authority* and *obedience* be justified at the same time. Hobbes has justified obedience admirably by stressing the dark side of human nature. Thus, the power accorded to those who govern finds a basis. But it is not right to justify every kind of obedience, every kind of power. Can it be possible to justify at the same time obedience and refusal to obey, authority and the limits of authority? This is the eternal political problem to which all regimes are the ever-imperfect solutions.

CHAPTER THREE

DIMENSIONS OF THE POLITICAL ORDER

In the preceding chapter, I have followed the transition from the philosophical quest for the best regime to the sociological study of regimes in their reality and diversity. My reasons for believing that the search for the best, abstract and universal regime does not lead anywhere are the following four.

1. It is doubtful whether the best regime can be determined by ignoring the way society is run: it is possible that the best regime can be defined only for a certain kind of social organization.

2. The notion of the best regime is linked to a finalistic conception of the human race. If one holds a deterministic conception of human nature, then one tries to find out which institutions are the best, the most suitable for the normal, spontaneous behaviour of men.

3. The objectives of political regimes are multiple and they are not necessarily in accord. The regime which grants the largest margin of freedom to the citizen is not always the most efficient. The regime based on the consent of the governed does not always give the power-holders sufficient room for manœuvre.

4. Finally, it is generally recognized that at a certain practical level, political institutions inevitably vary. The question of the best regime can be put only at a high, abstract level; in every society, the institutions must be adapted to the peculiarities of a specific historic constellation.

At the same time, we have tried to warn against the danger of a false positivism which does not distinguish between the sociological study of the political regimes and the adoption of a cynical political philosophy. I mean by a cynical political philosophy one which takes the struggle for power and for the spoils which power brings for the essence or the sole reality of politics. The struggle for power exists at least potentially in all known regimes. But the sociologist should not confuse objective study with a cynical philosophy.

First of all, if he takes it for granted that politics can be defined exclusively by the struggle for power, he will lose sight of the meaning which men themselves give to politics. Then, the sociologist who endorses a cynical political philosophy is led either to a pure and simple relativism, according to which all regimes are, as it were, interchangeable or, as is more often the case, he is led to an implicit conception of the best regime based on the notion of power. The best regime would be that which gives power to one or another kind of individual; hence, inevitably, in a philosophy of this kind, the swing between scepticism and fanaticism.

What we are saying here is not that the sociologist can solve in general terms the political problem as set by men (and men set it by giving a meaning to the notion of legitimate government, or of the best government), but that the sociologist must *understand the internal logic of the political institutions.* Political institutions are not an accidental juxtaposition of practices. Every political regime contains a minimum of unity and of meaning which the sociologist must uncover.

The political regime is formed by a given sector of the community, the sector which has the distinctive characteristic of ruling the whole. One can therefore conceptualize the political reality by using either specific notions of the political order or vast and vague notions of philosophy. Neither the juridical nor the philosophical concept answers to the needs of sociological interpretation.

The juridical concept with the help of which more often than not we try to understand the political order is that of sovereignty. This concept is applied to the holders of the legitimate authority who, it is clear, have the right to rule. But it is applied in two different ways. Indeed, he who possesses legitimate authority is the bearer of sovereignty, but he is not always the holder of the real power. Suppose in fact that a contemporary political regime is founded on the sovereignty of the people. It is obvious that a very numerous people has never governed itself. The people, the number of individuals who form any given community, is incapable of exercising all the functions of government.

The well-known saying 'government of the people, by the people, for the people' presupposes that the holder of legitimate authority and the holder of the real power are one and the same. But in a complex community, as are all modern societies, one must distinguish between the juridically legitimate source of authority and the holder of real power. Even in the smaller communities, where the assembly of citizens was in fact the highest institution, a distinction was drawn between the legitimate bearers of sovereignty and those who wielded one or another function of authority. This distinction is explicitly made by Aristotle.

When we come to modern societies, sovereignty is only a legal fiction. Is the people sovereign? This formula can be accepted equally by western regimes, by fascist regimes or by communist regimes. In fact, there is not a single contemporary regime which would not claim one way or another that it is based on popular sovereignty. The difference lies in the political or juridical procedures by which this legitimate authority is transmitted from the abstract people to real men. In the ideology of fascist regimes the genuine will of the people expresses itself only through the intermediary of a man, the Führer or of a Party. In the ideology of communist regimes, the legitimate authority expresses the will of the proletariat and this has as its organ the Communist Party. As for western regimes, they maintain that, the people being sovereign, the citizen should be free to choose between candidates for the exercise of power. In other words, what makes the difference between regimes are the procedures by which political leaders are chosen, the ways in which those who hold real power are appointed and the modalities which run between the fiction of sovereignty and the reality of power.

For the sociologist, the theory of sovereignty is not without meaning, but he is less interested in the juridical principle of sovereignty than in procedures by which authority, vested in theory in the people or in a class, is transmitted to a minority which exercises it in reality. It goes almost without saying that in complex and highly populated societies government is ultimately for the people and not by the people.

At the other extreme, political regimes can be defined by

notions such as liberty, equality and fraternity. Some students seem to believe that the sociological problem of democracy lies in finding out which regimes bring with them equality and which liberty. I would like to suggest briefly why such concepts cannot define the political regimes of our time.

We all know that there is no modern society in which individuals are equal from an economic point of view; hence, what does the equality of citizens mean? Generally speaking, it means two things: either a share in sovereignty, that is the right to vote, or equality before the law. In most modern societies, these two forms of equality simultaneously obtain; the citizens are equal before the law and possess identical political rights, because they are all entitled to choose their representatives.

These two forms of equality do not exclude forms of social and economic inequality. As we know from numerous examples universal suffrage does not always permit the citizen really to choose his representative, even if the vote is genuine. Or again, the citizen does not get the impression that he holds power simply because he votes every four or five years. If democracy is defined exclusively or mainly by universal suffrage, this is tantamount to admitting a discrepancy between the institutions of eighteenth-century Britain, where the right to vote was restricted to a small minority, and the institutions of today. In the same vein, one could add that a society in which women do not have the right to vote falls short of the first principle of democracy. Yet between the institutions of the aristocratic England of the eighteenth century and the institutions of the democratic England of today one sees continuity and many similarities, in spite of the past inequality before the electoral law.

Freedom is an even more ambiguous concept. A linguist would say that one can speak of freedoms but that the conception of freedom can be found only in a metaphysical choice. If indeed only the man who is not prevented by someone else or by social circumstances from performing an action is free, then nobody is either free or totally deprived of freedom. The margin of choice or of initiative given to the individual varies from society to society, and also from class to class within the same society.

Can we say that political freedom is defined by specific rights which are themselves guaranteed by institutions? If so, it is true to say that the rules of *habeas corpus*, universal suffrage, freedom of speech and of expression are the content of freedom. But this conception in fact implies, in the world of today, a political stance.

Indeed the Marxist-Leninists consider that these freedoms are mere formalities and that it is necessary to sacrifice them in order to obtain the freedom which they call real. What meaning can it have to take part in elections, if the elections are manipulated by trusts or by all-powerful minorities? What good is the right of free discussion to the unemployed or even to the industrial worker who is bound to a monotonous job which has been decided upon by those far above him?

Besides, it is a fact that the feeling of being free is not necessarily linked with the institutions which we in the west consider essential to political freedom. The worker who joins the Communist Party considers himself oppressed and exploited under western regimes and imagines that he would be free (or that he would have the feeling of being free) in a Soviet-type regime.

In other words, either one should surreptitiously infiltrate a philosophy through the adopted definition of freedom or one should acknowledge the ambiguity between what societies and what individuals mean by freedom.

I shall discard therefore for the time being the juridical conceptualization involving sovereignty and the philosophical conceptualization involving liberty and equality. The sociological theory of political regimes lays the stress on institutions and not on the justifications for or the ideas invoked by the institutions. The sociological theory is more relevant to the reality than to the idea.

What does one mean by reality? First and simply, the political realities which we all know, which we observe daily, elections, parliaments, the laws, the decrees; in other words all the procedures by which the legitimate holders of authority are actually chosen and by which these holders of authority exercise power.

Our task is to discover what is characteristic in each regime, what is essential to the regime at the institutional level.

One sociological theory follows the tradition of Montesquieu, who tried to define political regimes by combining a small number of variables. The variables by which he determined the essence of political regimes were, as we have seen, the number of holders of sovereign authority, the moderate or immoderate way in which authority is exercised and the psychological attitude which is considered to be fundamental to each regime and again the behaviour which is specifically adapted to each regime and without which the regime would be distorted. Over and above this theory of variables, Montesquieu established a relation between the political regime and the other sectors of the community.

What Montesquieu tried to do for the types of regime which he found in history, we shall try to do for the specific regimes of industrial societies. But in order to discover the essential variables of each regime we shall first have to discover which are the functions which can be found in all political orders.

The two aims of any policy, according to the philosophers, were internal peace and the defence of the community against other communities. The first aim of any political order is to see that men live in peace, to prevent violence from erupting between the citizens. From this, we immediately draw what Max Weber held to be the very definition of the state, to wit, the monopoly of the legitimate use of violence. In order that men shall not kill one another the state and the state alone must have the right to use force. The moment that particular groups within the community arrogate to themselves the right to use violence, peace is in danger. It is easy enough today to grasp the import of this general proposition. Special groups exist today in France which set up clandestine courts, which pronounce death sentences and carry them out; I am thinking of the North African minorities who, for political reasons which are not for us to judge, themselves carry out justice. When we say that the main characteristic of political power is the fact that it retains for itself the monopoly of the legitimate use of violence, we are trying to exclude precisely this kind of eventuality. In general, in communities which are thought of as civilized this monopoly is to be found, but often small groups claim to set up rival powers. What we call the underworld, which gangster novels describe so imaginatively, consists of small groups which do not respect the state-controlled monopoly of the legitimate use of violence.

If this is the first function of political power, it can be deduced that the sovereign power, as such, commands the armed forces, that is in modern societies, the police and the army. To present the sovereign as the chief of police is not to enhance his dignity or his prestige. The police should enjoy the respect of the citizens, because the police, as a body, has the legal right to the monopoly of the use of violence. No one else, in the community should use physical violence. To restrict the right to use violence to a particular body is a triumph of political civilization. Nothing is more admirable, nothing is more symbolic of the achievement of political civilization than the English custom by which the police is unarmed. Here we have come, so to speak, to the last stage of dialectic: the citizens are first thought to be dangerous to one another, hence the creation of the police, which is armed to prevent them from murdering each other; when pacification in the true meaning of the word has reached the final stages, then the police which symbolizes the legitimate use of violence does not even need to carry arms, the physical instruments of violence. French society has not yet reached this final stage. As for the armed forces, in states with a police force, they are designed only to defend the community against external enemies. Within the community, only the police can intervene.

The police, which prevents the citizens from fighting, can only intervene as the rules or the laws demand. This gives rise to another aspect of the political functions; to establish rules or laws regulating the relations of individuals. It is easy to enumerate the many different kinds of laws about exchanges, property, trade, production, which lay down what each one has the right to do or is bound to refrain from doing. Political power in some respects lays down the rules of existence in the community: at all events, it guarantees that the rules are respected.

Decisions relating to relations with other communities clearly are dependent on the sovereign power. It is impossible to adopt once and for all a permanent attitude towards foreign countries. Change is the essence of diplomacy. Even within the life of the community, the laws in certain domains cannot lay down in advance what must be done at a given moment. To understand this idea, we need only think of fiscal legislation. By definition, the state is obliged to draw upon the income of individuals in order to pay for the collective tasks for which it is responsible. In modern societies, the needs of the state change often because of changing circumstances. The taxing of part of the income of individuals is no longer simply a way of furnishing the state with the means to carry out certain services. The taxation of private income plays a part in the regulation of the functioning of the economy. According to whether there is inflation or deflation taxation will be heavier or lighter.

The sovereign, who brings peace, fixes the rules governing individual activities and takes internal and external decisions, needs the assent of the governed. This is not a question of a function in addition to those which we have just examined, but of an essential aspect of every political order. Every regime must exact obedience. The governed must accept it as it is: furthermore the regime must have the consensus of the governed for the particular measures which it takes. We can imagine a country in which the vast majority of the citizens accept the regime and do not accept the particular measures taken by the legitimate authorities. Possibly France represents a case of this not inconceivable paradox. Nothing is easier than for a citizen to say: I accept a regime under which the authorities are chosen by election but these people (whom I have chosen) are the 'lowest of the low'. A combination of respect for the system and disrespect for the men chosen according to the constitution is psychologically possible.

We have thus found three essential functions of the modern political order. The first, which I shall call administrative, tends to ensure peace between the citizens and respect for the laws. The second which takes in the legislative and the executive functions in the ordinary meaning of the word carries with it the conduct of relations with other communities, the decisions by which the laws are framed, promulgated or modified and, lastly, the measures which must be taken by individuals, according to circumstances. But as these individual decisions concern the whole, the regime must justify itself by being considered legitimate and winning the loyalty of the people. This is not all. Every regime bringing with it organization of authority and of relations between the people, must be represented by its own picture of itself. Every regime puts forward a goal in the moral or human order which the citizens must accept.

These functions have always been recognized by the philosophers, each of whom has laid stress on one or other of them. The philosophy of Hobbes is based on his obsession with civil peace. Having lived through a revolution, he was ready to subordinate all other conceivable advantages to the supreme advantage of peace among the people. Rousseau considered that the essential was to establish a legitimate authority because this, in his eyes, could only emanate from the consensus of the citizens. The *Social Contract* is, in its deepest meaning, an exposé of the conditions in which power is legitimate, that is based on the assent of or expressing the will of the citizens. As for Marxism, it subordinates not only civil peace, but also the legitimacy of power to a final end. It holds that the regime which brings us near to the end of prehistory, the suppression of classes, is legitimate in our time.

The ideal regime would be clearly one which would reconcile these different needs. Hitherto, they have seldom been reconciled. The particular regime which in our time wishes to bring about the classless society arrogates to itself the right to sacrifice the consent of the governed. It is more often a conservative who sets himself the supreme goal of peace among the citizens than a reformer or a revolutionary. One could sketch a typology of political temperaments with reference to political objectives.

Let us take again the aspects of the political order which we have distinguished; the administrative aspect, the governmental aspect which includes the legislative and executive power, that is, on the one hand, the decisions which lay down the laws, on the other those which concern relations with foreign societies or the measures to be taken outside the existing laws or in conformity with them.

The contrast which leaps at once to the eye is that between the civil servant and the politician, a modern transposition of the distinction between the administrative function as we have described it and the executive and legislative functions which we have simultaneously isolated and reconciled.

Civil servants and politicians are opposed in modern societies on all grounds. The civil servant is a professional, the politician an amateur, the civil servant is selected according to strict rules, the politician is elected. Western democratic regimes are regimes of experts, ruled by amateurs. This is not a paradox; those who give orders to the civil servants and the administrators are by definition not specialists. They can, of course, understand what exactly the question they are dealing with is. The official theory of the Third Republic held that the politician need not be an expert in the technical sphere for which he was responsible, provided he was a man of general knowledge and intelligence. This is not meant ironically: it is the basis of the contrast between the administrator and the politician. In a way, civil servants are more necessary than politicians; in a regime like ours the administration must be particularly stable because the politicians so often change their governmental roles. It has often been said that the modern state is first and foremost an administrative organization. When a new state is created it is not absolutely necessary to hold elections or to elect a parliament, but it is definitely necessary to find civil servants and to establish an administration.

This does not mean that we can do without politicians, because they represent another aspect of the political order, the relation with the governed. The civil servant is competent, he knows what can be done, but he has no right to decide; by definition he is neutral. The police arrests the traitor, but who is the traitor? Is he a collaborator or a member of the Resistance? The answer is not given by the police, which simply arrests those whom the political authority tells him are traitors. Hence, the possibility, in troubled times, that the same policeman would arrest consecutively a member of the Resistance and a collaborator. Political opinion is stirred in such cases and protests, but wrongly; in normal times, the police force confines itself to the execution, according to the law, of decisions which are laid down by the current legislation. During the nineteenth century we in France went from the Empire to the monarchy, then back to the Empire, then to a monarchy, then to a second monarchy, then to a republic, then to a second empire, and yet the French civil service continued to exist. At every change of regime, a certain number of leading personalities in the administration of the civil service were changed: the higher the civil servant is in the hierarchy, the nearer he comes to politics. The administrative function, be it a police or a fiscal one, is politically neutral. It consists of applying laws which in theory the civil servants have not framed.

There must then be a different kind of man in power, defined not by his competence but by his legitimacy. The cabinet minister knows no better than the civil servants what can be done; in the majority of cases, he knows less, he does not even know better what *must* be done for the community. The politician, elected by the governed, is invested with legitimate authority and his task is to set the sights of the legislation within the regime, and even to set the sights of the regime itself. The assent of the governed takes two forms: the governed must give their assent to the measures taken within the regime; and they must give their assent to the regime and to the idea with which the latter identifies itself.

35

The politicians, working hand in hand with the civil servants, govern and are as indispensable as the latter, because the civil servants have the competence but not the legitimacy. The politicians, the cabinet ministers, fulfil a function as necessary as that of administration, because no regime can exist without communication between governed and governors.

Perhaps here one should introduce some considerations on what is traditionally called the judiciary power. The independence of the judiciary has long been considered as the sole symbol of liberal institutions. In fact, the independence of the courts in the administration of justice remains a main feature of western regimes, even when the judges have a status comparable to that of other civil servants. If here I do not give to the law the full attention which it deserves, it is because I am trying above all to find the specific features of the two types of regime and that, from this point of view, the distinction between the political and the administrative is relevant to the analysis. But the constitutional exercise of political authority, the respect for individual rights, presupposes that the civil power is subordinate to the judiciary and therefore to the courts which can apply the law. In this sense, the subordination of the police to the law and of the administration itself to the courts (that is to administrative courts) is needed if a genuinely constitutional liberal regime is to survive.

Which are the major characteristics, on the one hand, of the administrative function and, on the other, of political functions in modern societies?

At first sight, the institutions by which these two functions are exercised have evolved differently. The civil service is more complex; it stretches over ever-widening sectors of the life of the community; it covers and conditions an ever-increasing number of the predispositions of individual activities. It becomes more and more difficult to distinguish between public and private affairs. Should the nationalized enterprises, for instance, be considered as a private concern of which it happens that the community itself is legally the owner, or as an expression of the state power itself?

In any case, one can maintain the abstract distinction between the general conditions of activity imposed on individuals by legislation and the concrete activities of individuals or of public bodies. The general tendency of modern administrations to enlarge the sector for which they are responsible is however undeniable; using the terminology of German sociologists, one can say that the state and the society have a tendency to become more and more indistinguishable.

At the same time, the features of the political institutions and of their evolution are entirely different. The political system within which and by whom are chosen the holders of authority becomes more and more autonomous and circumscribed by the social environment. Traditional legitimacy bestowed power upon men who stood together at the pinnacle of the social and political hierarchy. The sovereign in the past in France was really the first man in France both through his prestige and through his authority; today, the men who provisionally hold supreme authority in a western-type regime are not by definition at the top of the social scale. A president of the council of ministers is a former secondary school master; he was elected; he became the leader of a party; for a time he possesses sovereign authority through the rules of procedure of a given sector, the political one.

In other words, one of the peculiarities of modern political regimes (especially in the West) is that the political leaders are chosen by methods which separate the political élite from other social élites. The political personnel of a democracy represents a part of the social élite (of those who are at the top of the social hierachy) but this does not mean that it is higher than the best of the industrialists, of the scientists, of the intellectuals or of the businessmen. The holders of political authority in our societies represent a special category, autonomous in relation to the other leading categories, and are recruited by procedures which bring it about that small men, small from the point of view of wealth and of prestige, sometimes hold high office.

This peculiar feature which was seldom seen in past societies known to history is explained by legitimacy. This does not originate either in tradition or in birth, but in a certain method of selection. The fiction of the people's sovereignty means that authority is legitimate in the measure in which the people have chosen the representatives. Of course, the people can choose as representatives the small as well as the great in society.

The political personnel of modern societies is 'specialized'. Societies are governed by men whose job is politics. Here again, public opinion is wrong when it uses the expression politicians,

37

that is to say professional political men, pejoratively. Our societies are actually governed by professional political men, who in most cases have gone into politics relatively early and remain there as long as possible, usually for a long time, because the longevity of politicians is a quasi-universal experience.

Finally, modern politics entails not only a permanent but, at least in the west, an open rivalry between individuals and groups. What is at stake in the political struggle is not always linked to the framework of the existing institutions and the interrelation of laws; what is at stake in the conflict is sometimes the political regime itself. Modern regimes, at least in the west, allow themselves to be called in question all the time. They allow a faction of the governed to discuss the merits of the existing order, to challenge the legitimacy of the governors, or even to recommend violent change.

The question whether democracy can be defined by the acceptance of parties which do not accept it is often asked in our university seminars. I do not pretend to give the answer at once. But the fact is that one of the peculiarities of modern regimes is the almost constant controversy both about the decisions taken by the sovereign and the way in which power is set up and founded. On the one hand, the more the administration encroaches, the more the state become indistinguishable from society: the decisions of the state influence the day to day life of the people. On the other, the political order is organized within a special sector, that of parties, of elections, of parliaments. The combination of the extension of the administration and the specialization of politics leads to quarrels not only about changes in the temporary power-holders but also about the way in which the government and society are organized.

In the west, we have witnessed the simultaneous enlargement of administrative functions as well as the specialization of political procedures; this is perhaps paradoxical. At least one other type of regime exists in Europe which, because of the responsibilities assumed by the state, refuses to call power, that is the regimes and those who embody it, in question. On the other side of the Iron Curtain, the identification of society and state is almost complete; but then, there, there is no question of discussing the principles of the regime or the legitimacy of the governors or even the wisdom of the decisions of the state.

CHAPTER FOUR

MULTIPLE AND MONOPOLISTIC PARTIES

We are trying to find a theory of the political regimes of our time. By theory I mean something other than the description of regimes as they function. A theory implies finding out the basic features from which the internal logic of each regime can afterwards be deduced.

For this purpose, we have started with functions in the most literal meaning of the term.

The administration guarantees the execution of the laws and in this sense the judiciary and the police are representatives of the administration in its negative function: to avert open clashes between the citizens, to ensure that the laws concerning private and public life are respected.

Political power, in a narrow sense, is defined by the ability to take decisions: some about foreign relations, others about matters which are not laid down by legislation (for instance, the choice of persons to be appointed to certain positions) and finally about the formulation and the modification of the laws themselves. The political or executive function in a wide and formal sense covers together what the jurists call executive and legislative functions.

These two kinds of functions are exercised in our societies by two types of men. They are embodied in two types of organizations; on the one hand, the civil servants and the bureaucracy and, on the other, the politicians and the electoral system of a parliamentary or party type. It is the politicians who in modern societies exercise the essential function: they ensure that the governed obey the decisions of the governors and link the political sub-system with the higher values of the community – values which the regime is supposed to serve.

Which of these two functions, of these two types of men, of these two kinds of organisms will help us to discover the main variable, the fundamental feature of the regime? The answer is never in doubt. It is not in the administrative order that we shall find what goes to form the specificity of each regime. The administrative function presents, of necessity, great similarities between one regime and another. If society is of a certain type, a great many administrative functions will be the same whatever the regime may be. The political system, in the strict sense of the term, determines the relations between governed and governors, establishes the way men cooperate in the running of public affairs, guides the action of the state and the governors. It is therefore the political system in the strict sense which will enable us to recognize the original traits which are characteristic of each regime.

As for the criterion of discrimination, I shall select, by a decision which the rest of this analysis will confirm, the distinction between multiple and single parties.

By the fact that more than one party has the legal right to exist, the parties inevitably compete for the exercise of power. A party has in fact as its objective not necessarily to *exercise* power but *a share in the exercise of power*. Because there are more competing parties, there must be rules by which the game is played. Therefore, a multiparty competitive regime is constitutional; the different candidates for the legal exercise of power know what means they have the right to use and what they should not use.

From the plurality of the parties, the legality of opposition can also be deduced. If several parties have the right to exist, and if they are not all in power, inevitably it follows that some of them will be in opposition. Therefore, by taking as our starting point the legal plurality of parties, we have also evoked the legality of opposition. That those who govern can be legally opposed is a relatively rare phenomenon in history, characteristic of a certain type of regime, that of the western countries. Finally, from the legality of opposition one can deduce an even more general phenomenon, which is the moderate or legal form that the exercise of authority takes in such cases. The two adjectives *legal* and *moderate* are not synonymous. One can imagine the exercise of power which conforms to laws which are not moderate, if the laws themselves are based on such discrimination between citizens that their simple application involves an element of violence (as for example in South Africa). On the other hand, illegal governments can be moderate; we have seen despots, men who govern without being subject to constitutional law, who nevertheless do not misuse their power to bring to trial and execute their adversaries. What is true is that in the measure in which legal competition between the parties for the exercise of power takes place, the exercise itself has every chance of being restricted by the existing laws and, consequently, it tends to be moderate.

Thus we come to the following definition of the regimes which are characteristic of western countries: they are regimes in which *the peaceful rivalry for the exercise of power exists constitutionally.* It is *constitutional*, whether written or not, and rules lay down the modalities of rivalry between individuals and groups for the exercise of power. In a monarchical system, competition takes place around the person of the king, for his favours, but this competition is not constitutional. In the race for places and for honours all have free rein. Competition between individuals surrounding the king is neither constitutional nor organized. One can envisage forms of competition which are organized, but not strictly speaking constitutional. Within the British parties, the competition for high office is institutionalized; nominations are made according to a constitution, although this constitution is not authorized by the state. Within the French Radical party, competition is not laid down by a constitution and is barely organized; each discovers his own road to success.

The competition is *peaceable*. The use of guns or of a *coup d'état*, a frequent phenomenon in many countries, is contrary to the essence of western regimes. In a democracy, men quarrel about how to obtain certain benefits which cannot be extended to everyone, but they do not quarrel for the sake of quarrelling and if they overstep the limits, if they violate the rules, then the regime is no longer what we call today democratic.

The *legal exercise of power* differs in nature from what we call the *seizure of power*. The exercise of power is, essentially, temporary. The man who exercises power does not believe that he is destined to hold it indefinitely. It is a seizure of power when the man who has seized it will not give it back to his unlucky rival. According to the essence of democratic competition, the man who loses once is not doomed to lose for ever. When the winner prevents the loser from running again, we leave what we in the west call democracy because we have banned opposition.

The peaceable constitution of competition for the exercise of power finds its normal expression in elections. I do not mean to say that elections alone enable the idea of the peaceable competition for the exercise of power to become a reality; after all, in the Greek city states a different method of designation held sway which, according to Aristotle, was even more democratic, and which was the drawing of lots. One can, in fact, envisage that the ultimate form of designation of the power-holders would be the drawing of lots, all the citizens being held to be interchangeable and equal. But the drawing of lots, save for particular offices, such as jury-service, for example, is inconceivable in modern societies. It is, I believe, incompatible with the nature of modern democracies which are defined by the representative principle. Theoretically, the representatives could be chosen haphazardly, but citizens in modern societies differ too profoundly from one another to accept any method other than that of election.

The reference to the *legal* exercise of power calls in question an essential idea: the essence of the regime is not limited to the *method of designation* of the holders of legitimate authority. The *method of the exercise* of power is no less important.

What is the main difficulty in a regime thus defined? Orders are given to *all* in the name of *some*. Those who govern only represent at best a majority; sometimes they represent even a minority of the voters and yet all the citizens must bow to the will of the representatives of some. Logically, it is quite easy to reconcile this and Rousseau gave us the ideal formula. He wrote: when I obey the orders of the majority even if I do not agree with them, I am obeying myself because I have chosen a regime in which the will of the majority is law. In a sort of ideal theory, this presents no difficulty: what the citizen adheres to is the legal designation of legitimate governors. The fact that the legitimate governors are today the representatives of political adversaries is only an inevitable and secondary episode which does not change the essential. The citizen respects the essence of the regime which he has chosen, when he obeys orders given by the representatives of his adversaries. But it is none the less true, when we revert to the plane of reality and of psychology, that such a regime has it as its bounden duty to maintain a certain degree of national consensus about the regime or the community's interests, without suppressing the dialogue between the parties, that is to say the permanent controversy between rival groups about what should be done.

How can this national consensus and this permanent controversy be reconciled?

There are two possible methods. The first, which is institutional, consists in taking away from the contestation of the parties a number of functions, of persons or of decisions. In some western-type regimes[1] the president of the republic or the monarch is above the party struggle. In other words, we try to embody in one man the unanimous allegiance of the governed to the regime and to the country. The monarch or the president of the republic is the expression of the whole community.

The second method, which is more difficult and effective, is so to limit the activity of the governors that no group will be tempted to rebel rather than to obey. In abstract terms, the regime which in the west is called democratic is barely possible if one does not circumscribe the sphere within which the governors are enabled to take decisions.

The opposition accepts decisions which are taken legally by the government in power, or the majority, but if a time comes when these decisions endanger its most vital interests, its very existence, will they not try to resist? There are circumstances in which a minority chooses to fight rather than to submit.

It is here that we leave behind a western democratic regime. All democracies run the risk of crossing what we may call the threshold of violence. Let us take the case of the southern states of the United States; the decisions of Congress or of the federal government on racial integration run the risk even today of bringing about a situation in which the threshold of violence is crossed: we sometimes fear that the white minority in the South will try to defend by all possible means its way of life, its interests and privileges, even at the expense of the constitution.

The smooth functioning of a western regime depends then essentially on what the competing parties propose to do. The fundamental problem of western democracy, the combination of national understanding and contestation, is easy or difficult to resolve according to the nature of the parties, the aims

[1] But not in presidential systems.

43

which they set themselves and the doctrines which they preach. Let us pass on now to the other type of regime, the one-party regime.

I am chary of giving a name to this other type of regime. It is not certain that all one-party regimes have the same common denominator. There are two vast differences between them. At all events, I do not want to load with moral and political connotations an analysis which I want to be objective.

This second type of regime is characterized by the monopoly by one party of legitimate political activity.

By legitimate political activity, I mean participation in the competition for the exercise of power; participation also in deciding upon the plan of action, the plan of running the whole community. A party which has the monopoly of political activity immediately finds itself faced with a clear and difficult problem: how is this monopoly to be justified? Why has only one group of men, and one group only, the right to participate in political life?

The justification for monopoly varies with the one-party regimes. I shall take as an example the Soviet regime, which is the purest and the most developed of the one-party regimes.

The Communist Party of the USSR offers two systems of justification: one by the idea of genuine representation and the other by historic goal.

One can hold that the choice by elections of the legitimate power-holders is false, and unjust because this choice is manipulated by social forces. In order to ensure a genuine choice, a true representation of the popular or of the proletarian will, we are told that it is necessary to have a single party. According to this method of justification, the suppression of elections is the authentic condition of representation.

The second method of justification, still combined with the first, is attached to the historical goal. According to the communists, the monopoly of political activity by one party is indispensable if the entirely new society which alone conforms to the highest values is to be created. A homogeneous society cannot be forged and social classes suppressed if the rights of the opposition are respected. When fundamental changes are desired, it is necessary to break the resistance of groups whose ideas, interests or privileges are encroached upon. Thus, if the aim of a party is the creation of a society having nothing in common with existing societies, it is normal that this party should claim the monopoly of political activity, that it should refuse to restrain in any way whatsoever its freedom of decision and of action, in order to maintain its revolutionary power intact.

When a party, and one party alone, has the monopoly of political activity, the state is indissolubly linked to it. In a multi-party regime in the west, the state boasts of not being circumscribed by the ideas of any of the competing parties; the state is neutral through the fact that it tolerates a plurality of parties. Perhaps the state is not neutral in the sense that it exacts from all parties respect for itself, that is, for its own constitution but in practice, at least in France, it does not do so. The French state recognizes the legality of parties which make no secret of their intention to violate the constitution, should the occasion present itself. The multi-party state, which is not linked to a particular party, is ideologically a party of laymen. In a one-party regime, the state is a *party-state*, inseparable from the party which monopolizes legitimate political activity. If, instead of a *state of parties*, a *party-state* exists, the state will be obliged to restrict the freedom of political discussion. Since the state presupposes as absolutely valid the ideology of the monopolistic party, it cannot officially allow this ideology to be called into question. In fact, the restriction of the freedom of political discussion varies in degree according to the regimes of a single party. But the essence of a single-party regime in which the state is defined by the ideology of the monopolistic party, is *not* to accept *all* the ideas and to prevent some ideas relating to the party from being openly debated.

The logic of this kind of regime does not lie in the exercise of power being legal and moderate. One can imagine a one-party regime in which the exercise of power is subordinate to rules or laws. At least with regard to those who do not belong to the monopolistic party, the party-state reserves for itself almost unbounded possibilities of action. Besides, if the monopoly is justified by the vastness of the revolutionary changes to be achieved, how can one ask the exercise of power to be moderate and legal? The monopoly of political activity was granted to one party precisely because the reality was so disappointing. The single party is in its reality a party of action, or better still a revolutionary party. The single-party regimes look only to the future and find their ultimate purpose not in what was or what is, but in what will be. As revolutionary regimes they carry in them an element of violence. They cannot be expected to offer what forms the main feature of multi-party regimes, that is respect for the law and for moderation and respect for the interests and the beliefs of all groups.

Are the power-holders in a single-party regime chosen according to some rules or arbitrarily? In most cases, the single-party took over the state, not according to rules, but by force: even when it conformed on the surface with constitutional rule, which is almost true of the Nazi party in 1933, it distorted its meaning almost at once by the fact that it excluded the possibility of any further genuine elections being held. Inside the party, though, was no peaceful competition such as we see in western regimes between parties possible? Could there not be an organized and peaceful competition of individuals or of factions for the exercise of power in a single party and therefore, at the same time, for the exercise of power in the party-state?

In theory, this hypothesis is reasonable and possible. There is always on paper and sometimes in fact an internal legality in the single party. The party leaders are elected; in the Polish CP the present general secretary Mr Gomulka was appointed according to the constitutional rules of the party, through a decision of the Politburo. One can therefore imagine a political regime which bans all but one party, but which does not ban opponents within the monopolistic party; a regime which entails some legality in the competition for the exercise of power within the single party. But for ever-increasing reasons, this is a rare and difficult combination.

Let us take the communist parties. They have been, and they remain, parties of action, revolutionary parties and their structure is adapted to the need for strong authority. The Russian party was formed clandestinely, according to the doctrine proposed by Lenin in 1903 in his famous booklet, *What is to be done?*; a doctrine called democratic centralism which, in practice, gives to the general staff of the party almost unconditional authority over the mass of members.

Who, in the monopolistic party, elects the power-holders? All the members? Hitherto, no monopolistic party has dared to organize elections in which the members could vote as do the voters in western democracies. Within all the parties, even when there are elections and regular elections at that, as for instance within the French Socialist Party, the secretaries of the federations and the permanent officials wield a dominating influence. The more the secretaries of the regional organizations control the votes, the more the organization of peaceful competition within the monopolistic party becomes difficult, because the local and regional bosses are appointed from above; it is the general staff, it is the general secretariat of the party which selects the office-holders of the party. There can be no freely held legal and organized competition, if the voters are not at least to some extent independent of those whom they elect. But in all single-party regimes those who should be elected, i.e. the leaders, select those who elect them, i.e. the secretaries of cells, of sections, or of federations and ultimately the leaders at all levels of the hierarchy. This kind of vicious circle in the organization of monopolistic parties does not exclude a certain legalization of the struggle for power within the party, but entails the permanent risk of the substitution of violence for legal competition. In the Russian CP a general-secretary by the fact that he appointed the regional or local leaders gained the upper hand over the apparatus in spite of the fact that in theory there are electoral procedures within the party. But this procedure has lost all substance in the same way in which the elections to the assemblies are, in a monopolistic party regime, no more than a kind of ritual collective manifestation of enthusiasm and do not contain any of the features of a western-type election.

These are, it seems to me, in a nutshell the main features of the two types of extreme regime that we can observe in our time.

I would like to apply to these two types of regime Montesquieu's conception of the *principle*. What is the principle of a pluralistic regime? What is the principle of the monopolistic party? By principle, Montesquieu means the attitude projected upon an institutional organization which answers to the needs of power in a given regime. In a pluralistic regime, the principle is a combination of the two attitudes which I would call respect for legality and the respect for and the sense of compromise. According to Montesquieu, the principle of a democracy is virtue defined by respect for the laws and by concern for legality. I shall modify

Montesquieu's conception by relating it to the new phenomena of representation and of competition between parties. To be sure, the first principle of democracy is respect for rules and laws, because, as we have seen, the essence of western democracy is legality in competition for the exercise of power. A healthy democracy is one in which the citizens show respect, not only for the constitution which lays down the conditions of political struggle, but also for all the laws which form the framework within which the activity of the individual takes place. But this respect for rules and laws is not enough – something else is needed which cannot be written in and which is not strictly confined to legality – the *sense of compromise*. The notion of compromise is difficult and ambiguous; in some languages, it is a term of praise, in others pejorative. In Germany, an unpleasant word was long used to describe political compromises: *Kühhandel*, the approximate translation of which is 'horse-trading'. The English word 'compromise' on the other hand conjures up approval or praise. After all, to accept a compromise is to recognize the partial legitimacy of the arguments on the other side and to find a solution acceptable to all.

But it is not enough to say that the principle of democracy is at the same time respect for the laws and a sense of compromise; there is a good and a bad use of compromise. The tragedy of western regimes is that in certain circumstances compromise is disastrous. Very often, compromise does not lead to a solution in the conduct of foreign policy; there is a choice between two policies, each with advantages and disadvantages, opportunities and risks. Nor does the policy of the middle way reduce the dangers. It multiplies them. Sometimes it brings the worst of both worlds. Let us take an example old enough not to fan passions: when Mussolini's Italy started the invasion of Abyssinia, France on paper had two possible policies: one was to allow Mussolini to act and the other was to prevent him from acting, even if this meant the use of force, with the realization that the inequality between the forces of Italy alone on the one hand, and those of Great Britain, France and her allies on the other put a military conflict out of the question. The policy adopted was to invoke sanctions, but sanctions ineffective enough to avoid any risk of a military reaction from Italy. The consequence, which could have been foreseen, was that Italy was angered enough by the sanctions to fall into the camp of the Axis, yet her undertaking was not hindered enough to force her to call a halt.

The good compromise is often easy in economic matters; and is widely used. But even in economic matters, there are circumstances in which compromise is not possible; 50 per cent of command economy and 50 per cent of market economy do not make an economy efficient. This is probably the key problem of our western regimes; how can the compromise which is necessary if no section of the community is to be alienated, be used without depriving the action of effectiveness? It goes without saying that there is no definitive answer to such a question; but it can be said that the pluralistic regime works well if it can provide a 'good use of compromise'.

What is the principle of the monopolistic party regime? Obviously the principle which keeps such a regime alive and flourishing cannot be respect for legality or for the spirit of compromise. In all probability, a monopolistic party regime would die if it were infected by the democratic spirit of compromise. The principle of a regime of a monopolistic party lies at the other extreme.

Trying to find which could be the answers of a disciple of Montesquieu to the question of what the principle of a monopolistic party regime is, I found, without being entirely convinced, two attitudes. The first is *faith* and the second *fear*.

To say that one of the principles of a one-party regime is faith is to repeat, in other words that the monopolistic party is a party of action, a revolutionary party. Now, on what can a revolutionary party live, if not on the faith of its members? We have seen that it justifies its monopoly by the vastness of its ambitions, the glorious character of the end towards which it is working. For the party-members and the ordinary citizens to agree to follow a revolutionary party, they must believe in its doctrine and message. But, by definition, since the party is monopolistic, as long as the society is not homogeneous, there exist actual or potential opponents, traitors, counter-revolutionaries, foreign agents (it does not matter what they are called), all those who do not accept the party's message. The stability of such a regime must withstand the scepticism or the hostility of those who do not belong to the monopolistic party. What is the state of mind of those dissidents

49

most favourable to the security of the state? Fear. Those who do not believe in the official doctrine of the state must be convinced of their own impotence. Maurice Barrès, a little more than half a century ago, used a particularly unpleasant formula which ran something as follows: the social order is based on the awareness which the people have of their own impotence. Let us say, modifying Barrès's formula, that the solidity of the regimes of a monopolistic party demands, as well as faith and the enthusiasm of the faithful, the awareness that the unbelievers have and should have of their own impotence.

The unbelievers' feeling of impotence can be accompanied by resignation, by indifference, by fear, but the fear is necessary and inevitable. A revolutionary party, whether of 1789, or 1917 or of 1933 (for all revolutionary parties have certain features in common) cannot arouse the enthusiasm of a minority without frightening those who do not share this enthusiasm. A revolutionary party gives rise to violent feelings. If you do not share the enthusiasm which animates and spreads it, at least you should be silenced.

I have tried in this analysis to bring out some features of opposing regimes, starting from one variable taken as decisive. This deduction, starting from the natue of the regimes, has been possible because political systems are not a simple juxtaposition of institutions; they have an internal logic. This is a legitimate method, provided that it is not pushed too far. In this analysis, I am not trying to describe all the diverse, specific features of these systems; I am trying to outline an abstract type. Fortunately or unfortunately, the systems do not entirely realize their essences. Moreover, starting from one major variable, a great variety of institutions is conceivable. Everything, in a monopolistic party system, cannot be deduced from the monopoly of political action accorded to a single party; different kinds of single-party regimes exist in the same way as diferent kinds of multiple party systems do. What justifies the choice of the major variable is that this enables us to rediscover many of the important features and above all what is *essential*.

Starting from the notion of the unity or of the plurality of parties we have found the legitimizing formula specific to each regime, the style of allegiance to the state and to the government, the freedoms possible within each type, and the *principle* of the regime in Montesquieu's meaning of the term.

Political systems have a coherence and they become intelligible when that coherence is fully understood.

CHAPTER FIVE

THE MAIN VARIABLE

In the previous chapter I described two ideal types of political regimes, starting with the notion of the monopolistic party on one side and of peaceable and organized competition between several parties on the other. I described a regime in which precise rules lay down the conditions in which the governors are chosen and power is exercised. But I also described how one party, claiming the monopoly of political activity, can have as an objective the revolutionary transformation of society and, in the name of this vocation, exercise absolute authority lawfully, at least according to its doctrine. I specified equally that this is a question of two ideal types and not one of categories of political regimes. I should like, starting from these two ideal types, to outline possible categories of different political regimes in contemporary societies and to go on to justify the choice of the plurality of parties or of the single-party as a criterion.

In each of these ideal types, I have combined several variables. In the ideal type of the multiparty regime, I have brought in simultaneously the plurality of parties, constitutional rules about the choice of those who govern, the constitutional character of the exercise of authority. The characteristics are not necessarily linked. We can distinguish between regimes by showing how it is possible to separate their characteristics. The same method can be used with regard to the ideal type of regime ruled by the monopolistic party.

Lastly, we shall try to discover if there is not, as well as multiparty regimes and regimes of the monopolistic party, a third type of regime without party. The hypothesis, be it true or false, is reasonable. A few days ago I asked a Soviet sociologist the following question: In the communist regime of the future will there be one or more parties? He answered: Neither, there will be no party. In a sort of ideal representation, a third kind of regime is conceivable in the far-distant future.

Today I shall move backwards, and I shall start with regimes of a monopolistic party.

The ideal type of such a regime demands a perfect party, in the sense of the totalitarian will, animated by an ideology (I call ideology here an overall representation of the historical world, of the past, the present and the future, of what is and of what must be). This party wishes to bring about a complete transformation of society so that society conforms to the demands of its ideology. The monopolistic party nourishes vast ambitions. Ultimately, the representation of the future society implies an identity of the society and the state. The ideal society is classless, the non-differentiation between social groups implies that each individual should, at least in his work, be an integral part of the state. There is, thus, a multiplicity of phenomena which together define the totalitarian type; the monopoly of politics by one party, the will to stamp the whole of the community with the imprint of the official ideology, and lastly the effort radically to remake the society, so that the result will be in the end unity of the society and of the state.

I have chosen the 'perfect' party: in fact there have been, and there still are, parties which claim a monopoly of political activity and which do not take ideology so seriously or else have an ideology with more limited ambitions. Thus, there appears a second category of regimes of the monopolistic party. Let us take the case, for example, of the Fascist Party which retained for itself the monopoly of political activity, but which did not have an all-embracing ideology. Many activities were held to fall outside the ideological realm. The Fascist Party did not want from the first to overthrow the social order; what was essential in fascist ideology was the affirmation of the authority of the state, of the necessity for a strong state. During one phase, the conception of the strong state was combined with a leaning towards a liberal economy. A monopolistic party, with an ideology which differentiates between secular and sacred activities, between personal and collective activities and the state, does not go so far nor does it use such

53

violent methods, nor does it arouse the same degree of enthusiasm and of fear.

In the third kind of regime, the monopolistic party thinks of itself as provisional, charged with the task of bringing about a revolutionary change, but it accepts that, once this has been done, there should be a reconstitution of multiple parties or at least of a regime of electoral legality. We know of an example of this regime, of a single-party with a pluralist inclination – Turkey. Under the leadership of Kemal Ataturk one party made a revolution and from the ruins of the Ottoman empire erected a national state with separation of church and state. For a long time, the revolutionary party monopolized political activity; then, after the war, elections were announced and it was proclaimed, amidst general scepticism, that they would free. This scepticism was groundless, because the party gave proof of its sincerity by losing the elections. The result of the first free elections was that the opposition, the Democratic Party, came to power and remained there by means of elections; the authenticity of these elections was not demonstrated with the same certainty, because they were won by the party in power. The Democratic Party was afterwards overthrown by a military *coup d'état*, but the plurality of parties continued to exist.

One could ask whether, by definition, all regimes of the monopolistic party are not, according to their own doctrine, provisional? Because the parties are revolutionary, they proclaim that the task which they must accomplish will not continue indefinitely. As revolutionary parties, they must transform society, but once this transformation has been brought about, a new phase opens. I shall not push this reasoning too far; it would be only too easy to invoke the formula: 'Il n'y a que le provisoire qui dure' ('The provisional alone endures'). Orthodox communists do not say that the one-party regime is definitive, but that the definitive regime can be seen far off on the horizon. Furthermore, national socialism or fascism were authoritarian regimes *in the name of a principle of authority* when they arrogated to themselves the monopoly of political activity, but they invoked for doing so the legitimacy of this very monopoly. In contrast, the monopoly of political activity in communist regimes is held to be legitimate only because it has a task to fulfil.

I shall not go into the question of whether all monopolistic party regimes are essentially transitional parties. Let us say for the moment that one can distinguish between the different kinds of monopolistic party regimes according to the nature of their doctrine, the scope of their projects, the violence of their methods and the ideal image of the society which they want to create. The categories of single-party regimes divide themselves according to the respective degree of totalitarianism, which is itself measured by the more or less all-embracing character of the ideology and the more or less perfect identification of state and society.

Let us now take the possible and real kinds of multi-party regimes. In the ideal type, which I have constructed, there were many parties, authority was exercised according to constitutional rules, and all the citizens shared in the electoral competition which was observed with all fairness. We do not need much imagination, only a little observation, to realize that these different characteristics do not always occur together. Multi-party regimes with authoritarian intermediaries exist, for example, in South America; these are multi-party regimes in which the electoral competition is distorted by various kinds of governmental pressure; multi-party regimes in which a part of the population is outlawed and does not take any real part in the electoral competition. There is genuine electoral competition between the Whites in South Africa, but the Negroes do not share in it; the electoral competition is genuine in the southern states of the United States, but, through various procedures, many of the negro voters are barred from competing. When they are not legally barred, they are often able to exercise their rights only with difficulty. In certain, apparently multi-party, regimes plurality is a fiction. Multiple parties in such regimes conceal in reality a single leadership; the same is true of the popular democratic regime, in eastern Europe, but also of certain under-developed countries, in which the parties represent groups which are almost indistinguishable one from the other and are ultimately manipulated by a few tribal chiefs, great landowners and governors.

In abstract terms, one can distinguish three kinds of flaws which can mar the ideal type of multi-party regime. First: the regular non-application of electoral legitimacy, either through the exclusion of some of the voters, or by the manipulation of elections.

Then, the customary non-application of the rules of peaceful competition either between parties or in parliament. Lastly, the non-representative character of the parties; when these parties only represent a small minority of the people, communication between the social groups and the parties which claim to represent them is broken.

Let us now say a few words about the third kind of regime, in which we find neither a single party nor multiple parties, which have neither electoral legitimacy nor revolutionary legitimacy. These regimes, without parties, exact a kind of 'depolitization' of the governed. In France, we have experienced an attempt at this kind of order: the Vichy regime in its first phase, which could not be defined either by a single-party (there was none) or by multiple parties, which had almost completely disappeared. Those who governed widely repeated the words of Charles Maurras that the habit of the French people of voicing their opinion on all subjects must be done away with. The legitimacy resembled that of a good father, of an enlightened despot, surrounded by councillors, but not subject to the likes and dislikes of the governed. This non-politized authoritarian government could only have existed in France in the exceptional conditions of the occupation.

It is possible that such regimes can exist in our time, but hitherto they have hardly ever appeared in fully industrialized countries. They are only to be found in countries on the fringes of industrial civilization. The Portuguese regime is a case in point; elections are held from time to time, with a list approved by the government and a list of a timid opposition, but the regime does not rely upon a party of continued and intense activity. The government created a representation of the country, in an Assembly or a party, but what we can call a party in Portugal bears little resemblance to parties in democratic countries, even moderate ones. The guiding idea is to reserve for the governors, who are implied to be those most fitted to judge, the monopoly of decisions and political thought. Neither is the regime of General Franco in Spain a single-party regime, comparable to the national-socialist or fascist model. Nor is it a multi-party regime: it is authoritarian in the name of the idea which it has of Spain and of the doctrine of legitimacy which it preaches. It accepts organized groups but none of them, the Falange, the church nor the trade unions, is considered as the exclusive mainstay of the state.

If this analysis, brief as it is, is correct, an objection can be raised which has a bearing upon the method which I have followed; which was to start with two ideal types and then to establish a differentiation between the species within the types. Were we right to take as a starting point the notion of a single party or of multiple parties? After all, the parties are only one institution among many, they are not even an official institution in the French or English constitutions, which do not explicitly recognize them. The parties are a social reality in the limited sphere of competition which has for stake and for result the appointment of those who govern. Is it possible to reconstruct the ideal types of political regime in our time starting with a fact which is not even written into the constitution? I would like to justify my choice and thus to limit the scope of the categories which I have established.

I have chosen this criterion and contrasted monopolistic and multi-party regimes because this contrast is offered to me by the history which we live. The fact is that the contrast which seems to dominate Europe today is that between regimes in which a single revolutionary party claims the monopoly of political activity and multi-party regimes which accept the rules of peaceful competition. Furthermore, we were able to see in Hungary at the end of 1956 that the overthrow of a single-party regime immediately gave rise to the multiplicity of parties. It is thus a question of an alternative which we have seen in operation.

Parties are essential if one function common to all political regimes is to be fulfilled: the choice of those who govern. Traditional legitimacy, that which is founded on birthrights or on the past, disappears; the principle of legitimacy which nearly all contemporary regimes lay claim to is the democratic one. They repeat that power derives from the people; sovereignty resides in the people. Hence, what is above all important, in an age in which democratic sovereignty is taken for granted, is the *institutional modality of the implementation of the democratic principle*. A single party and multiple parties symbolize two characteristic modalities of the institutional implementation of the idea of popular sovereignty.

I had a second reason for my choice, drawn from the history of political ideas. Classic philosophy has always established categories of regimes according to the number of holders of sovereignty: monarchy – one man alone is sovereign; oligarchy – several; democracy – all of the people. At the final reckoning, I have intentionally transposed the arithmetical fiction. We cannot define the political regimes of our time by the fact that they are monarchical, aristocratic or democratic (the British regime is at once monarchical, because there is a queen, aristocratic because many of those who govern are drawn from a restricted class, democratic because everyone has a vote). It has thus seemed to me convenient to take up again the antithesis one-many and instead of applying it to the holders of sovereignty to apply it to the parties.

In one sense, this transposal is surprising since the party does not exist officially in the constitutions, but this does not mean that it is meaningless. The parties are in some ways the agents of political life; it is within the parties that the fight for the highest office takes place; it is through the parties that one arrives at power. Thus, in asking the question: are there one or more parties? I am applying to modern political life a classic proposition in the philosophy of the past.

Montesquieu recognized in his time the appearance of a new phenomenon, which was fundamental in relation to traditional philosophy, that of *representation*. He understood the importance of representation; the holder, formal and theoretical, of sovereignty was no longer identical with the real holder. When the Greeks spoke of democracy, the people actually exercised power. The assembly of the people took decisions. To be sure, the agents of execution, those who implemented the decisions, the officials, in certain political or military circumstances, were in command, but the holder of sovereignty was no less capable of exercising it effectively. From the time when the phenomenon of representation intervened, the theoretical holder of sovereignty no longer actually ruled. By the same token, the phenomenon of parties became essential since the unity or the plurality of parties determined the modality of the representation.

Yet another reason justifies this method. In the Soviet Union, we pass from one man to collective leadership and we return from collective to one man leadership without observing any essential changes in the regime. By contrast, the transition from the single party to multiple parties would entail a fundamental change. It seems to me, thus, that the phenomenon of the unity or of the plurality of the parties, the institutional implementation of the principle of representation is at least *one* of the essential aspects of modern societies.

I should like to add one final reason. The parties are the active element in politics; it is between the parties or within them that the political game is played and that the conflicts take place. One of the main features of modern systems is that conflict within them is seen as normal. Constitutional regimes accept the competition between individuals and groups for the choice of governor and even for the way the community is run. To adopt as a criterion the unity or the plurality of parties amounts to considering the *basic rules of the party struggle as specific to the political regimes of our time.*

This being said, I should like to pause a moment at the objection which could be raised by the categories of political regimes of modern societies proposed by Eric Weil in his *Philosophie politique.*

According to Weil, there are ultimately only two kinds of governments of modern states which he calls *autocratic* and *constitutional.* 'One speaks of autocratic government,' he says, 'where the government deliberates, decides and acts alone, without any other mandatory intervention on the part of other institutions, and thus defines the conditions of the validity of the acts of the government.'

In other words, this is the decisive criterion of the constitutional use of authority: there are on one side regimes in which the decisions taken by the governments are immediately valid, and on the other there are regimes in which if a governmental decision is to be valid, fixed precise rules must be established.

In order to discuss this opposition, which I do not intend to argue (for it seems to me acceptable on the philosophical plane of Eric Weil's work), we must study, even if summarily, the relations between *plurality of the parties, electoral legitimacy* and *constitutionality of the exercise of power.*

Historically, the essential phenomenon has been the gradual evolution towards constitutional forms, of systems which were originally authoritarian. The political struggle, for several centuries, has had as its stake the establishment of constitutional rules, designed to limit the arbitrariness of monarchical governments. This struggle broke out in England; it caused a revolution and gave rise to philosophical arguments which were centred on the concept of sovereignty; what are the respective rights of the monarch and of the assembly? Has the monarch alone the right to take certain decisions? The outcome has been the establishment of rules according to which decisions must be taken and the necessary intervention of other instances, for example Parliament, so that taxation may be legal.

Moreover, I shall add that power can be or could have been used constitutionally without multiple parties or democratization. In England, in the past, the government was constitutional although the right to vote was limited to a small minority and there were no parties taking part in electoral competition among the masses. A legal form of administrative action and a constitutional form of decisions of the executive power does not necessarily imply either universal suffrage or the establishment of multiparties.

Democratization, in the form of the extension of the right to vote and of the creation of parties followed in England upon the constitutional evolution of the exercise of power. The fundamental difference between political evolution in Britain and in France lies in the different relation between these two phenomena. The constitutional use of power in Britain came before democratization; in France it was delayed by revolutionary attempts at democratization.

The French Revolution tried first to introduce the equivalent of a constitution such as was already to be seen in Britain; with elections, a representative assembly, to lay down the precise laws by the power of which the king would be compelled to collaborate with the representatives of the people. Soon the constitutions were carried away by the storm and what followed was a succession of governments – republican, revolutionary, imperial – in which the exercise of power was arbitrary or despotic, but which claimed democratic legitimacy. The French liberals of the nineteenth century pondered constantly over the difference between the political evolution of Britain and that of France. In their eyes, the misfortune of France was to have first tried to create a republic or a democracy, instead of imposing the constitutional procedures which are necessary to safeguard freedom. Looking at the destiny of the two countries, they thought that the British had reached their aim, a constitutional regime and personal liberty, without revolution (the revolution took place in the seventeenth century) whereas France, invoking democracy and a republic, passed from crisis to crisis without reaching the same goal.

As for the past, it is undoubtedly true that monarchical regimes have managed to arrive at constitutional practice without mass political parties, such as we know them today, and without universal suffrage.

If we look back into history, the fundamental opposition is perhaps to be found between constitutional and autocratic regimes. On the philosophical plane, Eric Weil is possibly right. But if we try to carry out a sociological analysis of the types of political regime, the use of the constitution as a criterion presents difficulties.

The constitutional orderliness of the exercise of power is a matter of degree. All regimes imply legal rules, according to which the decisions of the government must be taken. The Soviet Union has a constitution, of which the government takes little account, but in the west, too, constitutions are from time to time distorted or manipulated.

Autocratic regimes, as Weil defines them, embrace simultaneously the traditional pre-democratic regimes and the authoritarian or totalitarian post-democratic regimes, contemporary with multi-party regimes. Must a regime of the traditional kind, such as those of Portugal or Spain, and a basically revolutionary and modern regime, like the Nazi or communist ones, be placed in the same category? They have some features in common, such as the denial of constitutional rules[1] for the exercise of power, but historically, sociologically, they are regimes which do not belong to the same type.

In contrasting constitutional with non-constitutional regimes, we at once make a philosophical choice between two kinds of regime. If single-party regimes are by their nature non-constitutional, the essential feature of the modern regime being constitutionality, then non-constitutional regimes are either leftovers from the past or temporary expedients. Such an interpretation rejects, from the outset, the ideological system on which the regime of the monopolistic party is based. On the sociological plane, we ought not to choose a criterion of classification which eliminates beforehand the justification which a regime gives to itself. Such a classification, according to Eric Weil, gives an unequivocal definition of the specific characteristics of the modern state.

---

[1] Even this statement is arguable in the case of Spain and Portugal.

Thus, the classification of regimes into autocratic and constitutional ones begs the question which is set in our times: the problem of the contrast between the total state and the limited state, of the identification or lack of identification of the society with the state. In Weil's political philosophy, the contrast between a planned economy and a market economy plays no part. No decisive importance attaches to the alternative of a society left to itself and separate from the state and a state which wishes to encompass the whole of society. I do not say that he is wrong on any of these points. These explanations tend to suggest that the distinction between the two types of political regime, based on the party system, was justified as one possible method among others. This choice begs the question which the classification by the antithesis of the constitutional and the non-constitutional regime answers in advance.

To finish let us think for a moment about the ultimate meaning of the contrast between multi-party and one-party regimes.

To choose this criterion is to consider that modern political regimes are characterized by the *modality of the party struggle*. Modern societies, we saw when we studied social groups,[1] are necessarily divided into classes or layers. They are not homogeneous; individuals organize themselves into subgroups inside the community and these subgroups compete over the distribution of the national income, over the hierarchy of incomes, for the idea they have of the community itself, for the establishment of one political regime rather than another.

Once the heterogeneous industrial society with multiple groups has been accepted, the meaning of the contrast between multiple parties and single parties becomes clear. There are two extreme ways in which this inevitable struggle can be organized.

The first is the open organization of the competition through the freedom given to pressure groups to manifest themselves, to political groups to form in order to win votes and come to power. In multi-party regimes, power in general is used in a constitutional manner. It is the combination of the plurality of parties and constitutional procedures which reveals the fundamental problems facing the regimes. The multi-party regimes derive from constitutional or liberal regimes; they wish to uphold liberal values in

[1] *La lutte des classes.*

democratic politics. Power must be exercised according to the rules, individual rights must be respected and those who hold power must have enough authority to act effectively.

The fundamental dialectic of the multi-party regimes is that of liberalism and democracy, of democracy and efficiency. We shall try to understand the fundamental problem of the multi-party regimes, which is dependent on the double tension between constitution and democracy, democracy and efficiency.

As far as one-party regimes are concerned, it is also by starting from the monopoly of the party that we can understand the problems which confront them. Either the single party does not have an ideology and it is a question then of a minority which holds power, forbidding those whom they govern to debate the problems of government; or it is a question of a single party, armed with an ideology, with the will radically to transform the whole society. But a party which justifies the exclusion of other parties by its will to revolution is faced with an alternative: either permanent revolution or, if it renounces permanent revolution, traditional stabilization or technocracy. The Nazi regime did not last long enough to come up against this alternative, the communist regime has lasted long enough to recognize it. In the present phase, and I do not know how it will be answered, the question arises: either the party must justify itself through a permanent revolution or else, its work being far enough advanced, it must agree to a pause and, thus, to the gradual re-establishment of the constitutionality of power. Is the gradual introduction of constitutionality compatible with the monopoly of the party?

In Poland, we have seen the beginning of this evolution. There the exercise of power within the framework of a single party has had to submit to rules. It is one possible modality. It is enough that the electoral rules should be respected within the party, that the rules for the exercise of power be imposed on the leaders of the party for us to have both the single party and constitutionality of power. But on the day when this happens, how will the monopoly of the party be justified? And if there are several groups freely competing within the party, why can they not be called parties?

In multi-party systems, the effectiveness of the state and the respect for the laws amidst the tumult of passions and competing interests must be safeguarded. In a single-party regime, the monopoly of the power by a minority must be permanently justified. Starting from this, I do not pretend that we perceive the essential *sub specie aeternitatis* of the political regimes in our time. But perhaps one can detect the dialectic appropriate to each type of regime, and perhaps one can also interpret intelligibly the dialogue between regimes whose rivalry characterizes an epoch.

PART TWO

CONSTITUTIONAL-PLURALISTIC
REGIMES

CHAPTER SIX

ANALYSIS OF THE MAIN VARIABLES

In this second part, I shall study western democratic regimes, or, as I prefer to call them, constitutional-pluralistic regimes.

The study of this subject presents us with an initial difficulty. These regimes are made up of many different institutions, practices and customs; it is therefore almost impossible to establish categories of the main kinds. Monopolistic regimes can be distinguished by the ideology and the objectives of the single party, by the methods it uses and the kind of society it wants to create. On the other hand, the diversity of constitutional-pluralistic regimes is so startling that one wonders which institutional peculiarities may be singled out to help to define the category.

All constitutional-pluralistic regimes, of course, have rules according to which those who govern must collaborate with other bodies, and conditions in which the people have the right to protest against the decisions of the administration or the government. But the combination of this fundamental identity and this diversity of institutions lends itself with difficulty to the identification of the category. In this chapter I should like to explain why this is so.

At the same time, I shall indicate the possible comparisons between different examples of pluralistic regimes. In doing so, I shall take the opportunity to review the main variables which we have to use in order to understand both the fundamental problems of these regimes and the actual regimes which we shall analyse in more detail.

Generally speaking, the description of constitutional-pluralistic regimes is made up of four main aspects:

1. The political system must be considered as being a special social system, from elections right up to the decisions taken by the government, including the structure of the parties, the functioning of the assemblies and the selection of ministers.

2. The political system is related to what can be called the social *infrastructure*. The exercise of power or decision-making depends on social groups, on their interests, their rivalry, their ambitions, their possible agreement and their permanent rivalry.

3. Our analysis must comprise the administration or the bureaucracy for it is at once the agent by which the decisions taken by the government are implemented, the government's technical adviser, and a body indispensable to the functioning of private activities.

4. Then we must study what I shall call, for want of a better expression, the historical environment of the political system. Every political system is in fact influenced, if not determined, by an accumulation of traditions, values, ways of thought and of action, peculiar to each country.

It goes without saying that these four aspects can only be separated in theory and not in practice. The way a particular parliament functions depends on the electoral and constitutional laws (this is part of the first rubric when describing a political regime), but the political struggle in parliament cannot be explained by reference to the rivalry of social groups outside the political system in the strict sense of the term. Furthermore, ministers are advised by the permanent administrative body. In fact, the methods of parliament are not decided exclusively by what is set down in the constitution, but are influenced by the idea the politicians have of what they have the right to do and what they do not have the right to do. An American sociologist has related the modalities of parliamentary competition in France to the modalities of competition in primary, secondary or higher education. There is, in France, a style of parliamentary battle which is to be found again in some ways in the scholastic jousts, in the universities, journalism and elsewhere. Every country has its own style; that of the United States is violent and friendly; that of the British moderate, aristocratic and formidable.

Political science studies the political system as it is; it tries to isolate the organs and the functions of the political system. I am going to run through the main variables.

The first, which at the moment is of most concern to constitutional lawyers, is the *constitution* itself, as laid down by a fundamental law and as it is observed by politicians.

A distinction is often drawn between the presidential and the parliamentary type of constitution. These two types, in almost their purest form, are to be found, on the one hand, in the United States and, on the other, in Great Britain.

The American system is defined by the separate election of the executive power, embodied in the president of the United States, and of the legislative power, represented by two assemblies, the House of Representatives and the Senate.

The President is elected by universal suffrage in two degrees, since, according to the constitution, the voters only elect those who will elect the president. Although we are now used to thinking that universal suffrage decides directly the choice of the president, according to the constitution, it is the presidential electors who are chosen on election day. In practice, the mandate which the vast majority of presidential electors receives is binding; it is agreed in advance for which candidate each of them will vote.

Consequently, provided that there is an absolute majority for one of the two candidates, the election of the president is assured from the moment the ordinary citizens vote. In the case in which neither of the two candidates obtains an absolute majority among the presidential electors, the House of Representatives will elect the president (most probably the candidate who has gathered most votes in the presidential elections). In practice, at present, the election is the equivalent of direct universal suffrage, in spite of the two degrees laid down by the constitution, but, on the other hand, there are two other degrees anterior to those in the constitution which are of real importance. In fact the American presidential candidates are elected through party *conventions*, the members of which are appointed or elected by methods which vary from state to state. Whatever the complication of these practices may be, the system finally ends in the choice of the holder of the executive power by all the people.

The president of the United States can only exercise his authority in agreement with the assemblies, the House of Representatives and the Senate. Yet the president's party in the United States does not necessarily have the majority in Congress. For the system to function, a Republican president must be able to co-operate with a Senate in which the majority party is Democratic. As for the ministers, they are chosen from men outside congress by the president and are answerable to himself. These appointments must in some cases be ratified by the Senate.

In Britain, the government, according to the constitution as it operates today, is the representative of the majority in the House of Commons. With two parties, the government relies on the majority of members, and the American combination, in which the president does not belong to the party which has the majority in the two houses, is impossible.

Both these systems entail, in the present state of affairs, two parties, although there are great differences between the British and the American parties. The two British parties are under party discipline; Conservative members when the whips give the order can only vote for the Conservative government; under the American system, the parties are not disciplined and the president usually governs with a majority of his own party and a minority belonging to the opposition party.

In the first case, discipline is the moral rule and in the other, there is a moral rule that a member votes according to his conscience and not according to party necessities.

These two examples present us with forms of constitution which are both akin and opposed. In both cases, several bodies must cooperate. We are told that in the United States there is separation of powers, which is in one sense true. The supreme executive, the president, is chosen in a different way from the holder of legislative power, the House of Representatives and the Senate. But if the system is to work, there must be cooperation between the president and congress. In the same way, the British system implies permanent cooperation between the government and the House of Commons. In both systems, power is limited because it is divided between a number of bodies. In the words of Montesquieu, 'power checks power'. The president of the United States disposes of very wide powers; he has a certain freedom in the conduct of foreign policy, but to declare war or to sign peace the approval of Congress is needed. At the same time, the two systems work in such a way that decisions can be taken; the aim of a consitutional regime is to limit power, not to paralyse it. In the American system, the president has the right to choose his advisers and to conduct foreign affairs. In the British system, the government relies on a parliamentary majority which usually approves its proposals and acts, until a time comes when such is the indignation that the prime minister is overthrown by his own party. Sometimes the members of the majority party would prefer to have new elections in order to approve measures decided upon by the government. Finally, in both systems the judiciary is independent, the citizen having the right to defend himself against administrative or governmental arbitrariness.

From the point of view of constitutional organization, one can therefore retain these two ideal types of presidential and of parliamentary government and believe that all the other constitutions of pluralistic regimes resemble one or the other of these two prototypes.

But the distinction between constitutions does not give, at the same time, categories of types of regime. The British and the American are more akin than the French parliamentary government and the British. The French system, in which the constitution is not so very different from the British, works in an entirely different way. Our system entails several, and not just two, parties. The British system lends great stability to the executive and the French great instability; across the channel, the electoral law, which is very simple, has not changed since the beginning. There is only one ballot and the candidate who wins the most votes is elected. France probably holds the world record, not only for constitutional changes, but for changes in the electoral laws.

Hence, if we were to classify constitutional-pluralistic regimes solely according to the differences between parliamentary-presidential types we would place in the same category regimes which, in practice, are essentially different. Constitutional distinctions, which are valid on the juridical plane, and are even sociologically useful to point the direction in which pure constitutional types are possible, are not sufficient for drawing the categories of the different kinds of regime.

The second variable in the political system is that of parties. Parties are, to use the simplest definition *'voluntary groups, some more organized and some less, which claim in the name of a certain idea of the common interest and of society to assume, alone or in coalition, the functions of government'*.

This definition brings the parties back to their objective. A party is a group of men who wish to perform the functions of government and who, consequently, must do their utmost to succeed, which means to win the maximum number of members in the assemblies and the maximum number of ministers in the cabinet. It is a voluntary grouping because in constitutional systems no one is forced to join a party. The vast majority of people in constitutional-pluralistic regimes do not belong to any party (the same holds good for single-party regimes).

It is not easy to apply this definition to monopolistic parties, once they are in power. The party, as we know it in the United States, in Britain and in France is, by its very nature, in competition with other parties. From the moment that there are no more rivals, its nature changes.

I have not used the word power or influence to define the party's objective. The professional trade unions undoubtedly want to influence the decisions of the government. They are not, however, made up of parties, according to our definition, because their aim is not to form a government. The old Maritime and Colonial League was not a party, even although it wanted to spread knowledge of the sea and of the empire. Neither is the League for the Welfare and Renewal of French Algeria a party; it is a voluntary grouping which aims at influencing the people and the government, but not at taking power. The exact definition of party must take into account the intention of its members.

These categories of parties are drawn from the sociology of Max Weber. Two ideal types, are situated between two extremes; on the one hand the organized mass party and, on the other, the parliamentary group.

The organized mass party is represented by the German Social Democratic party as it existed from the end of the nineteenth century until Hitler seized power. It included a great many (hundreds of thousands) members and received millions of votes in elections; its members, those who supported it and voted for it, were permanently organized into sections and federations and they obeyed a constitution which presides over the life of the party. The party endowed itself with a permanent bureaucracy which resembled those of great business concerns. In this way, the same members were both officials and party leaders.

At the other extreme, some members who have ideals or ambitions in common join together to have their own representatives in parliamentary commissions or to put forward candidates in the case of elections by common lists. The French Radical Socialist Party was an example of this type, in contrast to the organized mass party.

These two types are not mutually exclusive. Some organized mass parties are not bureaucratic in style. The party leaders are not permanent officials of the organization, but personalities or politicians who, thanks to their social position or to their parliamentary activities, have forged ahead. In Britain, the two large parties are admirably organized; they have features in common, yet the Conservative Party is profoundly different from the pre-First World War German Social Democratic Party.

As for the parties which are less well organized, they form a great number of variations; for example, in France they range from the Socialist Party to the independents and the radicals, passing through the MRP and the UDSR. The party which, leaving aside the Communist Party, bears most resemblance to the mass organized party is the Socialist Party. The SFIO has a constitution, full-time members, the sections meet regularly, delegate some members to regional congresses and others to national congresses. We can study the written constitution of the Socialist Party in the same way as we study the written constitution of the Fourth Republic. Fundamentally, they are the same kind of party; with the same organic law by which the party leaders are chosen and they themselves take decisions. The constitution can be manipulated just as the constitution of the French Republic can be manipulated. It is possible to study exactly how a party interprets its constitution just as one analyses the way in which the constitution in a republic works.

The sociology of parties which is to be found in most books derives from Maurice Duverger, who applies it to different parties in different countries. Duverger traces the birth and death of parties, describes the internal organization of each of them, shows how party constitutions are interpreted, manipulated, respected or violated. He tries to discover how authority is shared within each party and to compare the party system from one country to another.

Here again, partial comparisons are permissible. The two types of party system most often seen are the bipartite system and the multi-party system. This distinction, which is permissible, does not give us categories of kinds of regimes. In fact, multi-party systems can function in the same way as the British two-party system. On the other hand, two-party systems can function in quite a different way from the British one. The party system is one of the important variables, the consequences of which must be analysed in order to understand how a political regime functions; it is not an efficient enough variable to give us the key to categories of kinds of pluralistic regimes.

The third variable, within the political system, is the way the regime functions which, in its turn, is subdivided into three sectors, one can almost say into three stages, of a part of the electoral law and the elections, according to how the parliament works, i.e. relations between the assemblies and the governments.

The study of elections has been one of the most popular subjects in political science simply because it is one of the easiest. The study is quantitative, dealing with figures and comparing them. Note is made of how voters vote, according to country, circumstances, regions; thanks to scientific, sociological methods, relations between types of men, social position and ways of voting can be established. A vast amount has been written on the electoral results since the beginning of the Third Republic.

The second aspect of the way in which a regime works, that of discussing how parliament itself works, has been neglected because it is more difficult in that it does not end in a mass of figures. By this I mean the relations between the members of parliament themselves within the assembly, the way in which they cooperate and compete; how do they work together? In Britain there is a path to office and each member is more or less sure of his due – the straiter the path to office, the more ambitions are confined. The French case[1] is once more at the other extreme; one could say, with only slight exaggeration, that many of the deputies can lay claim to many of the honours. In any case, no deputy knows for certain what is beyond his reach. Do not let us exaggerate: in the French parliament there is also a path to office. No one can become president of the council without having spent several years in parliament, but from the Third to the Fourth Republic the path to office has acquired an additional suppleness and flexibility. Pessimistic theoreticians would say that this is a change for the worse; as man is by nature ambitious, a good constitution must set bounds to his ambitions.

[1] It must be remembered that we are speaking only of the Fourth Republic.

The relations between the government and the assemblies are laid down by law in the constitution or the regulations of the assembly. In fact, these relations vary and are different in each country according to the moment, the strength and prestige of the executive, the personality of the president of the council. Even in France, which is governed by what is wrongly known as a system of assemblies, many of the vitally important decisions are taken by the ministers without the approval of or consultation with parliament, and such governments – as for example those of Clemenceau or of Mendès-France – reduce the Chamber more or less permanently to the role of legislation or of approval.

A fourth variable, now in fashion, is what are called 'pressure groups'.

Pressure groups are organizations which try to influence public opinion, the administration or those who govern, but without assuming the functions of government. The trade unions are pressure groups, the unions of beet producers or the milk producers are also pressure groups. Whatever may be said to the contrary, pressure groups conform to the nature of constitutional-pluralistic regimes. It is impossible for the interests of the employers or of the workers not to be ventilated, not to find expression and to defend themselves; if once one agrees that the regime itself should be called in question, how can one not agree to question particular decisions relating to prices and to the allocation of the national income? How can the representatives of special collective interests be denied the right to put their case to those who govern?

The pressure groups are today a special study because of the dislike which they engender and because it is difficult to identify them. Parties work in the light of day. Of course, most socialist voters do not really know how the majority of mandates is decided at a socialist party congress, but the socialist party is visible, public, with its own newspapers, its representatives; it fights in the open. Pressure groups are little known or badly understood; they act in the corridors and it is always possible to think that from the shadows they exert undue influence. Of course they are influential. The problem, which we will study later, is to know what are the limits of this influence.

I would like, then, to say a word about the last political variable – a variable which is implied by all the foregoing and which concerns

75

the men who take a leading part in the regime, in short the minority which Mosca called the political class and is better named the political personnel. Who are the men who make policy? Who succeeds in so doing? This is a very absorbing piece of research which will try to explain the success of politicians with the reputation of being second-rate, until they have actually reached the first rank. Why have some men with remarkable reputations never succeeded in breaking through? What are the qualities which assure success in a given regime at a given time? In England before 1939, it was widely said that Winston Churchill was too intelligent to become prime minister, unless war broke out. This was only a witticism, but one with serious undertones; who are the men who are accepted as leaders in a particular regime, in peacetime and on the other hand in periods of crisis?

I shall pass more quickly over the three other aspects of the description.

Some think that the social structure provides a principle of classification. The Marxist-influenced sociologist would perhaps say that the study of the political system is secondary, that class relationships must be studied in order to discover the elements of a particular political system.

It goes without saying that the social infrastructure is not unrelated to the functioning of the political regime. It is common knowledge that one of the factors which decides the choice of the electors is precisely the economic-social position of the voters. Proportionately, there are more people who vote for the socialist and communist parties among the workers than among the non-workers; the structure of a society is revealed by the party system. The social origin and the economic conditions of the politicians are one of the factors in their behaviour, but the social classes, as such, are not the political actors. A social class has never appeared to be animated by a precise will, unless in the form of a party; yet, a party can never be identified with a social class.

Let us take the example of the party which now comes the nearest to representing a class. A little over half of the communist voters in France are workers; half of or even slightly more of the workers vote for the Communist Party. These statistics must be accepted. If we add that the Communist Party represents or embodies the working class, we are no longer dealing with a factual proposition, but with a theory. To what extent does the Communist Party represent the will of the French working class? The empirical and statistical answer is that it represents the will of half the workers. But in the same line of reasoning, in Britain it is the Labour Party which represents the working class and in Germany it is the Social Democratic party.

We can go further. A political party is always defined by an end or an ideal. The objectives of the Communist Party depend on an end or ideal as much as on the workers who vote for it. There are two possible conceptions of the interests of a social group. In a pluralistic-constitutional regime such as that under which we live, the interest of the workers is to enlarge their share in the national income or, again, to bring about the nationalization of some industry or to take a greater share in the life of the community. There is a second conception of the interests of the workers, the Marxist one, according to which the interests of the working class lie in trying to create a different society. In this case, it is no longer a question of the interests of the working class in the present system but of a system which, according to some, will conform most closely to the interests of the proletariat as such.

At this point, class interest is defined by a particular idea of the regime which is good for a given group. The social infrastructure does not enable us to decide which are the essential interests of groups. It is at the political level, that the ultimate meaning of the class struggle appears.

There are circumstances in which socio-economic phenomena do have an immediate and often decisive bearing on political events. The economic crisis of 1930 was the direct source of the increase in the votes of the Nazi party and of the overthrow of the Weimar republic. The analysis of the political regime demands a knowledge of the social infrastructure, but the latter, taken alone, does not permit, any more than does any other variable, categories of kinds of regime.

In a bureaucracy, too, one can draw distinctions between kinds, but these distinctions will be less striking, because the civil service carry out similar functions and have features in common. The bureaucracy, in constitutional-pluralistic regimes, must answer to three needs: it must be *efficient, neutral* in such a way as not to be entangled in the party struggle and lastly to make itself acceptable to the people, to appear not as their enemy, but as their interpreter or *representative*.

It is not easy to satisfy any of these three needs. A bureaucracy is not automatically efficient. There is a permanent danger, in all pluralistic regimes, that the administration will lose its neutrality, owing to the fact that each party tries to set up cells within it, and to find places for its own men. Lastly, the administration, and I am thinking of fiscal administration, runs the risk of appearing to represent a hostile state, instead of being accepted or recognized as the interpreter of the national will. But in constitutional-pluralistic regimes, the bureaucracy is not, and should not be, the instrument of powers, alien to the people, but at one and the same time the instrument of those who govern and the representative of the people.

Let us now say something about the social environment and the different variables into which the social environment can be broken up.

I can see at least three variables which are important if we are to understand the way constitutional-pluralistic regimes work and their degree of success.

The first is the idea that the people have of the merits of the regime. This is a truism, but truisms can be important. In countries in which the people think that a political regime based on the elective principle and on parliament is bad, this kind of regime can only take root with difficulty. By definition, a regime cannot work smoothly unless it is accepted by the people. The idea which the governed have of the good regime decides to a great extent their judgment of the existing regime.

I will devote one or two chapters to the study of the French regime which I think is better than the French themselves hold it to be, but they are all the more inclined to pass judgment in that they have never weighed up what all of them consider to be normal and legal. The constant questioning of the method of government weakens the government itself. A healthy regime is perhaps that in which the people are convinced that they are living under the best of all possible systems. Neither the Americans nor the British on the whole have any doubt about the superiority of their regime, although this does not prevent them from criticizing it in detail.

The second variable of the social environment is the method

by which it is formed or in other words the historical traditions. The French regime is still weighed down by its legacy from the successive revolutions through which it was constituted. The constant questioning of the constitution, a clear source of weakness, is partly the result of a troubled history. Whenever France faces a crisis, the constitution becomes the subject of widespread debate. If it is not possible to solve the financial or the Algerian problem, it is the fault of the constitution. This line of reasoning, which is taken as a matter of fact, is a daily occurrence.

The third variable is the relation between the party system and the Church or churches.

It is striking that the religious quasi-unity of France goes together with a multiplicity of parties and in the United States the taste for diversity seems to find expression in churches and sects rather than in parties. Do not let us push this suggestion too far; let us simply say that in every country, one of the most important variables in the social environment is precisely the relation between the diversity of religious beliefs and that of political ideas.

Let us end with the following remarks:

At the level of the political regime, we can find multiple distinctions which are applicable to particular aspects: a distinction between parliamentary and presidential governments, between the two-party system and the multi-party system, between countries with disciplined parties and those with non-disciplined ones, in countries in which the parties accept the rules of the game and those in which some parties are revolutionary or, in other words, refuse to play it.

Political science is in some respect weighed down by the accumulation of available knowledge, and the difficulty too of synthesis. The variables which I have listed must be remembered and analysed, but how can all this be brought together in a synthesis and what will be the principle of unification? The result of this uncertainty is that, in the search either for causal explanations or for advice for action, we hesitate.

Let us go back to the French case. What influence does the electoral law have on the party system and on the way in which the French parliament works? Would it be enough merely to change one particular variable, for example the electoral law, to modify one aspect of the French regime which is thought to be deplorable? Would parliamentary instability be avoided simply by changing the electoral law? A teacher hesitates to give a categorical answer because the phenomena under consideration – the plurality of parties, the lack of discipline of the parties, the instability of the governments – have been endemic ever since the French began to practise this kind of regime.

If one were sure about causal explanations one could in all probability advise a certain course of action. But each time we look at a particular phenomenon, we find that it is linked with a plurality of factors. In some ways, the instability of the French governments is a simultaneous expression of all the variables of a political regime, of the historical environment and of the social infrastructure.

It is still too soon to know if the Fifth Republic has opened a new chapter in the history of French democracy.

CHAPTER SEVEN

ON THE OLIGARCHIC CHARACTER OF CONSTITUTIONAL-PLURALISTIC REGIMES

In the preceding chapter I explained why it seemed to me impossible to draw up categories of the kinds of constitutional-pluralistic regimes. On the other hand, we cannot study every example of this kind of regime in detail. What then must we do?

In order to understand the essence of a political regime, we must grasp the problems which are characteristic of it: confront the principle of legitimacy with its practice, specify the difficulties to which the institutions give rise and disentangle the causes of strength and of weakness.

What are the fundamental problems of a constitutional-pluralistic regime?

The first seems to me to be clearly the result of the bringing together of the democratic idea and parliamentary practice; is it true that a multi-party regime is an accurate embodiment of the idea of popular sovereignty? Is it true that parliamentary practice gives the reality of power to the people as laid down by the doctrine? One could go further: who really possesses power in a constitutional-pluralistic regime?

The second question appears immediately in contrast to the first. The first, in fact, suggested the possibility that the multi-party system was merely a façade, and that behind this façade were concealed those who actually wielded power. The second question is: how can an efficient government be established on perpetual party strife? How can a power which stands in need of the constant approval of the people be effective?

The third question, linked to the second, is how, under a regime which permits perpetual strife among the citizens and groups, can one prevent the national unity, which is so necessary to the wellbeing of any community, from being upset?

The last question is as follows: 'Were constitutional-pluralistic regimes constitutional before they were popular?' In the nineteenth century formal respect for the constitution already existed in Britain and from time to time in France, but the electoral law was limited; the visible power was in the hands of a small minority. This gives rise to the question: can constitutional-pluralistic regimes be popular and remain constitutional? Is there not a contradiction between the rise of the masses and the nature of constitutional regimes which are drawn up and put into practice by the middle classes?

Were I to translate these questions into a vocabulary borrowed from Greek philosophy, I would say that the first is tantamount to asking whether and to what extent democracies are oligarchies; the second is whether democracies inevitably become demagogies or, in other words, how can effective administration be reconciled with constant anxiety about public opinion and the parties; the third, if and how can a democracy avoid the risk of degenerating into anarchy; lastly, the fourth, if and how one can avoid a democracy from degenerating into tyranny.

The problems set by a modern democracy have been familiar in societies with a fundamentally different structure.

We shall try first to answer the first question, which is to specify the oligarchic character of modern democracies.

To start this study, I shall refer to a theory which today is called Machiavellian and which is to be found in many books, Pareto's *Traité de sociologie générale*, Mosca's book on *The Ruling Class* and again in James Burnham's *The Machiavellians*. The main idea of these theoreticians is, in my language, but it is one which they would accept, that *every political system is oligarchic*. Every society, they say, at least every complex society is governed by a small number of men; the regimes vary according to the character of the men who wield power. Very often, at the centre, even of political parties, it is the minority which rules. The Italian sociologist, Roberto Michels, has written a book on the political parties in which he has tried to demonstrate and has succeeded in showing that in most political parties the minorities hold the key positions and keep them with the passive approval of the mass of members.

The Machiavellians have explained that regimes which are called democratic are really oligarchies of a special type – plutocratic oligarchies. The minority in power is dominated by the rich, the financiers, the business men, the industrialists. These men do not like violence and prefer to use guile. But in the end democracy is only skin deep because it is the minorities, often hidden in the shadows, which take the most important decisions.

Some of the facts on which the Machiavellians draw are irrefutable. It is true to say that in all societies it is a small minority which takes decisions. It is also true that in modern democracies oligarchy presents plutocratic characteristics; those who hold the means of production, the rich, the financiers, influence directly or indirectly those who direct public affairs.

To this demonstration of the oligarchic character of democratic societies there must be opposed not an objection but a fact (which the Machiavellians themselves accept). *It is impossible to conceive of a regime which in one sense is not oligarchic.* The very essence of politics is that decisions should be taken *for* and not *by* the community. Decisions cannot be taken by all. Popular sovereignty does not mean that the mass of the people itself takes directly decisions on public finances or foreign policy. It is ridiculous to compare modern democratic regimes to the utopian ideal of a regime in which the people govern themselves. This is to compare existing to potential regimes. The same observation is valid for the Machiavellian criticism of Soviet-type regimes.

A Yugoslav politician, Milovan Djilas, who at the present time is in prison, has published a book *The New Class* in which he develops a Machiavellian criticism of the regimes of eastern Europe; the new regimes which call themselves people's democracies are oligarchies in which a small number of privileged persons exploit the masses. To be sure, Djilas suggested that this new class is unfruitful, that it does not give back to society services commensurate with its privileges. But on this decisive point his argument is weak. I would make the same objection to Djilas as I do to the Machiavellians: regardless of whether the regime is called a liberal democracy or a people's democracy, does it not mask an oligarchy? The question is to know how they use their power, according to what rules do they govern, what are the advantages and disadvantages of this rule for the community? The problems present themselves in this way.

1. First of all: who forms the oligarchy? Who forms the dominant minority and how easy is it to enter it? Is the ruling minority open or closed?

2. What kind of man has the opportunity in each kind of regime to become a member of the political personnel?

3. What are the privileges enjoyed by the members of the ruling minority?

4. What guarantees does this kind of regime give to the governed?

5. Who, in a regime of this order, does in fact possess power and what does the notion, so frequently used today, 'to possess power' actually mean?

To what extent are the ruling minorities of constitutional-pluralistic regimes open or closed? It all depends on the species and the phases of development of these regimes. In the nineteenth century, in Britain and in France, it was difficult to break into the governmental minority, if one was not on the right side of the barricades (at least of a revolution). These minorities are today more open than they were in the last century, for reasons relating to the structure of industrial societies. The more democratic a regime becomes, the more the system of education is broadened, the more opportunities to rise in the social scale appear.

Constitutional-pluralistic regimes, combined with industrial civilization, do not give *all* the citizens the *same* opportunities to reach higher positions; the ideal of the equality of opportunity is never realized, but the politically ruling minority is no longer closed and there are several ways in which it can be reached. In France, one can become one of the politically ruling minority either through one's family or social position or through the trade unions, the professional groupings or the universities, etc.

Who then have the brightest prospects in constitutional-pluralistic regimes?

The Machiavellians have given us a depressing answer. They have said that those who succeed in parliamentary regimes are essentially those who know how to talk; orators are not necessarily competent to direct public affairs. Debating regimes oil the wheels for those who know how to use words. One does not need to be a profound sociologist to discover this. Barristers, lawyers, university professors have a good chance of making a political career. Even this statement, trite as it is, is not always true. There are countries in which good speakers are distrusted, sometimes even a kind of snobbery favours the 'bad speaker'. Some play on their lack of talent in speech-making to impose themselves as speakers. I know at least one recent president of the council who was completely without any talent for public speaking; other qualities can ensure promotion: the art of lobbying, the art of compromise, the art of pulling strings.

The Machiavellians say that the members of the assembly, the speechmakers, do not know how to act, which is often true. Someone who can succeed in a profession, a trade union or in the Communist Party is not the same kind of man who succeeds in parliament. One can speculate indefinitely about the advantages and disadvantages of different kinds of success. Peaceful regimes, inevitably, benefit those who possess the qualities of peace. The world today is ruled by two kinds of men, those who have won success through war and those who have been successful in peace-time. Under the Weimar republic, Hitler could not satisfy his ambition; he needed a regime which was non-parliamentary; it is doubtful whether his regime, which was non-parliamentary, represented an advance for the governed. Here the third question appears.

What are the privileges given to the ruling minority in a constitutional-pluralistic regime and what guarantees does it give to the governed?

On this point, I think that constitutional-pluralistic regimes are easy to justify. Not that the members of the ruling minority do not enjoy privileges. Leading personalities in the party who are defeated in elections move freely towards another assembly (to which they are *appointed* by the prime minister). In the case of an electoral setback, they find 'second lines of defence' and ways of falling without hurting themselves. Nearly all the governing minorities – especially in pluralistic democracies use the closed shop system, the trade union of mutual help. Nevertheless the publicity given to these privileges tends to keep them within bounds. As long as men are not governed by saints, those who take part in government will profit from it.

Lastly, and this is an essential point, the constitutional-pluralistic regime is the one which gives the maximum guarantees to the governed. Not that persecution and injustice are impossible. In France the purge in 1944–5, McCarthyism in the United States, gave proof that constitutional-pluralistic regimes do not always practise what they preach. (But the regime was not yet stabilized in 1944–5 and McCarthyism entailed more social than state-controlled persecution.) All in all, it is enough to have lived under various kinds of regime to realize that there is a difference in nature between the safeguards given to the citizens by a constitutional-pluralistic regime and those given to subjects in an unconstitutional one.

The Italian sociologist, Mosca, spent most of his life in expatiating on the baseness of democratic regimes, which he called plutocracies. He invented the theory of the system of privileges, of particular interests which hide behind big words. Towards the end of his life, he stated with a mixture of irony and bitterness, that the constitutional-pluralistic regime gave more safeguards to the citizens than any other regime in history. But a word of warning! I said *safeguards for the governed*. The variable 'safeguards for the governed' is not the only criterion by which the respective merits of regimes can be judged.

Constitutional-pluralistic regimes can superimpose themselves on societies in which elections, even if free, only give power to the representatives of privileged minorities, in the aristocratic manner. A regime of competition between parties does not imply that the ranks of the ruling minority can be breached and runs the risk of consolidating the power of an anachronistic minority. What the history of Europe for a century has revealed is the transformation of society in a given direction, from restricted franchise to universal suffrage, from aristocratic parliaments to parliaments, elected by universal franchise, of leading figures, professional politicians and mass leaders. We have seen in Europe the gradual change in the way in which politicians are recruited; at the beginning those who were elected were usually aristocrats, members of the upper middle class, well-known figures, lawyers; then came the professors; today we find in the assemblies, members who have made their way in the trade unions, in the professions and who represent the masses more directly.

This kind of regime has been contemporaneous with a revolution in social and economic life which brought about a rise in the standard of living, the spread of employment and, perhaps even more important, the destruction of traditional hierarchies. Individuals live crowded together in cities, and vote spontaneously for the leaders of the masses or for professional politicians.

Another political mechanism has led to this evolution in the popular meaning of constitutional-pluralistic regimes; I mean the logic of elections and ideas. The regimes which I call constitutional-pluralistic call themselves republican or democratic, those who govern treating those whom they govern as their sovereign. It is difficult to situate popular sovereignty, unless mythically, in the people, without gradually extending the right to vote, and without generalizing the concept of who is a citizen. In conjuring up democratic ideas, we hasten the transformation of societies. When those who rule are elected, they are always worried about their popularity, the approval of the governed: here lies both the greatness and the slavery of this kind of regime.

We come now to the last question which I asked: who *actually* holds power under this system?

I take no longer as my reference Machiavellian criticism but Marxist criticism.

According to the Marxists, especially Marxist vulgarizers, the regimes which I call constitutional-pluralistic are bourgeois democracies in which parties and parliaments provide camouflage for capitalist rule. This is not the whole of the Marxist conception; we shall consider only the purely political thesis: the economically ruling class holds the actual power. Is it true that in these regimes the parties are only a façade and that the real power is held by a few men who possess, control or direct the means of production? To what extent are the economically dominant classes identical with the politically ruling minority?

Let us say at once that the Marxist hypothesis is not completely false; it can be true in certain circumstances and false in others. The minority which wields political power through electoral and parliamentary machinery can at the same time be the class which possesses the reality of economic power. In fact, the coincidence of the economically privileged ruling class on the one hand and the politically ruling minority, on the other, has much less chance of being maintained when 80 per cent of the population earn their living in the cities, in which there is no natural aristocracy comparable to the landowners or the leading personalities in a village. The votes of town dwellers cannot be so easily pressurized: they vote for the representatives of parties which are not or which they think are not the power bases of the economically privileged class.

There was a time when parliamentary oligarchy was both economic and political. In England in the eighteenth century, and even in the first half of the nineteenth century, the situation resembled not only the Marxist version of the 'monopolists' who manipulated elections, but a definite meeting, the coincidence in the same ruling class of economic and political power. Today, in all the constitutional-pluralistic regimes of western Europe and in the United States, we can see a physical dissociation, if I may use the word, between those who exercise political power and those who exercise the ruling economic functions. In the United States and in Britain, the big business men often hold important political office. The case of the secretary to the American Ministry of Defence who was the director of one of the great business concerns and who said 'What is good for General Motors is good for the United States' is not forgotten. He proclaimed the pre-established harmony of interest between a business concern and the national interest as a dogma to which an acceptable meaning can also be given. But it has been used as an example by the most popular Marxists. It is a symbolic illustration put forward, it goes without saying, by an honest man quite honestly convinced that he was not criticizing but praising his country. Perhaps he was not altogether at fault. Suppose that we were on the other side of the Iron Curtain and instead of saying 'what is good for General Motors is good for the United States' we said 'What is good for the Putilov factories is good for the Soviet Union' would not everyone agree? Once this has been said, how different is at this point the meaning of the two statements?

To come back to our question: what is the nature of the power which the directors of economic concerns possess? What is the power which the economically privileged minority possess?

We mean by the word power (perhaps it would be better to say strength) an individual's ability to influence the behaviour of one or more of his like. In this sense, everyone or nearly everyone has some power.

But the power which interests us here is that which arises from the institutions themselves, from the place which each one holds in the social system, either in the partial system of the business concern or of the economy, or in the overall system of the whole society. In this course of lectures on the political regime, it is power at state level that is above all important.

The directors, naturally, have power in their business concerns. They take decisions affecting all the workers. The authority of a director of a nationalized firm is not essentially different from the authority of the director of a private enterprise. This authority is legal, entails real power, and is subject to technical necessities, administrative needs and social habits. The power of big business men can be greater or less according to the country or the industrial sector, but it is not based fundamentally on the law of property. The directors of the Renault works are the representatives of the community, those of Citröen of a company; but both hold the same kind of power and exercise the same sort of authority.

There is a second sort of power which is of greater interest to us: what is the relation between the power of the leaders of industries and the decisions taken by the administrators or by the politicians? The directors of limited companies are not distrusted because they have power in their enterprises (this is natural and legal), but because they are thought to bring pressure to bear, often secretly, on officials and on politicians in the interests of their own concerns. There is no doubt that the leaders of industry influence some of the decisions which the public authorities take. Let us pick out three aspects or three methods: the pressure, often hidden, on the officials, propaganda through professional journals or the national press and lastly direct action on the ministers.

It is necessary to distinguish between the action of economic leaders on political power in order to obtain administrative measures or legislative decisions favourable to the enterprise or the industrial branch in question and the action which tends to impose on those who govern certain decisions relating to high policy. The second is the essential problem; in fact, the first entails, before anything else many special studies, of the kind much in fashion today, largely because it is difficult to conclude them. Pressure groups do not, in fact, exist officially, except in the United States, where they speak of the French lobby or the China lobby, meaning organized groups whose object it is to bring pressure to bear on congressmen to further the interests of Chinese or French policy. It goes without saying that industries can form lobbies.

Such actions are often effective in constitutional-pluralistic regimes. A producer or a group of producers can obtain a subsidy for export, a protective tariff which is open to criticism from the point of view of the general interest. Thus, the representatives of private interests succeed in wresting from the administration or from the political leaders concessions which enlightened despots would refuse. In relation to the optimum of rational administration, constitutional-pluralistic regimes are certainly wanting.

The real question goes further: to what extent do these economically dominant minorities dictate the general policy of the regime?

Are social reforms paralysed by the action of the economically privileged minority? We have something by which we can judge; it is enough to look around, to observe the social evolution of the last fifty years, to see that these economic minorities which are thought to be omnipotent have not been able in any of the countries of western Europe to avert changes to which they have always been thought to be hostile. They have not been able to prevent the nationalization of some industries in France and in Britain. They have certainly been unable to prevent the extension of social legislation.

A communist would reply that these minorities have nevertheless prevented the destruction of capitalism. Without doubt, in constitutional-pluralistic regimes the right to own the means of production has not been eliminated. The policy of these regimes has not fatally wounded the interests of those who are thought of as the economically privileged minority. In the only known example of the complete destruction of capitalism, the constitutional-pluralistic regime itself disappeared at the same time. When the right to private ownership of the means of production has been completely suppressed, the rivalry of the parties is suppressed at the same time. Within constitutional-pluralistic regimes, there are still limits to socialist reforms. But these limits have been less narrow than we might imagine. Many socialist theoreticians proclaimed that the so-called capitalist class would never accept passively reforms such as those passed by the Labour Party in England in 1945.

In the order of internal policy, reforms which are possible despite the economically privileged minority, or thanks to it, are far-reaching. It is still impossible today to set the limit beyond which the privileged minority will not be pushed without reacting by violence.

This is still probably not the decisive question. Do those who are commonly called 'capitalists' secretly dictate the policies of various states?

This is a vexing question. Many who listen to me or who read me are convinced beforehand that this is true. I cannot shake their conviction, since their system of interpretation gives the explanation for my error. Having a certain picture of the way in which constitutional-pluralistic regimes function, they consider that my eyes are blinded to certain realities, not by a conscious denial of the truth but as a result of my social position.

This being said, this is how I see the problem.

For about ten years, the vicissitudes of my career have led me to follow French policy more closely than during my youth at the university. One of my disappointments has been to realize that those who, according to the communist picture of the world, determine the course of events are very often men without political ideas; it is impossible to say what the French capitalists (by this I mean the middle classes) wanted on most of the great questions discussed in France in the last ten years. I have met some representatives of capitalism, the 'cursed race', and I have never known them to hold firm and stable opinions about the policy to be followed in Indochina, in Morocco or in Algeria. I am ready to admit that a man with interests in a particular part of the world was open to argument. In matters concerning Morocco the 'great French capitalists' divided into two groups, one of which thought that they would fare better in an independent Morocco, and the other fearing the worst should this come about. On an equally fundamental question, what colonial policy is best suited to capitalist interests, the capitalists themselves are divided.

I discovered among the group of 'big industrialists' or of 'big capitalists' the same uncertainties, doubts and disputes as are to be found in the market square, in the newspapers or in Parliament. In order to imagine that they direct French policy, I would have to suppose that some of them are able to impose their policy.

Is an experience of this order open to generalization? It has not been proved that the same is true in all countries. In the United States, at the present moment, the directors of the great business concerns influence the leaders of government; they exert even more influence on the Republican administration than they exerted a few years ago upon the Democratic one. No matter what the administration may be, they always have representatives in Washington who attend official or unofficial functions, who talk, advise and act.

Do they represent one predetermined policy? Here too I have doubts. I do not think that one can say that the American capitalists are all agreed upon a particular foreign policy. In so far as they do have a preference, it is, in my experience, very often the opposite of the one attributed to them. For example, the representatives of American capitalism have never been wholly convinced that the anticommunist passion was entirely justified. Many businessmen tend to be in favour of an agreement with the Soviet Union rather than of an aggressive policy. In one of his books, James Burnham has an ironic chapter entitled 'The suicidal tendency of American capitalism'. He blames the capitalists for wanting above all to do business, even with their enemies. American industrialists contributed greatly to the success of the first Soviet five-year plan; lacking foresight, they are always ready to subordinate long-term political interests to the desire to make profits.

I do not say that this is the permanent state of mind of every economically privileged class in the capitalist world – I would say that in most of the cases which I have been able to observe directly the representatives of capitalism are less 'politicized' than one would imagine. Their political convictions are less directly linked to their business affairs than current interpretation admits.

You could object that I have taken special examples to make my point. The examples are all taken from after the Second World War. But, since the Second World War, the capitalists have discovered that imperialism does not pay. The state of mind which I observe is born of recent reflections: war has become too costly, the underdeveloped countries no longer enrich the metropolitan which must invest in them. Does this hesitation arise from the fact that the ex-imperialists are divided amongst themselves on the best way to maintain or to liquidate imperialism? This objection does perhaps contain a grain of truth. In the past, in certain circumstances, the intervention of great economic interests in politics was more clear cut. However, books about the role of the great economic interests in colonial conquests do not lead to these simple conclusions. There have certainly been cases in which the incitement to conquer came from the economic world, but very often the initiative is political. There is a famous saying of a German chancellor before the 1914 war: 'Every time I talk about Morocco, all the bankers threaten to strike.' The Wilhelmstrasse, the German Ministry of Foreign Affairs, was more concerned about Morocco than were the great capitalists. The economic leaders, both in France and in Germany, were ready to compromise on the Moroccan question.

When Italy launched the campaign in Tripolitania, it was the government which forced the Bank of Italy to acquire interests there and which gave it, in return, the monopoly of issuing bank notes.

I do not deny that on some occasions the representatives of capitalist interests have brought pressure to bear on the politicians. What I say is that it is not true that the minority which directs the great industrial concentrations constitutes a unique group, having representatives in common throughout the world and one political will. Never and nowhere has this crystallization of the rulers of economic organizations into a class aware of itself been proved.

Nor is it true so far as we can judge by experience that these representatives of the great economic interests 'tyrannize' over the political leaders and impose their own decisions on them. Those who direct the great industrial concentrations normally and legally exert influence on the policy of the country. To describe them as despots is to sacrifice truth to mythology. The representatives of the great economic interests do not deserve either so much praise or so much blame.

It is praising them too much to credit them with a superior intelligence and to believe that they are capable, because they are leaders of industry, of manipulating the press, the political parties and parliament. The leaders of industry are like other men. To imagine that the political game is simply a screen behind which their omnipotence is concealed is only an emotional aberration which is explained by hatred of the economic system. One must really detest the great enterprises to credit their leaders with such an evil quality. Anyone who has not very strong feelings about them judges them to be nearer to the general run of mankind, occupied above all with their business, anxious to obtain something or other from the politicians, but without a vision of the world, and still less an organization which enables them to rule.

Nor do they deserve so much blame; they are not diabolical despots who would drag humanity into war through greed for profit. Many people in the past thought that peace could be secured simply by nationalizing armaments. Nationalization has at least the virtue of dispelling these illusions. Relations between nations are not rendered peaceable because some of them are deprived of the opportunity to enrich themselves by making guns.

The minority which directs the economy in constitutional-pluralistic regimes wields an influence which is greater or less according to the country and to the time; they have no ultimate power – either for good or for ill.

CHAPTER EIGHT

IN SEARCH OF STABILITY AND EFFICIENCY

Constitutional-pluralistic systems are oligarchic as are all political regimes, but they are less so than most. It is true that, in our time, the economically ruling minorities in these regimes are always linked to the politically dominant circles, but the most characteristic fact about them is the dissociation of social or economic power on the one side from political power on the other. Those who exercise the most important functions politically are not the same as those who occupy the most important social positions.

This duality between the social or economic élite and the political personnel has resulted in a division of power; as power is not concentrated in the hands of a small number of men, it is more difficult to find out who really makes the decisions in constitutional-pluralistic regimes. As this diffusion or dispersal of power is intellectually unsatisfactory, myths proliferate according to which a few men in the background have the real power, which is looked for in vain in the open. In this way the myth of the Jesuits, of the freemasons, of the oil companies and lastly, at a higher level, of the trusts is born.

I myself do not believe that these regimes are more unified or more intelligent than they seem to be. The 'operators' are figments of their enemies' imagination.

If my analysis is accurate, the real problem of constitutional-pluralistic regimes in our time is not, or is not only, the problem of watering down the oligarchic character of government, but also and above all of attenuating the risk of power becoming dispersed and those who govern becoming impotent.

The second argument, which is complementary to the one

against oligarchy, is directed against the instability, the weakness or the ineffectiveness of these regimes. True, regimes of this kind are unstable and restless, and sometimes one does not know who is in power, or for how long. Every government has usually two aims; the first is to remain in power and the other is to use power in the common interest. In constitutional-pluralistic regimes, the anxiety to remain in power sometimes seems to be greater than the desire to serve the collective interest (but does any government exist of which this is not true?).

If one imagines the perfect governor (the counsellor of the prince or the philosopher), a minister of the French Republic, anxious not to put weapons into the hands of the opposition, bears little resemblance to him. Moreover, those who exert authority are perpetually hampered by various rules of the constitution and of the administration. They are subjected to the influence of pressure groups and exposed to the illwill of the press. It is easy to represent the governors as paralysed by the checks which all regimes of this order seem to consider as their main duty constantly to multiply.

I agree with the idea that the lack of constitutional and administrative rules can in some cases make action easier. It has taken several years to erect a building intended for the faculty of science on a site formerly reserved for something else. It should not be necessary to change the essence of a regime in order to attain a higher degree of administrative efficiency.

The second remark which I should like to make is borrowed from Montesquieu. In *Les Causes de la grandeur et de la décadence des Romains* he says:

Every time we see everyone at peace in a state which calls itself a republic, we can be sure that there is no freedom. What is called unity in a body politic is a very delicately balanced thing; true unity is unity of harmony which results in all the parties, no matter how opposed they may seem to be, working for the general good of the society just as discords in music work for the whole harmony. There can be unity in a state in which there seems to be nothing but friction, that is a harmony from which happiness, which is the only true peace, results. It is like the parts of the universe which are eternally linked by the action of some and by the reaction of others.

I do not mean to say that the well-being of the citizens can be measured by the intensity of political troubles felt by the polity, but neither is the quality of a political regime measured by the apparent peace.

After these preliminary remarks, let us try to find the regimes which try to attenuate the consequences of the defects, instability and inefficiency, which lie in wait for them.

First of all, I shall risk a general statement. Stability seems to have as its fundamental condition the agreement between the constitutional rules and the party system, and secondly, the agreement between the whole of the constitution and the parties on one side and the social infrastructure or the wishes of the community on the other.

In practice, we can see two directions in which the executive power, whose source is the party struggle, can be made stable and effective.

The first direction is the one taken by the United States: to cause the executive power to emerge from a consultation, more or less direct, of the sovereign power according to a different procedure from the one by which the members of Congress are chosen. The American constitution carries this principle to its limits. The executive power is stable because the supreme executive is elected every four years and cannot, unless physically incapacitated, be deprived of his mandate. He represents the whole community, and he enjoys, through a constitutional decision, a higher prestige and authority than do the elected representatives, who only represent part of the community.

The second way in which the executive can be made stable and efficient is that of Great Britain, where the government is the expression of a parliamentary majority. The government lasts for as long as this majority does, generally as long as the parliamentary term itself, and it is able to act since it can almost certainly count on the approval of parliament.

These two constitutional systems only ensure stability and authority in the extent to which they fit the structure of the party system.

Let us imagine that in the United States there are parties which are under the party whip, as are those in Britain; the system could no longer work. The system works in the United States even when the president belongs to one party and the majority in both houses to another. The cooperation between a democratic president and a republican majority or the other way round demands that the senators or the congressmen who belong to the Democratic Party can approve a proposal put forward by a republican president; in other words, there is no party discipline. If there were the presidential system and disciplined parties, the regime could only function on condition that the congress and president belonged to the same party.

On the other hand, the British regime can only function today because of party discipline. If you imagine free voting in the House of Commons, the much vaunted constitution ceases to be a model. Furthermore, the two main parties must be sufficiently close to one another. Think of two parties, one of which is extremely liberal in the economic sense, and the other resolutely set on a planned economy; their alternation in power would mean an overthrow of the laws.

These remarks illustrate the general statement. It is not constitutional rule as such which ensures stability and efficiency, but the agreement between this rule and the structure of the party system, the nature of the parties, their programme, and the way the political game is played.

The American regime clearly involves one danger: not only that it may be paralysed by opposition between the president and congress, but also that there may be a *coup d'état*. When American influence spread the system which had taken root in the United States to other countries, the result was a proliferation of *coups d'état*. In one way, the American system is perpetually balanced between the threat of *pronunciamento* and that of paralysis. When we cite the American presidential government as a guarantee of efficiency, we are forgetting that it was conceived to have the very opposite effect. Those who drew up the constitution tried to limit the government's possibilities of action, because they were inspired by the liberal pessimism which believes that those who have power always tend to misuse it.

In the same way, the British regime presupposes not only that cooperation between the parties is possible, but that the power which each receives in turn can be limited. Had the Labour Party wanted to misuse the opportunities which the electoral victory of 1945 gave it, the conservatives would have thought that the system itself was dangerous.

In both cases what we see is that one of the conditions necessary if a constitutional-pluralistic regime is to work is that ambitions should be disciplined. In the British as well as in the American regime, there exists a ladder to office, and successive rungs to be climbed. The number of those who can climb to the highest office is limited.

Is authority implied once this stability is assured, either by the legal term of office under the presidential system or by the coherence of the majority in parliamentary government? In other words, has a government which lasts the necessary freedom to act? The immediate reply is that it certainly has not. Those who want to reform the institutions should notice that it is not enough for a government to last a few years for it to have freedom of action.

What gives the ability to act in the American regime? The president is only able to impose his will according to the prestige which he enjoys and the resolution which he shows. It is not the American institutions which guarantee sufficient authority to the executive power; they merely give to those who hold office the *opportunity* to exercise the necessary authority. What is essential is that the president should succeed in getting his proposals through Congress. He is not always successful in this. With elections every two years, there are many months during which the president is unable to act.

In the British type of system, the government, which has a working majority, can in theory do almost anything. But here another characteristic of constitutional-pluralistic regimes intervenes. What the government can do is not defined by the institutions as they are laid down in the documents, but decided by and limited by what is called, for want of a better expression, public opinion. A constitutional-pluralistic government is constantly aware that it can do some things and not others.

What can it really do? No one can answer this question positively. The possibilities depend largely on what the governments themselves believe. The impossibilities are created by lack of confidence on the part of those who govern.

In France, what those who govern can and cannot do is spoken of in private, but never in public. They freely tell those who question them what they consider to be possible in the given state of mind of the members of parliament and of public opinion.

Could the government in Britain, after 1933, have rearmed more quickly than it did? Did public opinion prevent the successive governments between 1933 and 1939 from preparing effectively for the war which most of them felt was coming? The fact is that most of the governments thought that the measures which they knew privately to be necessary would not be approved by the public. Today in Britain a question of the same order is raised; this is not a question of rearmament, but an economic one. In private and even in the newspapers the question is asked in the following terms: can the government, in order to maintain the value of the currency and stabilize prices, agree to a percentage of unemployment? What is the number of unemployed which public opinion, the press, the trade unions and the public in general would accept? This is the kind of question which decides the freedom of action of constitutional-pluralist governments.

The kind of system is defined by the constant struggle between private interests and private-collective interests. The interests of the community as a whole run the risk of disappearing in the din of party propaganda; hence the necessity arises to create bodies which are exempt from the rivalry of parties or of groups. In the abstract, the remedy is simple: for the impartiality or depolitization of the administration to be ensured there must be a press which is as free as possible, not only in relation to the government, but also in relation to the parties and the interest groups, a press in which those who write have the right to say what they deem to be useful to the whole community. Lastly, there must be commissions of the type of the British royal commissions in which men who are thought to be impartial are given the task of studying objectively and scientifically some administrative problem. Advice does not free politicians from the burden of choice, but it brings moral pressure to bear on that choice.

One last remark can be added: as well as an impartial administration, an objective press and commissions of inquiry, those who take part in the party struggle, the parties and the interest groups, must not push the defence of their particular cause too far and must keep the sense of the collective interest as well as the interest of the politico-economic game itself. It is easier to ensure that a constitutional-pluralistic system works well when the unions of employers and of workers have a double function, one of which is to put forward claims and the other to restrain the claims. I mean by the function of putting forward claims the function which all trade unions perform in the interests of their members, by the function of restraint, a subtle and camouflaged action to discourage excessive claims while at the same time obtaining satisfaction of moderate ones.

This applies to the realities which we can observe. In Britain, the trade unions are as much institutions of restraint on the people as institutions of claim. Claims in the pure state threaten to become revolutionary and to break the framework of the constitutional-pluralist system.

Are these regimes necessarily inefficient?

The first difficulty in answering this question is that the regimes are only factors of the efficiency or inefficiency of those who govern or of the country. When we ask whether constitutional-pluralistic regimes are efficient, we must immediately ask whether non-constitutional regimes are efficient. There is no reason why the same answer should hold good for the present Spanish regime, the German regime of the Third Reich and the Soviet regime. In other words, any general statement about the efficiency or inefficiency of regimes of this kind is risky: it presupposes that the results of a regime can be determined in the abstract, made up of the real nature of the country and also of the men who are to make these institutions live.

We must ask therefore what are the factors making for inefficiency, which are linked to a constitutional-pluralistic regime. What are the inefficiencies which threaten a regime of this kind?

The first danger, as we well know, is the risk of conservatism or of paralysis, through excessive concessions made by weak governments to private interests.

The second arises out of the perpetual temptation with which those who govern are faced to yield not to particular claims, but to the general desire for ease; by this I mean to sacrifice the need for military preparedness to the desire for prosperity, which is normal to all men, regardless of the regime.

Lastly, the third danger is the sacrifice of economic prosperity or of the whole community through inability to choose a coherent policy.

All constitutional-pluralistic regimes are threatened by conservatism; I remember that before the war I shocked some of my colleagues in the *Societé Française de Philosophie* by saying that democratic regimes, what I call here constitutional-pluralistic regimes, were essentially conservative. This statement is an exaggeration; but it is true that every constitutional-pluralistic regime, in our day, is threatened in time by the paralysis of power. This gives rise to the phenomenon of revolution or of pseudo-revolution which rejuvenates power and gives it back the ability to act. In regimes which work well, we find pseudo-revolution. Members of Parliament or ministers, suddenly, for some reason or other, are given greater power than those who govern usually have and use it to put through rapid reforms. We experienced a pseudo-revolution in France in 1936, at the time of the Popular Front, and we experienced a second pseudo-revolution in 1945 after the liberation. The British experienced a pseudo-revolution in 1945. Every regime of this kind swings between phases in which those who govern have little authority and are checked on all sides by the resistance of particular groups and movements of opinion, some violent, some not, which give freedom of action to those who govern.

Perhaps this is not even peculiar to constitutional-pluralistic regimes. The *ancien régime*, before 1789, was also paralysed by the proliferation of privileges and acquired rights which in the end weakened the monarchy, although it was not a constitutional one. The French Revolution has been interpreted by some as an extreme form of rejuvenation and of strengthening of power.

Further, in periods during which in principle nothing is happening, many things may be taking place. For example, in the ten years after the end of the last war, one of the most frequently used words was inactivity, but during the same ten years society in France changed far more radically than in the previous decades.

In other words, the difficulty which those who govern have in taking action is not an exact gauge of the degree of conservatism of the society. Society can change despite governments with very limited means of action and on the other hand, society can change very little even when governments are able to take action. The government is not necessarily the driving force of change. Paradoxically, it can be said that regimes often work well when the driving force is to be found in society and the checks in the government. Society changes rapidly because of the vitality of the economy and the government intervenes largely to cushion the shock to groups or individuals of the changes which the growth of the economy makes necessary. Do not forget that I am speaking of regimes in the industrial civilization which we studied during the previous course. But in an industrial civilization changes come of themselves. Only an extraordinarily effective resistance by those who govern can prevent economic change. In most cases, the paralysis which threatens the constitutional machinery is not enough to avert economic and social change, the driving force of which is in the society itself.

Regimes of this kind bring with them the advantages and disadvantages inherent in the dispersal of power and of the explicit protection of private interests. By definition, they can neither perform actions as striking as those of regimes in which those who govern know no check, nor can they commit mistakes of the same dimensions. Nothing comparable to the collectivization of agriculture from 1929–35 in Russia is conceivable under a constitutional-pluralistic system.

Let us not forget, however, that even in regimes of this kind, we have witnessed events in some ways almost as terrible: for example the crisis of 1930–3. Such regimes are capable, not of committing monstrous actions, but of passively suffering the consequences of monstrous phenomena.

In order to come to a provisional conclusion, let us say that on the whole in most cases a constitutional-pluralistic regime is more likely to produce a healthy economy than a regime of the monopolistic party.

Let us pass on now to the second danger, the sacrifice of the community to the citizens.

I am thinking of the distinction which Pareto established in his *Treatise on General Sociology* between the good of the community taken as a unity, an entity, and what is good *for* the community, that is for the individuals who compose it.

Pareto thought that the greatest good for the members of the community is not reached as long as the well-being of some can still be increased without diminishing that of others. But this highest interest, if it corresponds to the highest well-being, is not necessarily the same as the good of the community taken as a political unity. The greatest well-being for the individual sometimes jeopardizes the defence of the community itself.

The first observation to be made on this point is obvious: such a regime is in its essence peaceable. No one in a war-orientated community thinks of institutionalizing permanently the competition between interests and parties. If the competition between interests and parties is accepted it is because peace is desirable. Again, such regimes, as contrasted with regimes which are essentially different, are oddly embarrassed. Let us take examples far enough away in time to allow us to be objective. Between 1933 and 1939, the constitutional-pluralistic regimes seemed to be decadent because they were at grips with regimes embodied by men whose ways of thought and action differed fundamentally from the way of thinking and of action of parliamentary leaders. Parliamentary leaders believe in compromise and do not like violence. The leader of a monopolistic party believes in force and despises compromise. The leaders of fascist regimes think that war is a law of history and that conquest is the normal goal of all vital collectivities. Constitutional-pluralistic regimes in the twentieth century are ill suited to conquest, and even to some extent to preparing for war.

Of course, the regimes which we are studying conquered great empires in the nineteenth century (and lost them in the twentieth). But the problem is to know exactly why this same kind of regime was able to conquer so much in the last century and to lose it so rapidly in this one. To say that, generally speaking, such regimes are unable to conquer is a statement refuted by the experience of the last century; to state that they are unable to keep their conquests in the twentieth century is a different matter.

Let us confine ourselves on this point to one remark only: such regimes are increasingly deprived of the ideological justification for their empires, and they possess neither the ability to use force nor the necessary hypocrisy to carry out permanently a policy which runs counter to their ideas.

Such statements are only true in the long run. In the short term, and by accident, many events may take place which will refute the statements which I have just made. Conquest, in the last century, was easy because of the military superiority of the Europeans; on the other hand, they were to some extent justified by the doctrine of a 'civilizing mission'. In this century, this no longer holds good.

But if we want to demonstrate the relations between a regime of this kind and war, there is another aspect of the problem which must not be forgotten; once engaged in war, such regimes sometimes go further than regimes of a different type. I have a particular example in mind: the mobilization in Britain between 1939 and

1945 compared to that in Nazi Germany. The mobilization of men and of resources was more widespread in democratic England than in the Third Reich. It is easy to answer that, in time of war, the nature of these regimes changes. This is partly true; the party struggle is suspended in time of war. Great Britain's experience is a confirmation of a statement in *La Democratie en Amérique*.

Tocqueville wrote that regimes which are called democratic have the double peculiarity of finding it difficult to prepare for war and even more difficult to stop, once they have embarked upon it. There is a link between these two phenomena; they have difficulty in preparing for war in peace time because in democracies, which are peaceful systems, those who govern want to follow what they think the people want. After war has been declared, a kind of reversal takes place. The regime, such as it has become once the guns have been fired, is so different from the peace-time system that the government is tempted to go beyond victory and to put an end once and for all to disagreeable necessities and to revert as quickly as possible to a state of peace. This is the root of the reluctance to prepare for war and the inability to stop.

Let us come now to the third danger; to what extent are such regimes capable of taking on the functions which are indispensable to the collective good?

Are constitutional-pluralistic regimes inefficient in economic matters? Judging by experience, it is impossible to say that this is so. All in all, such regimes exist in the richest countries, with the highest standard of living. It is in the United States, in Britain and in western Europe that economic well-being is most widespread.

At certain epochs, in particular during the economic crisis of 1930 to 1933, such regimes seemed unable to work a modern economy. But knowledge of the facts has revealed something which is, perhaps, a little disappointing; there is no clear-cut relation between the quality of the institutions and economic administration. Countries in which the institutions work well, as for example Britain, have made grave administrative mistakes, and possibly countries in which the institutions normally work less well have made fewer mistakes.

In other words, the essential phenomenon of the period 1930–3, during which there was a tendency to believe that such regimes could not survive, were the mistakes in economic administration; mistakes which are hardly, if at all, linked to the competition between the parties and the party struggle. The clearest example is that of France.

From 1930 to 1933, France pursued a policy the result of which was that on the eve of the war industrial production was about 20 per cent lower than it had been in 1929. But the decisions which gave rise to this decline cannot be put down to the instability of the governments or to the lack of authority, which are the defects commonly attributed to the French system. Mistakes committed by officials, by representatives of private interests, just as much as by members of parliament, were the reason why the French crisis was prolonged for ten years. The refusal to devalue the franc from 1931 to 1936 played no part in the violence of the party conflict, since by a kind of miracle the majority of the politicians rejected a measure which all the world now knows to have been vital if the French economy was to recover.

As for foreign policy, I hesitate even more to make a categorical judgment. It cannot be denied that the foreign policy of constitutional-pluralistic regimes between the wars was peculiarly ineffective. But British foreign policy was no better than that of France. Perhaps it was even worse, and more vacillating, between 1920 and 1939. In the first phase, Britain thought that France was more to be feared than Germany – a strange illusion to say the least; in a second period, that is after Hitler's coming to power, those who conducted British policy thought for a long time of an agreement with the Third Reich and of the possibility of putting an end to Hitler's ambitions. Once again, in some cases of inefficiency, we cannot be sure of a link between the way the institutions worked and the decisions taken.

What does remain true is that the foreign policy of constitutional-pluralistic regimes will always run the risk of being ineffective in certain circumstances, that is whenever they confront regimes of a fundamentally different nature. Parliamentary regimes will always find it difficult to understand the mentality of men formed in a different world, accustomed to different practices. This danger of misunderstanding is increased by the reluctance of such regimes to face unpleasant facts and to take risks when action is called for.

The propensity to refuse to face facts and the reluctance to take risks are, you will object, characteristics of the human race rather than of a type of regime. Up to a point, this is true; men, no matter who they are, prefer to imagine that the world is as they want it to be and not to see it as it is when things go wrong. There is also a category of men, and it is not entirely composed of neurotics, who have a different tendency; they always see disasters on the horizon and not the things which could turn to their advantage. All the same, in the press, in political life, it is more usual to see the world as we want it to be rather than as it is.

Regimes built on words and on debates will always find difficulty in making a radical choice and will always be inclined to prefer compromise. But in foreign policy a choice, and a quick one, must often be made. Remember the occupation of the Rhineland in March 1936; the choice was clear: military reprisal or acquiescence. An armed reprisal was difficult on the eve of elections; passive acceptance was made difficult by the importance of the event. A middle course was chosen, that is a solemn declaration that what had in fact been accepted would never be accepted.

This example is a caricature, but a symbolic one. All regimes of this order will always tend to substitute verbal for effective retort and to believe that the world is other than it really is.

CHAPTER NINE

ON THE CORRUPTION OF CONSTITUTIONAL-PLURALISTIC REGIMES

Everybody knows the saying that the Republic was beautiful under the Empire. This ironic phrase, very characteristic of the pessimism of the French, seems to me to be profoundly true. Constitutional-pluralistic regimes which today are known as democracies cannot fail to be disappointing, both because they are pedestrian and because their highest virtues are negative.

Pedestrian, because by definition they share in human fallibility; they accept the fact that power emerges from the rivalry between groups and ideas; they try to limit authority because they are convinced that men who have power misuse it.

Such regimes also have positive virtues, if only that of respecting constitutionality and individual liberties; but perhaps their highest virtues are negative ones, which are only fully appreciated once they have been lost. Such regimes are able to avert what others cannot.

This being said, a regime which permits permanent conflicts of ideas, of interests, of groups and of individuals must reflect the character of the men who make it work. It is possible to imagine a constitutional regime without any flaws, but one cannot imagine a regime in which the politicians are all aware that as well as their own particular interests, they also represent and must serve the collective interest – a regime in which the conflict of ideas is unfettered, but the press is objective, and individuals have a feeling of solidarity despite the differences of opinion which divide them.

If the analyses which I have developed in the last two chapters are correct, it may be asked whether it is possible to distinguish between corrupt constitutional-pluralistic regimes and healthy ones. Are we not tempted to answer that, in its essence, this kind of regime is always to some extent corrupt? I am perfectly prepared to recognize that such regimes never fully realize their potential, that they never solve completely the problems which confront them. But there are differences in degree which justify us in speaking in some cases of healthy regimes and in others of corrupt ones. I am speaking here of different kinds of corruption in constitutional-pluralistic regimes.

First of all, the degrees of corruption can be distinguished by their main cause. This is to be found either in the political institutions, in the narrow sense of the word, or in the social infrastructure.

The corruption of political institutions appears when the party system no longer corresponds to the different groups of interests, or rather when the party system works in such a way that no stable authority emerges from the rivalry of the parties.

The second kind of corruption is that of the public spirit. Montesquieu called this the corruption of principle. Different modalities of corruption of principle can be imagined: either devotion to the party obliterates in the end the awareness of the common good or else the spirit of compromise, which is a necessity if the regime is to work, ends by preventing any clear decision from being made and any firm policy from being embarked upon.

Lastly, corruption can originate from the social infrastructure when the industrial society is no longer able to work, when social rivalry becomes so intense that the political power, emerging from the parties, is unable to dominate them.

Such categories are useful, but they cannot be used as a basis for our study because very often it is impossible to say what the main cause of corruption is.

A second, and simpler, kind of classification is based on the distinction which I made in the previous two chapters between oligarchy and democracy.

Constitutional-pluralistic regimes can be corrupted by too much oligarchy or too much democracy. In the first case, they become corrupt because a minority manipulates the institutions and prevents them from reaching their highest form, which is government by the people.

The second kind of corruption appears, on the other hand, when oligarchy is too eroded and the different groups push their claims too far and no authority able to safeguard the general interest remains.

This, too, is useful. Corrupt regimes can in fact be the result of too much oligarchy or too much democracy.

But this distinction is both abstract and general; it is not always easy to know to what category a particular case belongs. Also, I prefer to use another simple distinction, that of 'not yet' and 'no longer'. There exist constitutional-pluralistic regimes which are corrupt because they have *not yet* struck deep roots in society and there are constitutional-pluralistic regimes which are corrupted by time, by wear and tear, habit and which *no longer* work.

By and large, most corrupted regimes in the sense of *not yet* suffer from an excess of oligarchy; in contrast, regimes which are corrupted in the sense of *no longer* suffer more often than not from an excess of democracy.

I shall therefore study first the difficulties in taking root and then the risk of decomposition or of dissolution.

The first difficulty, the most usual and the best-known one, to be overcome before roots can be struck, is the failure to respect the constitutional law. After all, the characteristic of this kind of regime is the establishment of laws within which the rivalry of individuals, of groups and of parties takes place. Every violation of the law by force is a breach in the very essence of the regime.

Many such regimes have difficulty in asserting themselves. For long periods the constitutional working is interrupted by *coups d'état*. France tried to introduce a constitutional regime at the end of the eighteenth century, but the regime only began to be established and to enjoy general respect in the last years of the nineteenth century. Between 1789 and 1871 none of the systems was considered valid by the whole nation.

More generally, it can be said that Latin countries had and still have great difficulty in making constitutional-pluralistic regimes work in a permanent way. Why this should be so is open to argument.

Some obvious reasons can be suggested in a brief analysis.

The first is the part played by the Catholic faith and the Church in the life of Latin countries. How can a regime of this order be established and accepted by the whole people, if the greatest moral and spiritual force does not support it, if the Church is, or appears to be, hostile to the political institutions? The phenomenon is clear in the case of Spain; it played an important part in French history up to 1855 and has overshadowed the history of Italy.

In all Latin countries, many, if not all the parties have put forward extreme claims. Now, if such regimes are to live, the parties which have given birth to them must abide by the rules. In France, the moment a democratic or republican regime is established, some parties appear which are hostile to it and blame it for its moderation and conservatism.

The third reason appears to be that industrialization has not made so much progress in Latin as it has in Protestant countries.

The second difficulty to be surmounted during the period of taking root is the manipulation of constitutional practices by an oligarchy. It is not necessarily a bad thing that during an initial phase a ruling class, aware of itself, should assume power. After all, this is what happened for a long time in the history of England. But for such regimes to take root under cover of oligarchic power, the oligarchs must be really favourably inclined to the institutions and must help to modernize the society and rationalise the economy. What is to be feared is that the institutions will be manipulated by oligarchs who are hostile to genuine party rivalry and at the same time against any encroachment on their privileges.

I have the countries of the Middle East in mind. In Egypt, before the recent revolution, a constitutional-pluralistic pseudo-regime was completely manipulated by an oligarchic minority, made up mainly of great landowners. They were plutocrats, as well as oligarchs, who were more anxious to maintain their power and wealth than to transform society.

Constitutional methods, the pseudo-respect for individual liberties, run the risk of being degraded into instruments by which anachronistic privileges are preserved. The regime is corrupted, or rather it does not rise to its full height because the absolute power of the ruling minority militates against this.

The third difficulty is linked to the second. The differences between the groups and especially between the different groups which form the ruling minority reach such proportions that the regime is doomed.

I am referring to France. The divorce between social strength and political power has, in one form or another, always been endemic in France. The same can be said of the countries which are today called underdeveloped. Sometimes the old oligarchies dominate the elections and use constitutional practices as a kind of camouflage. In so doing they force the representatives of the middle classes, who want to speed up modernization, into a kind of extremism. Sometimes, on the other hand, intellectuals, professional revolutionaries or soldiers seize power and use it arbitrarily in order to do away with the old privileges.

France is an instructive example of this. The constituent assembly did not contain a single republican. The idea of a republic was thought to be impossible in a country as vast and as populated as France. The monarchy was overthrown because the old principle of legitimacy was weakened and the disputes between the different factions, all part of the old order, were too violent to allow genuine competition to function. The form the revolution took was directly caused by the failure of the attempt to introduce parliamentary practices, modelled on those of England.

This failure had lasting results, since before the end of the nineteenth century no regime was really deeply rooted and accepted by the whole population. Sometimes the faction in power came from former privileged classes; sometimes on the other hand the victorious faction threw the descendants of the aristocracy into internal emigration.

These new élites, often composed of officers or of intellectuals, have become in our day, according to circumstances, either fascist or communist; the two formulae sometimes spring from the same source, i.e. a will to break with conservative or pseudo-democratic regimes which are manipulated by the representatives of the traditional élites.

What is necessary to the process of taking root is that the élites thrown up by the development of industrial society should be able to find a place in the system.

The fourth difficulty is to limit the claims of the people during the first phase of a constitutional system. I am thinking of France in 1884. To replace a monarchy with a republic does not mean that from one day to another the resources of the community or the productivity of the economy is increased. A regime does not distribute more wealth to the masses simply by calling itself republican or democratic. Revolutionary changes give rise to hopes and claims; how then can the regime avoid becoming the scapegoat for the inevitable disappointments?

There is a case which is of even more interest to us today. This is the case of India. The survival of a constitutional-pluralistic system in India depends, on the one hand, on the maintenance of the coherence of the ruling group in the new state and, on the other, on a degree of passivity among the masses, or again on the maintenance of traditional social discipline in spite of economic changes. If the political consciousness of the masses in India is awakened too soon, it is doubtful whether the constitutional-pluralistic system will survive. No matter what regime there may be, because of the lack of resources, it will be a long time before it will be possible to satisfy grievances, even legitimate ones. Democracy exists in India, which is a poor country, because two infrequently found conditions are simultaneously present – the resignation of the crowd and the coherence of the élite.

Here we come to another difficulty about which I shall only say a word because it is such an obvious one. This is the dearth of administrators.

We are studying primarily how constitutional-pluralistic systems function politically, but the quality of the administration is just as important as are the purely political factors. If a constitutional-pluralistic regime is introduced into a country which is almost devoid of administrators, it is unlikely to function. Would any other kind of system work better? To be sure, no regime will function well if there is a dearth of qualified administrators. But the fact that to this can be added a constant conflict of interests, of ideas, of men and of parties increases the difficulties of the administrators. Take Indonesia, for example; this is a country with no unity of language, of religion, of nationality, in which the number of qualified administrators is derisory and to which a regime modelled on the constitutional-pluralistic systems of the West was introduced. It is hardly surprising that after a few years both the regime and the national unity fell apart. It is not the function of democratic regimes to create states or to unite nations; what it can do is to enable the unity of the state and of the nation to resist the permanent rivalry of men and ideas. No one has ever created a nation by telling men to go and debate. Sometimes the West seems to be advising the liberated countries to create power out of their divisions.

If I had to sum up the various difficulties which must be overcome before a constitutional-pluralistic regime can take root, I would sum up in the three following formulae:

The gap between social strength and political power must be fair, i.e., according to the old bourgeois wisdom, neither too great nor too small. If the gap is too great, an explosion is almost inevitable. The social forces will try either to get rid of or to manipulate the political leaders. If there is dissociation between those who exercise political power and those who possess social position through money or tradition, then the regime is pseudo-constitutional and the strings are pulled by the oligarchs.

The formula which serves as a foundation for the regimes must be respected, the institutions accepted in principle, and the spirit which is needed if these regimes are to function must animate at least the ruling minorities, if not the masses.

Lastly, the third necessity is that the regimes should be effective enough. Efficiency is measured by two objectives: the first is to safeguard the unity of the community, in spite of the multiplicity of conflicts, and the second is to modernize the economy, in spite of the conservative tendency of the interest groups.

I shall examine the risks of dissolution: first, at the level of political institutions; secondly, at the level of the principle or of the public spirit; and thirdly, in relation to the social infrastructure or more generally in relation to the tasks which these regimes must accomplish. (I shall deal later with the third point.)

1. At the level of political institutions

Let us take once more the case of France.

What today threatens the regime is not the violence of ideological passions, hostile to the regime. On the whole the French today are more inclined to accept the existing regime than at any other time since 1789. Perhaps this is because they are weary after so many vain experiments. Nevertheless the regime is thought to be in danger. And if it is indeed threatened, it is purely and simply because many people feel that the constitutional law, the party system and the discrepancy between the constitutional law and the party system is responsible for a weakness and an instability in the executive which is incompatible with the common good. Any system which is accepted as legitimate can be threatened by its own weaknesses.

2. Corruption of the principle

I am using the word 'principle' in the sense in which Montesquieu uses it. Men today are no longer of the kind that such a regime demands; they no longer possess the qualities necessary to keep alive a regime of freedom.

What kind of men must there be in a constitutional-pluralistic regime? Let us discard the word *virtue* used by Montesquieu; the societies in which we live cannot be virtuous in the sense in which Montesquieu used the word. Virtue, according to him, was made up of a will to equality and frugality which is contrary to the essence of industrial societies. Be they communist or democratic, our societies are not virtuous in this sense, for the simple reason that their aim is to produce as much as possible and as well as possible. One cannot imagine a society the aim of which is to produce as much as possible and to distribute as little as possible. Men cannot take frugality as the highest virtue in an economy which is trying to create affluence.

These statements are obvious, although many of those who criticize democracy persist in believing that the virtues of modern democracies can be the same as those of former ones.

They do have one feature in common, and that is respect for the law. Citizens in constitutional-pluralistic regimes must possess three qualities:

They must observe the laws and especially the constitutional law, because it is the charter at once of their conflicts and of their unity;

they must put forward their claims, have opinions, I would even say that they should have strong party feeling so that the regime can be enlivened and the torpor of uniformity avoided;

they must not push party passion to the point at which any possibility of agreement disappears, that is to say that they must have the feeling for compromise.

Undoubtedly, there is a risk that one or other of these qualities will be lost. It is difficult to maintain a balance between these three qualities so that people have the right amount of all three. When men have strong party feelings, they tend to lose the sense of compromise.

Sometimes when political passions run high men lose their respect for the law or for the constitution. Regimes are always threatened either by excessive partisanship or on the other hand by too great a feeling for compromise.

Regimes of this kind must beware of the strong party emotions which are fatal to the national unity, but they must also beware of too much feeling for compromise; because, if, when they are faced with a problem, their first reaction is to try to bring the parties of the right and of the left together, the solution will in all probability be a bad one. An excess use of compromise is shown, in a corrupted regime, when a parliamentary solution rather than a solution to the actual problems is sought.

Every policy is faced with problems which it must solve. The status of some overseas territory or the policy to be followed if the deficit in the balance of payments is to be made good, must be decided upon. The decisions must be the result of an analysis of the situation. This analysis does not dictate what measures must be taken. But it does suggest the different directions which it may take. All these directions have advantages and disadvantages, risks and opportunities: choose one and you may win.

This is what lies behind the objective study by the counsellor of the prince, that is by the officials. These men are charged with saying to the politicians: here are the facts of the case. Then the politician has a different duty: to amass, in support of a possible solution, a parliamentary majority. The search for a majority is not to be scoffed at. But when this search becomes in itself a solution then we can deduce that the spirit of compromise has reached the point at which even if the regime survives it will be paralysed.

This danger cannot be avoided. By definition the best decision, if the majority refuses to support it, is excluded. The objection which can be made to an intellectual who proposes a solution to a difficult problem is not without weight: 'It is easy for you to talk. You are not in power and therefore do not need to amass a majority.' It is easy to solve problems if you ignore the wishes of the citizens or of their elected representatives. For the essence of constitutional-pluralistic regimes is that problems cannot be solved without the consent of the elected representatives. But when the people's representatives forget the problems and only think of their own game, there then occurs the corruption which strikes at the very heart of the system. The intellectual and moral attitude vital to the system has vanished.

This corruption of principle has nothing or little to do with demoralization in the sense which moralists give to the word. This corruption of principle can infect virtuous men, good fathers, good husbands, good tax-payers. It is a purely political corruption, the causes of which can be linked to the system itself.

The corruption of principle and the corruption which the classical writers described when writing about democracy have something in common. Plato, for example, thought that democracy began to degenerate when the governed behaved like the governors and the governors like the governed, when the citizens lost the habit of obedience and despised discipline, when the rulers seemed to look for the applause of the ruled. What I have just described is after a fashion the transposition, in our modern societies, of the double corruption of the ruled and the rulers. The citizens make claims which are too vast and the rulers are not decisive enough. Now the governed must make claims, but before accepting a decision taken by the majority, the governors must take into account the preferences of the citizens, but not yield to every vociferous minority.

The decomposition of the spirit which is necessary to a constitutional-pluralistic regime sometimes contaminates the institutions themselves. When the structure of parliament is such that the rulers are constantly obliged to obtain the assent of their adversaries, the problem which must be solved is forgotten and attention is concentrated solely on the single problem of the majority.

I should like to finish by taking a particular example of corruption, the perfect example of corruption of a constitutional-pluralistic regime, that of the Weimar Republic.

I say the perfect example in the way in which one says the perfect crime. The different factors are nearly all present. We can follow at least one perfect pattern of the decomposition of a parliamentary regime.

A constitutional-pluralistic regime has, by definition, two kinds of enemies. This is because it has two kinds of flaws. It has enemies in those who denounce the dissolution of the national unity through the party system, and in those who dream of social unity and of the liquidation of the oligarchs, who, behind the scenes of parliament, pull the strings.

In order to simplify we shall call these two ideological oppositions the revolutionaries of the right and the revolutionaries of the left. The first denounce the threat to national unity inherent in the permanent conflict between the groups and the parties, the second denounce the 'monopolists', the party struggle, the social heterogeneity and dream of a homogeneous society. These two schools of revolutionaries exist, virtually or potentially, in all modern societies. It is easy to understand both sides of the argument and even to see similarities. Nothing is more attractive at first sight than to dream of a society in which class differences have disappeared; nothing is easier than to criticize the regime in which power emerges out of the conflicts themselves.

Both kinds of revolutionaries have a common aim, in certain circumstances, which is to destroy the pluralistic regime which, seen from the two extremes, is an evil, as it embodies the camouflaged capitalist oligarchy in the eyes of the revolutionaries and because it brings social disintegration and gives the revolutionaries of the left an opening.

In the Weimar republic, these two kinds of revolutionaries, of the right and of the left, were active. Both mobilized the masses. Nazis and communists were at one in opposing the existing regime.

The rightist opposition was strong in the Weimar republic because the constitutional-pluralistic regime was a new phenomenon, and enjoyed no prestige as it was a symbol of defeat. The rightist revolutionary exploited the national resentment or enthusiasm. In order to recruit the numerous cohorts in support of the 'national unity', this unity had to seem weak or the destiny of the community had to appear to be threatened.

The revolutionaries of the left, in the Weimar republic, were strong because the economy passed through an exceptionally severe crisis. Thirty-five years after, it is difficult to understand why the leaders of the capitalist world allowed the crisis of 1921 to develop until sixty million workers were unemployed.

It was then that the constitutional-pluralistic regime lost the necessary support of the masses, as to some it seemed unable to ensure national unity and to others unable to give the minimum of well-being or prosperity without which no modern society is possible.

These were the basic facts: what more could have been done if the constitutional-pluralistic regime was to survive?

These two oppositions had only to unite to make it impossible for the regime to function. It was sufficient only to have a majority of the regime's enemies in parliament. From then on, the regime was doomed to a *coup d'état*. By definition, the regime which we are studying is based on majority rule; if a majority in favour of the regime no longer exists, no constitutional-pluralistic regime is possible. In 1933, the National Socialists, Communists and a fraction of National Germans together had a parliamentary majority. It was necessary either to govern by means of a majority, which would have ultimately and inevitably ended in a *coup d'état* in the long run, or once again to hold general elections, which would probably have led again to a majority hostile to the regime.

This is a perfect example of the corruption of a constitutional-pluralistic regime. Not only was there a majority hostile to the regime itself, but within the regime the corruption had infected all the parties, taking the form of what I have called excessive devotion to the party. The regime presupposes parties, but the party must not become an absolute. In the Weimar Republic all the parties tended to become totalities, each having its own ideology and its own troops.

What was the outcome? Two outcomes were possible; the first was that parties which favoured the regime should themselves take the initiative and govern in violation of the constitution; the other was to give power to one of the groups hostile to the regime.

Looking back, we can see which would have been the better solution; with hindsight, one can say unhesitatingly that a *coup d'état* by those who supported the regime would have been better. If we imagine that the parties of the centre had governed by decree for several years, the consequences would have been less terrible than those of Hitler's coming to power.

But things turned out differently, for many reasons, particularly for the important ideological one of the quasi-solidarity between the revolutionaries of the right and the traditional conservatives. They both constituted distinct groups; their ideologies were profoundly opposed, but, before the Second World War, the traditional conservatives believed that they belonged to the same party as the revolutionaries of the right while in reality they were only inspired by the same hatreds. A traditional conservative in France for example was a member of the Action Française. Now a member of the Action Française – let us use the past tense so as not to offend anyone – before the Second World War disliked the radical or socialist leaders just as much as the fascists did. In reality a traditional conservative is very far removed from a revolutionary of the Nazi type, but he is not always aware of this. The National Socialists came to power as a result of a plot by the National Germans, and thanks to Hindenburg's decision.

It is in this way that, in a typical idealist manner, the corruption of a constitutional-pluralistic regime came to an end; the opposition to the regime won an absolute majority and the leader of one of the oppositions came to power and liquidated in semi-constitutional ways the existing regime.

The example is a telling one. A regime which we call democratic loses contact with the masses. Many of the citizens apparently end up by willing the destruction of their own freedoms. No regime can be sure that it will endure simply through the state.

CHAPTER TEN

IS CORRUPTION INEVITABLE?

Is the corruption of constitutional-pluralistic regimes inevitable? How does a regime become corrupted? Can it prolong its existence or is it inevitably destroyed by a revolution? These are classic questions in political writings; all the philosophers, from the time of Greece and Rome onwards, have pondered the predestined or accidental corruption of regimes.

The meaning of the question becomes clear when we turn to the economists. The economists ask the same question, first of all about crises, and then about the unique evolution of a given regime. There are three schools of thought about economic crises: the first holds that there is an endogenous causality of crises, the phase of prosperity creating the causes of the crisis which follows; the second school affirms not an endogenous causality of crises, but what can be called an endogenous *causality of the vulnerability to crises* – an economy at the height of prosperity is vulnerable to any incident which will bring about a depression, without the depression being absolutely inevitable; lastly, according to the third school, the crises are determined by exogenous accidental causes, and one can at the same time envisage and realize continuous economic growth without alternating expansion and contraction.

When it is a question of the irreversible evolution of the economic system, we find almost the same three schools: the first affirms the endogenous causality of the progressive paralysis of the system; for example, the theory of Marx, the law of the constant lowering of the rate of profit; the second school is represented by the work of Keynes who stated, not that the capitalist system can no longer work after it has reached a certain point of development, but that in proportion to its growth, it becomes increasingly vulnerable to depression or to chronic unemployment; the opportunities for investment diminish, the outlets for profit are no longer the same; lastly, according to the third theory, throughout all the phases of the capitalist system, the danger or the possibility of crisis exists, and the crises are neither more nor less to be feared in a phase of maturity than in an initial phase of development.

Let us refer these three ideas to the problem which we are looking at today, that is the problem of the corruption of constitutional-pluralistic systems; we can find their equivalent at two different levels. At the political level, it can be said that a constitutional-pluralistic regime destroys itself by continuing to exist, or becomes increasingly vulnerable the longer it lasts. The second level is that of the economic infrastructure: it can be said that the probability of corruption in these systems does not increase because of purely political factors, but that the changes in the economic and social structure are such that the system is either completely paralysed or finds it more and more difficult to function.

Do constitutional-pluralistic regimes destroy themselves simply because they continue to exist? Is there a growing probability of paralysis and of corruption in these regimes the longer they endure?

The argument which is most often put forward in favour of this thesis runs as follows: the essence of this kind of system, it is said, is that power is to be found in the divisions between the groups and the parties; all the parties are compelled to exploit the divisions which exist in any community. Now if the parties exploit the divisions permanently, the probable result is the gradual disintegration of the national unity and the appearance of the two phenomena which I analysed in the preceding chapter, excessive devotion to the spirit of compromise (the parties obsessed by the need to surmount their differences stop thinking about the problems in order to concentrate only upon coming to an agreement) or, on the contrary, an excess of devotion to the party, as we saw in the Weimar Republic.

Many countries have recently won their independence; India has been independent for ten years; the struggle was led by the Congress Party which owed its unity to a great extent to its resistance to the occupiers or the British overlords. The unity of the Congress Party will probably grow weaker with time, as the memory of the coherence needed if independence was to be won fades. But to return to France: the first generation of republicans under the Third Republic, was more united, or less divided, because it remembered the past struggle against a common enemy, the enemy of the republic itself.

The erosion by the passing of time of the unity either of the majority or of those engaged in politics, is a phenomenon which can be seen in many cases. But one cannot deduce from this that the regime degenerates inevitably, for at the same time other phenomena are produced which tend to strengthen the regime in the second or third generations.

The first factor which helps to strengthen it is the weakening of parties which are opposed to such regimes, a decline which goes hand in hand with the gradual decline of traditional forces. The republicans were more divided after the second generation of the Third Republic, but the traditional forces, hostile to the Republic during the first generation, rallied round it from the time of the Second. Every system grows stronger simply because it endures. Men become used to institutions and, as no system is perfect, an established regime reaps the benefit simply by existing.

Which of these two arguments – erosion through demagogy and strength through habit – is the stronger?

No general statement is possible. Demagogy cannot be said to weaken the system more than it strengthens it; it all depends on the phases, the cases, the countries.

What are the changes, linked to the development of an industrial society, which influence constitutional-pluralistic regimes in one direction or the other?

The current formula which is used in the press and in sociological textbooks is that of mass culture. On all sides, the question is asked if a mass culture can include political institutions which were formed in the last century. What we call mass culture is essentially the concentration of population in cities, the multiplication of collective organizations, interest groups and parties; individuals taken separately have less and less opportunity to act in relation to the groupings; crowds are manipulated or conditioned by the means of communication, the mass media. In the cities, individuals are bombarded by the press, by the radio, by the television and by all the procedures which claim to instruct – more often to distract – and for the most part to give them a more or less imaginary picture of the world in which they live.

Are these different phenomena, which are loosely called mass culture, favourable or unfavourable to constitutional-pluralistic regimes?

Twenty years ago, during the thirties, the answer would have been almost unanimously negative. Today, at the end of the fifties, the tendency would seem to be positive; sociologists are victims of fashion just as other men are and they tend to extrapolate the events which they observe and to believe that what is characteristic of one phase is prolonged indefinitely. During the thirties, we saw the disintegration of constitutional-pluralistic regimes beneath the blows of communist or fascist movements. Since the Second World War, to everyone's surprise, such regimes have become relatively stronger, at least in Western Europe and in North America.

What are the changes which operate in such regimes because of the general social evolution?

Respect for the traditional social hierarchies tends to disappear. A wave of thought which is called rationalist and materialist is widespread. The privileged groups which belong to the past, those which propaganda today calls feudal (it is a long time since there were feudal lords in the strict meaning of the term in the West), the traditional aristocrats have lost prestige and authority. Those who think that such constitutional-pluralistic regimes only exist because there is an aristocracy conclude that they are doomed. In fact, the situation is more complex. The traditional aristocrats see their influence diminishing, but it still exists and is made up of minorities which possess social prestige, moral authority or economic and political positions.

In modern industrial societies, in the United States or in France, there is no self-aware closed minority, which can be called an aristocracy and which possesses both social importance and political authority. Our societies are élites or ruling minorities, but not in most cases, *a* ruling class, which is coherent, and has a goal. As for the categories of directors, I listed them in my course last year:[1] *mass leaders*, that is secretaries of the trade unions or leaders of political parties, parliamentarians, professional

[1] *La lutte des classes*, chapter 15.

politicians or elected *functionaries* who often, in the background, wield great authority, directors of business concerns or *employers* and lastly *intellectuals* who enjoy a degree of prestige which is almost always too small in their own eyes, but which is in fact relatively great. These different minorities are not united and it can even be said that the essence of our societies is that the élites are rivals. In countries in which the struggle is a peaceable one, Britain or the United States, the trade union secretaries, the heads of mass parties do not think that the directors of enterprises or the directors of the economy are their enemies. They take part in a permanent competition which to them is normal. This rivalry would be incompatible with the existence of the regimes if the political directors, thrown up by an industrial society were in themselves hostile to parliamentary procedures and to the representative traditions.

The outlook, the inclinations of those whom the masses choose as leaders, constitutes perhaps the most important factor. In a system of free elections, inevitably the parties for which the underprivileged vote are directed by trade union secretaries, professional politicians and intellectuals, not by the representatives of old or new oligarchies. If the leaders of the masses are in principle hostile to representative institutions, then these institutions are sooner or later doomed.

But this is not generally so. In some countries many mass leaders are hostile to parliamentary procedures because, in their eyes, they paralyse social or economic change, but in the countries of Western Europe most of the popular mass leaders are still half favourable to them. In two European countries only, France and Italy, a great many, if not the majority of the mass leaders, are hostile to such institutions. This dissidence is not yet so great that constitutional-pluralistic regimes cannot survive.

Another argument, apart from the hostility of the new managers to parliamentary institutions, is that the latter are paralysed, deflected from their purpose by external pressures. How many times have we not heard the argument that the regimes which are usually called democratic have ceased to be what they should be; they are now only a tilting yard, in which those who represent private interests joust with one another and forget, despise and distort what should be the common interest. The answer to this argument is always the same: an existing system should not be compared to an ideal one which has never existed; to say that in a constitutional-pluralistic regime the interests, grouped together and coalesced, should have no say, is not to imagine a model of democracy, but an impossible and contradictory system. It is a question of deciding whether the private-collective groupings – for example the trade unions of workers or of employers – through the pressure which they exert on the administration prevent the constitutional-pluralistic regime from functioning. It is true that the pressure groups do succeed in seizing advantages which seem excessive to the ordinary citizens and to those who do not benefit from them. But for the time being, it is not true that in the main regimes of constitutional-pluralism they prevent these institutions from functioning. Let us take Britain as an example of an apparently extreme case: the organization of the trade unions is very powerful, all the unions being grouped in a single organization and the Labour Party, which is one of the two main parties, is financed by the central trade union organization. One might suppose that a system in which the workers' trade unions are directly linked to one of the two main parties would make it impossible for a regime which is based on the alternation in power of the two big parties to function. But in fact, over the years this has not proved to be so. The trade unions, in Britain would prefer up to a point to have the Labour Party in power, but when the Conservative party is in power, they do not oppose it systematically. If they were to try to engage in systematic opposition to the party chosen by the voters, the workers would not support them in the last resort and public opinion would be against them.

In the United States, the workers' unions have real power, but they are not linked to either of the two parties; nearer to the Democratic Party than to the Republican, they nevertheless do not always campaign for the Democratic candidate rather than for the Republican one. The candidate of their choice is not elected simply because they campaign for him. The influence of the unions is not so extensive that it commands the vote of the workers; the workers distinguish between the professional groupings which claim to promote their professional interests and the political parties between which they choose freely.

Lastly, according to others who reason from the experience of the corruption of the Weimar republic, in a mass culture in which propaganda is a permanent, almost inevitable, phenomenon, the parties become increasingly totalitarian; the devotion to the party spirit causes them to lose sight of the feeling of interests common to all the competing parties and consequently extremism in the end prevents the regime from functioning. The experience of the fifties is just the opposite of that of the thirties. It in no way confirms that the tendency of the parties to become totalitarian is irresistible. The only case which we have known is that of the German parties; neither the British nor the American parties become totalitarian and, as we know, the parties in France are not at all totalitarian. The French parties suffer rather from too little discipline. It would be rash to conclude from the role of propaganda in industrial cultures that the inevitable evolution of the parties in such cultures will lead them towards a totalitarian model or towards extremism.

What argument remains in favour of the theory that the very evolution of an industrial society is detrimental to the constitutional-pluralistic regimes?

The most serious and the most striking argument is that the tasks with which the modern state is faced are too difficult for a regime of this kind. The argument takes various forms which I shall discuss briefly. What are the 'tasks of a modern state' which are so frequently spoken of?

Social legislation, in our societies, is essentially an administrative affair. Any kind of administration can put through, always imperfectly but for the most part adequately, what is called social legislation. French legislation is among the most complex in the world because the French wanted to avoid wholesale state control and at the same time to safeguard the special regimes which existed before the general one. The French regime is an example of the dangers and defects of complex systems. It is not a question, however, of a parliamentary system which hinders the development and functioning of a welfare state or of the social services.

The second kind of task which faces the modern state is the direct management of a part of the economy, in particular of a sector of industry. In France, for example, an important sector of our industry has come under state ownership. But here again the difficulties which this creates for the functioning of a constitutional-pluralistic regime are much exaggerated. All in all, parliament is barely aware of what happens in the nationalized industries. I do not mean to say that this is an unmixed blessing, but the fact remains that the competition of the parties is extended to the nationalized industry. Those who lead the nationalized industries are appointed more or less directly by the state. Sometimes the appointment is in the hands of an administrative Council in which the state representatives are not in the majority. Differences of opinions about the choice of the director can arise between the various representatives of the state because they themselves are appointed by various ministries. However that may be, once an enterprise has been nationalized, it is administered by someone who is appointed in a different way from the directors of great business concerns, but afterwards his activities are of the same kind as those of a head of a private concern. The directorial board of Renault is subject to the same considerations, and submits to the same laws as that of Citröen. The government interferes only a little more in the administration of the Renault works than it does in that of the Electricity of France.[1]

Some difficulties over the financing of investments do possibly arise from this, but they are less important than one might think. After twenty years of trial and error, there is no reason to believe that nationalization, at least as long as it does not suppress the machinery of the market, is incompatible with the maintenance of parliamentary system.

The third kind of task which faces the modern state is the management or semi-management of the economy by the public powers. Here a number of difficulties do undoubtedly arise. In a mixed economy such as ours, the political managers and the administration take measures which directly affect prices and profits, and the allocation of this income between the members of the community, between private and collective interests. The decisions can either be arbitrary ones or inhibited by the traditional administrative regulations. For the direct management of the economy to be effective, the directors must be able to see what is expedient and impose their will. The semi-management of the economy is perpetually exposed to a double risk; either the administration is arbitrary and rides roughshod over the rights of the individuals or, on the contrary, it does not succeed in realizing its projects.

There is another way of presenting the problem: the ideal theory of the constitutional state is that the authorities formulate

[1] The Minister in charge controls the prices.

the laws, the general rules, which individuals must obey, but do not take particular decisions which affect private interests. But when half the economy is planned, many general decisions have neither the character of laws nor of application of the laws, purely and simply.

Under the French system, the greatest danger is not one of arbitrariness but of paralysis. It is true that we often complain about the risk of arbitrariness and it may be that some individuals are the victims of the administration. The wine growers hold that the building of the faculty of science on the site of their market is an arbitrary act which violates ancient rights, based on documents dating back for more than a century; the other party to the debate sees it as a typical example of administrative paralysis, a measure in the common interest being delayed because of respect for title deeds and privileges. Let us take a more serious problem: an economic crisis threatens and it is important to put in hand quickly a programme of public works; now in a regime such as ours this entails a long legal process, if only for the expropriation of the land on which the building can be put up. Constitutional tradition does not easily adapt itself to the need of economic management.

This is a genuine difficulty, but it does not mean that we must come down on one side or the other. There is a dialectical relation between a system of political competition and a purely competitive economic system. The system of political competition gives rise to protests by individuals and groups against the repercussions of economic rivalry. When these repercussions are too painful, the system of political competition tends to muffle the effects of economic rivalry. In other words, constitutional pluralistic regimes favour the evolution of the economy towards a semi-socialist system, towards a semi-planned regime in which an attempt is made to prevent the mechanism of the market from striking too drastically at any particular group.

We are governed by these regimes of attenuated economic rivalry and of permanent political competition. There is no reason why they cannot continue to exist in a more or less modified form. It is true that they are threatened by pressure groups, by the loss of the legislative monopoly of parliament, by the paralysis or arbitrariness of the administration: but all systems lead a precarious existence.

Who are the irreconcilable enemies of constitutional-pluralistic regimes?

The first category of enemies is composed of the traditionalists, of those who remember and regret an entirely different kind of system. This first opposition is usually weakened by the development of the industrial society.

The second category of enemies is made up of the economically privileged, who feel that they are threatened by the socialist trend of the regime. This second group resembles those whom Aristotle called 'the rich threatened by taxation', and whom he saw as one of the factions supporting tyrannical regimes. This rallying of the privileged to the enemies of the pluralistic regimes has already become familiar to us, between the two world wars, especially in Weimar Germany. In Germany, too, it seems that, at least in the present phase, the danger is less. The privileged seem to have understood, in most cases, that revolutionary regimes, either of the right or of the left, are more hostile to them than are pluralistic regimes. The managing directors who, like a recent parliamentary candidate, see no difference between a socialist and communist candidate are few and far between. In order not to see the difference, one must either have very strong convictions or a very narrow point of view.

The third kind of enemies are those who recruited from among the sub-proletariat or the sub-proletarians, those who feel that the functioning of the present regime is unfavourable to them. In all regimes of pluralistic democracy, some minorities are the victims of laws imposed by the economic groupings. For example, in France, the victims are the homeless or the badly-housed (victims of laws made to protect those who live in flats). In France, there are at least two or three sub-proletariats of this kind. But these sub-proletarians are hardly ever stronger than the groups which are reasonably satisfied with, if not actually enthusiastic about, the existing regime.

A fourth category remains: the popular masses who adhere to a class ideology, and who are hostile to pluralistic regimes because they dream of creating a homogeneous society in which classes will have disappeared. These masses, inspired by class consciousness, continue to exist but, in most of the regimes in a developed industrial civilization, they are decreasing rather than growing.

It is true that, as well as the social groups hostile to the regime, there are three groups of leaders or of men who are hostile to pluralistic regimes because of their ideology or temperament. For want of a better term I shall call them the *pure*, the *violent* and the *Utopians*.

The pure are appalled by a system in which everyone talks about allowances, incomes, subsidies: they have a horror of the 'economic jobbery' which is the inevitable characteristic of all parliamentary regimes. Let us remember, in semi-literary language, the anger of the centurion against the parliamentarian, of the parachutist against Clochemerle. This revolt against materialistic regimes, which has a noble inspiration, exists and will continue to exist, but only a minority is affected by it.

The *violent* are those who, in the manner of Georges Sorel, despise compromises and think that it is deplorable to obtain by negotiation what can be seized by force and who look back with nostalgia to a different kind of regime.

Lastly, the *Utopians*, conscious or over-conscious of the imperfections of party systems, who dream of completely different systems.

These three categories of temperamental or ideological opponents, are rather weaker today than they were a generation ago, but in certain circumstances they could become stronger. Here, too, there is no clear-cut evolution in one direction or the other. For such regimes to be definitely established, they must have no enemies, and there must be no dangers inherent in the difficulty of governing modern industrial societies; loyalty to the regime, instead of being simply a matter of course or of reason, must be enthusiastic. Now this is not so – the regimes are accepted, but not popular. Perhaps it is better so – if they were popular with some, they would be unpopular with others. They must be accepted as a matter of course. Accepted as a matter of course, they are sometimes at the mercy of violent forces which exceptional circumstances throw up.

Once again, it all depends on the circumstances. When profound changes are taking place, it is difficult for this kind of regime to function. Constitutional-pluralistic regimes need the groups in a society to reach agreement through their differences. If violent changes modify fundamentally the situation of some groups, agreement, based on a moderate formula or a pondered decision in favour of a compromise solution, is difficult. Periods of upheaval jeopardise pluralistic regimes. Germany went through such a period in the thirties, when the traditional enemies were still strong and the Utopians were already strong. It is possible that France is passing through just such a period.

To end, I should like to say a few words about the passage from corruption to revolution.

A corrupted regime is not necessarily on the brink of destruction. It can last for a long time. I would even go further; it is possible, in some cases, for a corrupted regime to be the less bad solution to a given problem or the best answer in the circumstances. Let me return to the Germany of the thirties. Given the division of the German masses, the fanaticism of the extremists, the totalitarianism of the parties, the Weimar Republic was a corrupted regime. But the best solution would perhaps have been to have helped this corrupted republic to last for as long as possible. It is dangerous to say that because a regime is corrupted, it must be destroyed. Corruption can be independent of the will of the people; it can reflect the economic and social situation or a deep division in public opinion. In such circumstances, the only choice is to prolong the corrupted regime or to give to one man or to a group of men or to a party the discretionary right to impose its will on all. Sometimes it is better to give absolute power to a group rather than to remain in the paralysed anarchy of parties at loggerheads with each other, but in the long run, absolute power may finally exact a higher price than paralysing anarchy.

How do we pass from a constitutional-pluralistic regime to another kind of regime? There are, in fact, three modalities of this transition.

The first is the *coup d'état*. The South American republics offer many examples of the transition from a constitutional-pluralistic regime to a more or less dictatorial one. The passage is defined by the violation of constitutional legality, a group of armed men seizing the state. In general, in the South American republics, it is the army or a party of the army which makes or favours the *coup d'état*.

The second modality of transition is the legal or semi-legal accession to power and, in the last phase, revolutionary upheaval. Hitler came to power, the President of the Republic called him to the post of Chancellor; then, once master of power, Hitler made a *coup d'état*. The same thing happened in our history. Napoleon III began by being a constitutional president, he prolonged his term as president by a *coup d'état*, which made him Emperor.

The third modality of transition to another kind of regime is military defeat, invasion from abroad or at least action from abroad. In his *Politics*, Aristotle recalls that internal regimes change under external pressure. When Athens took a city, it put democrats in power. When a city fell into Sparta's zone of influence, oligarchs were installed. Many constitutional-pluralistic regimes, in our century, have given way to authoritarian regimes of one kind or another under external pressure.

We have not, hitherto, evoked revolution properly speaking, on the model of the revolution of 1830 or 1848, but it is difficult to conceive of a revolution of this type against a regime, founded on constitutional or electoral machinery. The opponents in a parliamentary regime can be many or few, but how could the voters in a majority be passionately against a regime which is the outcome of their own votes? A revolution against a constitutional-pluralistic regime is normally made by a minority, with at most, the acquiescence of the majority.

For the minority to carry out a revolution, it must have either the help of the army (and this is the first possibility) or the support of the established authorities (and this is the second possibility) or the action of a foreign army (and this is the third possibility).

Once the break is made, what kind of regime will emerge from the disintegration of the constitutional-pluralistic regime? All the regimes can emerge which we shall study in the second part of this course, that is to say – all kinds of non-constitutional-pluralistic regimes, authoritarian regimes, which try to be limited or authoritarian regimes which try to be totalitarian.

THE CORRUPTION OF THE
FRENCH SYSTEM

In the previous chapter, I studied the problem of the corruption of constitutional-pluralistic regimes and I took as a starting point three hypotheses: *self-destruction, the growing vulnerability of the regime* and *the lack of change, oriented in a given direction.* In conclusion, I kept the third hypothesis. Not that the germs of corruption are not present in such regimes, but the tendency towards striking root is as strong as the tendency towards dissolution. At the political level, regimes are weakened by wear and tear, but strengthened by habit; the unity of the nation threatens to dissolve, but there is a chance that the revolutionaries will rally to its aid. As an industrial society develops, it creates fresh administrative difficulties, but the ever-rising standard of living inclines the masses to accept the existing regime. Constitutional-pluralistic regimes in a mass society must recruit political leaders who believe in parliamentary institutions and who stand fast by constitutionality. In spite of growing materialism, the people must be able to make sacrifices for the community. But although none of these conditions is impossible, none of them is guaranteed. This strictly abstract conclusion, is not the same as a forecast of the future of constitutional regimes. The capitalist system can disappear, without corruption having been fatal to it, and the same perhaps holds good for constitutional pluralistic regimes.

Today, I shall examine the French regime. I do not presume to teach you either what you should think or what should be done to improve our system. But in order to remain within the framework of a sociological analysis, I will try to test the concepts defined in the previous chapters.

In the preceding chapter, I said that the French regime was corrupt. You can object: how do you know? Why is it corrupt? My first answer is that it is corrupt because everyone says so. In a country in which, every day, the newspapers state that the regime has reached the last stages of decomposition, a crisis point has undoubtedly been reached. In matters of this kind, opinion is a reality and creates, in part, reality. The opinion which the people have of their regime is an integral part of the strength or weakness of the regime itself. A regime which all the people say is bad offers at least one characteristic trait of corruption; it does not hold the allegiance of those it governs.

In the second place, the people's lack of support for the regime is shown by the considerable number of votes cast for parties which are defined by opposition to the existing regime. In the 1951 elections, the total number of votes cast against the regime was 46 per cent, if the Gaullist votes are counted with those of radical opposition. If the 1946 method of voting had been applied in 1951, the Communist Party and the *Rassemblement du Peuple Français* together would have had more than a majority. In the last elections of 1956, the percentage of votes which I shall call technically 'revolutionary', meaning simply votes against the system, was slightly lower, but it nevertheless reached about 40 per cent. A regime in which at every election between 40 per cent and 45 per cent of the votes are cast against it offers again one of the characteristic features of any corruption, the breaking of the link of solidarity between the people and those who govern.

The third characteristic of corruption, which we can all see, is the instability of the government. It is a fact that the average duration of French governments is less than a year and that all Frenchmen agree that the short-livedness of the governments is one of the fundamental causes of the crises in which we are floundering.

These three characteristics of corruption seem to me to be all three objective and free from any value judgments of any kind.

Another question immediately arises: how serious is the corruption of the political regime?

The reply to this second question is not an easy one. Judging by experience, I would say that the years 1945–58 were, for France, from the demographic, economic and social point of view a period of rapid recovery; the mortality rate fell, especially infant mortality which is a sign of the increase of public health; industrial production grew rapidly; for the last four years it grew at about 10 per cent annually, which is an exceptional rate of growth for France and for other countries; even agriculture, which for long has been hidebound, is beginning to be modernized; the yield of wheat per hectare has grown in the ten years since the Second World War as much as it did in the previous fifty years. In many respects, the period 1945-58, which is generally thought to be a period of decadence, was at the same time a period of economic expansion and of social progress. This is not to say that there was no corruption of the political regime, but it proves that the latter, whether good or bad, does not exert a decisive influence on other phenomena. Nations can be strong with unstable governments. Strong governments can preside over the decline of a nation.

What are the consequences of the corruption of the political regime?

To judge by what the French themselves say, the effects of political corruption are essentially as follows:

1. The administration of economic affairs is, in many respects, lamentable and is at the root of the inflation which lasted from 1945 to 1949, and since then has caused the crises in the balance of payments; twice, at the end of 1951 and at the end of 1957, the reserves of foreign currency were almost exhausted and France had to ask for foreign aid.

2. Lacking a firm hand at the head of the state, pressure groups succeed in wresting from officials or politicians benefits which were not in the common interest; or again, certain groups are able to maintain outdated structures of production or of organization by obtaining subsidies from the public authorities.

3. The corruption of our regime has resulted in what is called the break-up of the French empire, of the French union, the 'loss' of Indochina, Tunisia and Morocco.

The first two complaints are, to some extent, well founded; economic affairs in France could have been better conducted and could still be improved. There is a relation between the weakness of the public authorities and the inflation of 1947-8, the crisis of the balance of payments of 1951 or 1957. What exactly is the link between the corruption of our regime and financial crises? They are open to debate – the periods in which the finances of France have been badly conducted are more numerous than are those in which they have been well conducted; inflation and devaluation are not something which the republic or democracy discovered. Many of the French kings discovered the art of manipulating the currency; the manipulation was a little more complicated than it is today but the results were not always different.

As to the weakness of the state in the face of pressure groups, the complaint is just as valid, but to what extent is this more true of France than of any other constitutional-pluralistic regime? In any regime of this order, we know that private interests have the right and the power to be heard and to defend themselves; hence the risk that the private-collective interests wrest from the authorities advantages which are partly illegal. Are the pressures much stronger in France than elsewhere? It is not easy to make a comparison because this entails a detailed study; what is certain is that they give rise to far more comment in France, that instances are widely reported (this is true of wine and alcohol because France usually produces too much of these) but such phenomena exist in all the western countries. Mistakes in administration did not prevent the development and modernization of the French economy in the years after the Second World War.

There remains the third complaint, which has been more resoundingly reported in the French press, the loss of the French Union, i.e. of the French empire.

Here again, it must be remembered that all the European countries since the Second World War have, in one way or another, lost part of what they called their empire. The British way of retreat can be thought to be more graceful than the French style, but if the independence of a colony or a protectorate is seen as a loss for the mother country, it must be remembered that countries enjoying a regime which is universally approved suffer the same misfortune. Even supposing that our institutions are the cause of events which we deplore, they are not their only cause.

These remarks are supported by the evidence; there are too many people in opposition and there is too great an instability in France. Let us come now to the second stage of this analysis.

Let us say first of all that there is a link between the excessive number of revolutionary opponents and the instability of the governments. In the present Chamber, out of rather less than 600 deputies, nearly 200 do not play the game. Once more, it is a question of a technical term; by 'not playing the game', I mean that they are indifferent to the way in which the regime functions and are systematically hostile to the policy of the regime. The English term is in-game member and out-game member. 400 out of 600 can constitute a governmental majority. As more than 300 deputies are clearly necessary for a permanent majority, the only coalition possible in the existing Chamber must include both the extreme left and the extreme right among those who take part in the game; the socialists and the independents must combine, if a governmental majority is to exist. A cabinet, in which the representatives of parties which differ about most subjects coexist, is by definition divided, and is therefore weak and ineffective.

A second consequence of this structure is that the extreme minorities in the governmental coalition have an influence which is out of all proportion to their size. When nearly all the deputies who 'play the game' are needed to constitute a majority, the 70 most vocal deputies, whether of the right or of the left, are indispensable. The tribute payed to the hotheads mitigates against the efficiency and stability of the government.

This explanation of the present instability is true up to a point, but it is not satisfying. At a time when the number of deputies outside the system was insignificant, French governments were not any more stable. The analysis which I have just outlined is valid for the present Assembly but it does not hold good for the whole of the historical phenomenon. Governmental instability in France antedates the development of the communist, poujadist or extremist vote. Governmental instability seems to be a characteristic of all French parliamentary regimes.

As for the structural causes of the instability of governments here, to my mind, are the main reasons: they are tightly linked together. It is simply a question of all the characteristics of the French party system.

1. French parties are numerous and have always been so.

2. The French parties are heterogeneous, some voting as the party line dictates (the communists and socialists), others boasting of their lack of discipline, like the Radical Party or the Party of Independents. It is easy enough for a system in which all the parties are disciplined to work; it is equally possible for a system in which all the parties are free from policy discipline to work, but the combination of disciplined and undisciplined parties is an additional factor of instability since to *constitute* a government the

parties must first of all reach an agreement and then after that the deputies, individually, must be in agreement.

3. The parties originate from and are founded on traditional ideas; they are often divided when it comes to a question of vital interest. The Socialist Party is usually a disciplined one, but when the CED (European Defence Community) was discussed, factions were set up and the unity of the parliamentary group was undone.

4. To the opposition between the parties and within the parties, a series of oppositions bequeathed from the past must be added; the Chamber contains at the same time opposition between the right and the left (without it ever being very clear which is the right and which is the left) and opposition within the right and within the left.

All these characteristics define what we may call a *structure of the French parliamentary game*, which resembles the *structure of the game within an American party* at the moment in which the presidential candidate is about to be chosen. The Chamber is divided into groups, some large and some small, some disciplined and some not; inside each group, new oppositions spring up, rivalry between individuals combining with the agreement on ideas; coalitions are always temporary and can break at any time.

This structure of the game, when it is a question of choosing the presidential candidate in the United States, only happens once in four years. We watch then a scene which is in some ways comparable to that afforded in a quasi-permanent manner by the French parliament. French observers, when they follow the game of an American party when a candidate is *nominated*, find little to edify them in the scene. Even the structure of the game implies procedures which do not all conform to the rules of fair play. But once the candidate is elected, everyone rallies round him, so that he can at least be elected, even if they break with him later. In the French system, the game is not halted after a cabinet has been formed and this can only make for governmental instability.

Hitherto, we have restricted ourselves to a simple description. If we want to go further we ask: Why has the game this particular structure? Here we are presented with various explanations which are all true and all unsatisfactory.

They are all true because they show that if the French politics is like this, it is because we are as we are. They are unsatisfactory because we want an explanation which would help us to change the world. All these explanations presuppose so many phenomena from the past and the present that we tend to become disheartened. All the realities of French life find expression in the regime.

The explanations fall into three orders: either we evoke the economic and social structure or else historical traditions or lastly the national psychology, going back, naturally, to Julius Caesar's description of the Gauls.

1. There are many parties and the parties are heterogeneous because France itself is heterogeneous. ... In some regions, nearly all the industries are concentrated; in others, the west for example, industry has barely penetrated and consequently the traditional forms of community life have been maintained. The strength of the different parties varies according to the province; even if a party represents all the provinces, those who vote for it differ from one region to another and the unity of each party is tenuous. A socialist from the industrial region of the north bears little resemblance to a socialist from the winegrowing region of the south nor does he resemble the socialist from the west of France where the clerical question still dominates the political battle. The social heterogeneity of France is one of the causes of the plurality and of the lack of discipline of the parties. The MRP, after its dazzling successes in 1945-6, has become once more a regional party with three powerful strongholds, in the west, the north-east and the north.

One condition necessary to the existence of a small number of great organized parties is a sufficient socio-economic homogeneity of the country itself; if the country is too diverse, this diversity will be reflected by the parties.

2. The right as well as the left still remembers the troubled episodes of French political history during the last century and a half. No government of any kind since 1789 has been universally accepted by the whole country; every time a crisis arose, no matter what the cause, the regime was blamed. In some parts of the country, historical quarrels such as the question of disestablishment, still arouse passion. The French continue to fight the battles of the Revolution, of the Dreyfus affair, of the armistice and of the liberation; and they still fight the battles of economic expansion and of overseas policy. Finally, they quarrel about the consequences of possible policies.

3. Why is this so? Let us leave tradition and pass on to psy-

chology. In France economic, social or technical discussions have always tended to become ideological conflicts. After all, economics are boring; the question of how inflation can be controlled has never interested in theory more than about thirty economists; on the other hand, the discussions about disestablishment or abstract questions such as, Do *raisons d'état* justify the condemnation of an innocent man? are *par excellence* exhilarating. They can be endlessly pursued; by definition, agreement is impossible; each camp has convincing arguments and the abstract level of the dialogue enables it to be carried on endlessly. de Madariaga wrote a book called *Frenchmen, Spaniard and Englishmen*; in which he describes the French as reasonable beings; he analysed the way in which such men engage in politics. The French engage in politics with a marked preference for theoretical problems. The most hotly debated controversies are those with the most negligible material consequences. de Madariaga takes as an example the Dreyfus affair.

It is not difficult to use and combine the three kinds of explanation and to come to the conclusion that France being as it is, it is not surprising that French politics is as it is. Once again this is a disappointing but incontrovertible fact. I have put forward these various explanations somewhat briefly. But they can all be elaborated in detail. The way of thought, the style of action, historical traditions, the economic and social structure find expression in politics. If all these interpretations are combined, we will have done almost all that we can to *understand*, which clearly leaves out the question of knowing what can or should be done.

Let us now go on to the second question; why are so many in opposition?

The three kinds of explanation of the number of opponents are exactly of the same order as the three kinds of explanation for the governmental instability, by the economic and social structure, tradition and psychology.

1. The French working class has never been entirely integrated into the regime; because of the slow economic progress in the last century, it has never received the integral benefits of the economic expansion; it is beginning partially to receive the fruits but it is not yet aware of this, because of the general climate of inflation. Lastly it remains faithful to a tradition of hostility to the state, of revolt against the capitalist system.

As for opposition to the state on the point of another section of the voters, that is the opposition of the right, the socio-economic explanation runs more or less as follows:

The number of Poujadists in the last elections is explained essentially by the rapidity of economic progress in the last ten years. All rapid economic expansion creates difficulties for some groups of the population which cannot adapt themselves to it. Rapid progress is unequal progress. There are regions and groups which benefit from it and others which do not. In a stagnating country, the groups accept the way in which they are treated; in an expanding country the groups who do not get their share in progress revolt against the set-up. They do not blame economic progress, they blame taxation (which is always resented).

The socio-economic explanation of the two extremes in France today are roughly as follows: the French working class remains for the most part hostile to the regime because, in the past, it was not integrated into the state; to this is added opposition at the other extreme because expansion strikes, absolutely or relatively, at the groups which do not succeed in swimming with the tide.

2. *Historical explanation.* For more than a century and a half the French have had doubts about their regime; they still have and will go on having them because they think in political terms. It needs time for a regime to be taken for granted. It is only stabilized when it is no longer called in question. The regimes in Britain and the United States are stable because they are intertwined with national values. The number of revolutionary opponents springs from attitudes moulded by history; the French seek fruitlessly for a constitution which will improve administration, by reconciling them with each other.

3. The third kind of explanation, which uses the argument of the national character, holds good equally in the same way for governmental instability and for the questioning of the regime. What is more stimulating for intellectuals than to discuss the regime and for the ideologically minded than to ponder about the advantages and disadvantage of any kind of constitution?

Let us now turn to an entirely different question, the question of reforms.

The kind of explanation which we have sketched does not lead to the drawing up of a plan of constitutional reform. Explanations of this kind tend rather to discourage the will to reform. The more the number of factors which decide the way in which the existing regime functions is insisted on, the greater the temptation is to say that everything must be changed in order that something be changed.

I will quote here an extremely interesting phrase from an article by the economist Pierre Uri which illustrates the kind of mistakes made in good faith and lucidly by intelligent people:

How can we overlook the fact that the difference which separates the Weimar Republic and the Bonn Republic; the opposition between the crumbling and the concentration of parties, between the recurrent crises and governmental longevity, rests on two small clauses; the vote of constructive defiance and the adjustment of proportional representation by the refusal of seats to parties receiving less than 5 per cent of the national vote.

If one takes the formula literally, the difference which separates the Weimar republic from that of Bonn rests on two constitutional clauses, the first according to which the government cannot be overthrown when the name of the President of the Council who will take its place has not been agreed on and the second which consists in refusing representation to any party which does not receive 5 per cent of the national vote.

These two clauses may perhaps be useful but in Germany today it is difficult to judge.

Conditions are such that the clauses have only played a small part. The Christian Democratic Party has permanently so many members in Parliament that they are always masters of the game; the chancellor towers over his colleague. Even without the 5 per cent rule, the crumbling of the parties which we saw in the Weimar Republic would not be produced.

The main difference between the two republics is that in the Bonn republic the revolutionary opponents are few and the large parties are unified and coherent; the national psychology has completely changed. I could list other changes.

It cannot then be stated that the main difference between the two republics lies in the constitutional clauses; perhaps one day they will play a part. But let us imagine that in the French parliament a large number of revolutionary deputies have decided to overthrow the government. They vote for the candidate for the succession to the Presidency of the Council even if they are against him. What would prevent the Communist Party and the Poujadist Party from combining for the elections? Constitutional rules can always be distorted.

What reforms can we imagine which would modify the functioning of the French constitution? Either the substitution of the presidential for the parliamentary form or the reform of the electoral law and of the right of dissolution within the framework of the present system.

Two objections to the presidential government are raised; if the presidential government is to be a solution, a majority of deputies prepared to vote for it must be found. This majority only exists in exceptional circumstances. We are going round in circles. The members of parliament must be in favour of or resigned to the introduction of this reform.

Would a presidential system help the institution to work better? Perhaps, but the diagnostic must be a cautious one. A presidential system does not give great scope to the executive; the executive is stable, but not efficient. The President of the United States is assured of a term of four years (this is not always a matter for congratulation) but he needs the approval of congressmen and senators who are elected in a different way. In the United States, and in every presidential system the majority in the two houses is not always made up of those who elected the president. Cooperation between an executive of one particular political colour and a legislative of another is necessary. In the United States, this cooperation is fairly successful; the Americans are pragmatists in politics and not extremists, they have little taste for ideologies and their parties are not under the party whip. Each congressman or senator votes, without taking much account of his party's orders. But would he behave in the same way in a French-style parliament? The freedom from the party whip of the parties is the condition of existence of the American system, just as the discipline of the parties is the condition of the functioning of the British system. What would happen with parties like ours, some disciplined and some not? The executive is stable, but a president chosen by the parties because he was inoffensive as many of our Presidents are would be weak. An energetic president, in conflict with the legislative bodies, would provoke a constitutional crisis, a common enough phenomenon in countries with a presidential system.

In the framework of the present regime, the possible reforms which are endlessly discussed in the newspapers and in parliament are without any great import. They evoke an electoral reform designed to reduce the number of revolutionary members. In France a 'revolutionary' deputy is not necessarily a deputy who wants to make a revolution, but simply a deputy who does not want to become part of the regime as it is at present. An electoral reform would easily reduce from 200 to 100 the number of revolutionary deputies without modifying the number of voters who vote for them. It is simply a manœuvre. It is harmful also to be too ambitious and to combine a method of election party by majority and party by proportion in the style of the German system in order to create more disciplined or less sectarian parties.

The second kind of reforms which are envisaged touch on the question of confidence and the rule of dissolution.

Some propose automatic dissolution in cases of ministerial crises, convinced that if the dissolution is optional it will not be decreed. Others reply that automatic dissolution may do more harm than good. Dissolution has a purpose in the English regime where the elections give clear and distinct results, but not in a regime in which the relative strength of the parties is not perceptibly modified from one election to another. One answer can be that automatic dissolution would avert governmental crises. The threat of dissolution would prevent crises and this would mean that the governments would last longer. But it is not enough simply for the governments to last longer, they must be able to act. The rule of automatic or semi-automatic dissolution gives the governments a chance to last longer, but does not guarantee that they would govern efficiently.

One last question remains and it is hotly debated: how to prevent the revolutionary opponents from blocking a measure without proposing either a substitute government or a solution? Many systems are imagined. The difficulty is always the same: the government must have the right to demand a vote of confidence, as this is the only way open for it to force parliament to vote certain measures. But if a vote of confidence is asked for too often, there is a risk that the government will be overthrown on a minor question. None of these reforms would change fundamentally, in the short run, the way the French regime functions.

Here we must ask a last question. In what sense is constitutional reform really, as everyone says, the vital question for France? France is passing through a political crisis which is caused by the Algerian war. The obsession with constitutional reform is a way either to shelve the problem which must be solved or to find an essentially different government which would be able to solve it.

PART THREE

A MONOPOLISTIC PARTY REGIME

CHAPTER TWELVE

THE SILKEN THREAD AND THE SWORD'S EDGE[1]

In the previous chapter I dealt with the French regime, taking it as an example of a corrupted one. A large proportion of the voters vote as though they owed no loyalty to the institutions, which in turn lend neither authority nor longevity to the governments. I then outlined the consequences of this corruption and in the last part I examined briefly the proposals for constitutional reform, about which I expressed a certain scepticism. It is unlikely, unless one takes into account the possibility of a revolution, that any of the structural features of the French regime will be modified. Finally, I ended by indicating that this obsession with constitutional reform possibly springs from the difficulty of the problems to be solved. Perhaps the regime is no worse and no better today than it was five, ten or fifteen years ago, but the task of reforming it is an exceptionally difficult one.

The French regime is such that the divisions which exist within the public opinion and within the governing groups are reflected and eventually even magnified in political circles. Every regime finds it difficult to create a unity of will and of action, when there is no such unity among the people; after all, even the British system which is always held up as an example does not easily create a common will when opinion is divided. In the years before 1939, Great Britain preserved the outward appearance of a homogeneous government, but it was paralysed by conflicts

[1] In the French edition this chapter is entitled *Fil de Soie et Fil de l'épée*. This is a double play on words. *Le fil de soie* is an expression used by the Italian historian Ferrero to denote the belief in the legitimacy of power, the existence of which makes the use of force unnecessary; *le fil de l'épée* is the title of a well-known book by General de Gaulle. [Translator's note.]

within the governing minority. One difference does, however, remain; more often than not, the British system is successful, thanks to party discipline, in keeping a government in power which is able to act, when possibly if the opinions of members, taken individually were counted, no majority would appear. France pushes the democratic idea to extremes, asking that every voter vote for the party of his choice, and then that each deputy be free to vote as he thinks fit. The result of so many questions, put to so many people, some well informed and some not, clearly does not result, if the nation is divided, in a common will.

The problems which faced France overseas after the second world war were not in themselves essentially different from those across the Channel. Great Britain had, by and large, some idea of what had to be done. Independence had to be granted to all the Crown territories in which the nationalist movements seemed to be strong. Even in Malaysia, where she fought and finally won a war against the communist guerillas, Britain ended by giving independence to moderate governments. In France the choice lay between two kinds of policies – a British-style policy which accepted the formation of independent states in the territories of the French empire or of the Union Française and a policy of reform leading to autonomy, but maintaining as far as possible French sovereignty. Neither of these two policies was clearly formulated and rationally elaborated; nor was either of them carried out with determination. After twelve years (in 1958) the first became a fact; Indochina is today composed of three or four independent states, Tunisia is independent, so is Morocco, and the territories of French Equatorial Africa have received through the intervention of the 'loi cadre' an autonomy which in all probability will become independence, whenever the will to independence shows itself strongly enough.

Here one comes to the real, pressing and tragic problem of Algeria, where both policies continue to be hotly defended by representatives of those who, twelve years ago, could have formulated one or the other. It is here that it is particularly difficult to arrive at the creation of a common will. Those who were against the complete independence of the territories of the Union Française are violently opposed to the continuation of the policy pursued in Tunisia and Morocco. The reasons for this opposition are understandable: it is a question of the last ditch. If Algeria is independent, like Tunisia and Morocco, the movement will spread irresistibly to the rest of the Union Française; the French minority is too important to submit to or freely to become part of an Algerian republic. Supporters of this policy do not accept that part of the French minority should return to France or be repatriated. They think, and in this they are right, that the nationalist movement in Algeria burns more fiercely and is more dangerous than in any other part of the Union Française, because in Algeria a nationalist revolution is combined with a social one. The greater part of the privileged class in Algeria is made up of Frenchmen. A nationalist movement drawing its supporters and leaders from the people is of necessity socialist as well as nationalist. Finally, those who defend the formula 'Algérie française' hold that French sovereignty in Algeria is indispensable if the links between the mother country and the other African colonies are to be maintained.

Those who press for independence for the territories of the Union Française are more than ever convinced that this is the only possible policy. There is an irresistible logic in history. It is inconceivable they say to give to Madagascar tomorrow the right to set up an independent state and to refuse the same right to Algeria. Finally, how is the war to be brought to an end, as long as the 'nationalists' or the 'rebels' in Algeria are given the external support which cannot be prevented?

Faced with this alternative, no party in the French Chamber is really united; every party has supporters of both policies.

The policy which has in fact been followed, at least since 1956, is that of the first school, which holds that French sovereignty in Algeria is indispensable to French security and to France's future in Africa. It is unjust to accuse the French government, as is done every day, of inactivity. It carries out a policy which has the support, if not of the whole country, then at least of a majority of the deputies. And yet there is clearly general dissatisfaction among the opponents as well as among the supporters of the policy which is being carried out. Supporters of the present policy want reinforcements to be sent eventually or at least that propaganda against French action in Algeria be forbidden. The radical choice which the upholders of the present policy demand would entail a disciplined effort by the nation to carry out the policy of the government. As for the other school, it speaks of inactivity because it does not believe that pacification can succeed.

Under the French system, I doubt whether in the immediate future any policy other than the present one is possible, for it reflects the country, parliament and the regime.

What is the solution? There are three possible ones: the first is tyranny, the second is dictatorship in the classical Latin meaning of the word, the third is to wait until events, in one way or another, bring the debate to a close.

The tyrannical solution is one which we all dream about during sleepless nights, provided that power is in the hands of those with whom we agree. We are all convinced that any policy would be better than the present one. The policy that each of us wants could be imposed by a group of men seizing power and compelling the obedience of those who disagree. This is the solution which has come about in many countries, riven by faction or by irreconcilable parties: one party or faction has swept away the others.

The second solution to which appeal is so often made is the appeal to the legal saviour, or, if you prefer it, to a dictatorship modelled on that of Ancient Rome. We all know what it is called today. The press, of every shade of opinion, recommends this last hope. But many who hold different views think of it when forced to take account of two eventualities. The arbitration of the legal saviour will inevitably disappoint all of them, because representatives from every camp appeal to it. At least, and this is the second hypothesis, this saviour will not invent a miraculous solution which will reconcile all the warring factions. We all imagine a policy so grandiose or so subtle that it combines the advantages of opposing solutions, without the inconveniences of either of them. Such a miracle seems, to say the least, unlikely. The problem which must be solved lies with Algeria and not with France. Even were our opposing parties to agree on the name of the saviour, our adversaries would not so easily rally to it.

The third solution, or absence of one, is that which we are experiencing. The government steers between contrary pressures and each of us, in private, waits for some unforeseen event to bring about the decision.

The present crisis has only been analysed here to show one feature of the French regime. This regime permits in every period of crisis part of the population to refuse to submit to the national discipline; the Communist Party, for example, makes no secret of its subversive aims. One can almost go so far as to say that the

French regime is characterized in every epoch by the treason of one third of the population, or at any rate by the fact that one third of the population acts in such a way that the supporters of official policy consider it to be composed of traitors.

In the last century Renan spoke of the 'internal emigration'. Under every government, part of the nation refuses moral allegiance to those who govern and takes refuge in an attitude of systematic hostility. In every one of the major crises of this century, a section of the people has rejected the decisions of the governments and refused them in spirit, if not in deed.

Does this refusal of loyalty conform to the essentials of constitutional-pluralistic regimes? Certainly not. It is possible to ban parties which do not play the game or whose practices and intentions are tyrannical. The Bonn government has banned revolutionary parties of the extreme right and of the extreme left, but it has not ceased to be constitutional-pluralistic by so doing. Such a regime, like any other, has the right to defend itself against those who would destroy it. But the condition which is indispensable if they are to remain constitutional is that they act within the law, without giving a free hand to the police, or in other words, that they safeguard the constitutionality of their acts and the control of the judiciary.

I do not want to suggest that those who disagree with the government's policy or who are communists should be banned in France. I have the best reasons for not holding such an opinion. Apart from personal reasons, there is a more general argument: when the number of dissidents or separatists, of those who are not morally loyal to the government becomes too great, there is a risk, if they are banned, that the constitutional-pluralistic regime itself is destroyed. When a country is too divided over the best regime or over the line to be followed in any given situation, it is often better to accept a state of semi-paralysis. When we are disappointed in the government, let us try to hear in its proposals the echo of what Jean-Jacques Rousseau called 'the sovereign people', so that its voice is changed and becomes our own, because in the last analysis it is we who elected it. So long as the laws of the constitution are respected, something is salvaged. It is in abiding by the law in times in which men are carried away by their passions that civil peace at least is preserved.

This is why I would say, borrowing an expression from Ferrero, that the constitutional regime is that in which, when all is said and done, the last barrier is the silken thread of legality. If this silken thread is broken, the sword's edge looms up on the horizon.

Passing to the third part of this course dealing with regimes of the sword's edge,[1] I shall take as examples of the three kinds of regime of the sword's edge, the Spanish revolution, the Nazi revolution and the Russian revolution which, despite their differences, have in common the fact that they were the result of a seizure of power by an armed minority.

In contrast to the constitutional-pluralistic regime, three other types can be distinguished. The first is opposed to the *pluralism* of parties rather than to *constitutionality*. The second is hostile to pluralism, but favours a *revolutionary party* which is identified with the state; this was the case of Nazism. Finally there is a third type which, like the second, is against the pluralism of parties and favours a revolutionary party, but the aim of this revolutionary monopolistic party is, in theory, the unification of society into a single class.

The Portuguese regime is an example of the first type. Of course, Salazar does not accept a parliamentary kind of constitution, but he does limit the powers of the State and guarantees the autonomy of social bodies. A regime of this kind tends to create a different type of representation from a parliamentary one. It rules out competition between the parties, the permanent competition for power, but it affirms that those in power are not and should not be omnipotent and that they are subject to law, morality and religion. It claims that it has a traditional basis and that it has done away with the unrest of parties and of parliament without as a result having created confusion in society and in the state. It tries to be liberal, without being democratic, but unsuccessfully.

The second type of regime which is usually called fascist has in common with the preceding one the fact that it rejects democratic ideas and parliamentary practices, but with some differences. The government of Salazar tries to 'depolitize' men, that of Hitler or of

---

[1] I have borrowed this expression from General de Gaulle in order to differentiate it from the silken thread of Ferrero, but Gaullism is not a regime of the sword's edge in the sense in which I use the term.

Mussolini to 'politize' or fanaticize them. Salazar's regime has no state party, those of Mussolini or of Hitler had.

The Spanish, Italian and German governments all had in common the fact that they rejected what they called the ideas of 1789, that is democratic and liberal ideas. All three relied upon the principle of authority, but they preached different doctrines. The Spanish regime would seem to be a middle way between the first and second type; it claims that it upholds the role of the Church; it declares that authority comes from above and should not be subject to the will of the citizens, but it is hostile to a totalitarian state. The Spanish regime is less conservative than that of Salazar: it contains several elements of modern fascism and the phalangist movement presents similarities with the Italian fascist movement. The Italian regime was based on a state party; it preached a doctrine of state control, but it was not very revolutionary when compared to that of the Germans. It tried to safeguard traditional structures, while giving to the government the discretionary authority to suppress parliamentary assemblies and the support of a single party.

The regime which represented the second type in its purest form was that of the National Socialists. The movement was anti-democratic and anti-liberal, but also to some extent revolutionary, in the true meaning of the word. It tried to overthrow the social and ideological structure of the Weimar republic. The unifying principle was not the state, as in Italian fascism, but the nation, or rather the race.

The third type of regime, the communist, also suppresses the plurality of parties, but it presents a first fundamental difference to the second. Far from repudiating democratic and liberal ideas, it claims to fulfil them by eliminating competition between the parties. It justifies these claims by an analysis of pluralistic regimes; it claims that constitutional-pluralistic regimes are only a camouflage for a capitalist oligarchy and that therefore capitalist oligarchy must be suppressed and a unitarian classless society must be established if true freedom and true democracy are to be brought into being. The monopoly of one party does not seem to it to be contrary to freedom and democracy, because this regime sees itself in an historical perspective. In order to reach its highest goal, a classless society, the absolute power of one party, which is the expression of the proletarian class, is an essential means.

These three types of regime can be grouped in different ways. From some points of view, there is on the one hand the first type of regime, which is conservative in the Salazar style, and, on the other, the second and third types, which are both revolutionary. On the one side a restoration of the traditional society, with a limited but absolute state, and, on the other, revolutionary parties, a party-state, that is to say a state identified with a party. According to this classification, two revolutionary systems are contrasted with a conservative system.

A second kind of grouping is possible, according to ideology. Here, the first and second regime are contrasted with the third. Salazar, General Franco, Mussolini and Hitler have in common the repudiation of liberal, democratic ideas. The authoritarian-conservative or revolutionary-fascist regimes are anti-1789, anti-rationalist and all preach an authoritarian doctrine. Here we have types 1 and 2 opposed to type 3, because the latter declares itself to be the child of ideology while the other two are its negation. Type 1 is the non-dialectic negation of the constitutional-pluralistic regime, while type 3 wants to be the dialectic negation, that is, a way of repudiating but at the same time preserving, thus of surmounting.

Lastly, according to another classification, the three regimes should not be grouped two against one. They should not form a group at all, as they each represent a different idea.

Every regime can be defined by the way in which it combines social differences with one single political will. The first kind accepts the natural differences in families, corporations and regions, and upholds unity through a strong, but not absolutely unlimited, state.

The second type is built on national or racial unity, based on a single party through which the diversity of social groups created by industrial civilization can be overcome. According to the fascist or nazi idea, the classes, left to themselves, would bring about social disintegration and it is necessary for one group, among the many, to overcome this difference and assert, by force if necessary, the collective unity, the unity of a will under state control.

Lastly the third type asserts that class warfare is linked with a particular economic system. If the diversity of classes or at least the antagonism between them is suppressed, unity will appear in the community itself. The state will be led by a single party because there will be no antagonistic classes in the society.

According to this last analysis, each of the three regimes is defined by a different relation between the inevitable differences and the necessary unity.

This classification of the three types makes no claim to be exhaustive and there are mixed or composite or equivocal regimes, which do not fit clearly into any of the three categories.

In the world in which we live, traditional legitimacy is on the way out. The rules of constitutional-pluralistic regimes are difficult to apply and presuppose a national discipline – in other words wisdom on the part of the parties. Therefore in most countries regimes are being established which are defined by the fact that one group imposes its will upon the others: it is possible that this group does not fit clearly into any of the three ideological or institutional categories which I have indicated.

One hesitates before stating into which category the present regime in Egypt fits, for it is revolutionary rather than conservative, in the sense that it sees itself as having a great task to fulfil, the task of bringing about Arab unity, but this idea is a myth. For the present, there reigns a popular charismatic leader, to use Max Weber's term – an officer who does not want to be thought of as a soldier. If he were a civilian, he would give himself a military rank, as did Stalin. But as he is a former officer, he is head of state. A pretence well suited to the world today.

In South America there are many regimes which are neither fascist nor conservative; they simply represent the seizure of power by a group of armed men under cover of circumstances. Further, the composition of the parties and the attitude of the masses are different. Argentina is a striking case of this for there the institutions, which are apparently constitutional-pluralistic, were defended by the privileged class and the great mass of the people were profoundly hostile to them. A popular and tyrannical leader, Colonel Perón, had the support of most of the trade unionists, even of the free unions. This alliance between a popular and tyrannical leader and the working masses has never taken place in Europe; it is the product of South America, where the institutions known as constitutional-pluralistic were a foreign importation and were monopolized and exploited by a small fraction of the ruling classes. In other words, to use my own expression, the constitutional-pluralist regimes in the Argentine were so oligarchic that they stirred up the anger or the opposition of a great part of the popular masses.

I have made a study essentially of the third of these three types of regime, that is the communist regime. The reasons for which I shall not deal with the first two are as follows:

The first, which is authoritarian-conservative has only been established in Europe in countries which are on the verge of industrial civilization; now, as you know, I am interested above all in political regimes which constitute the superstructure of industrial civilization.

Further I am attached to regimes which claim to be democratic: the fascist regimes, with a frankness or a brutality less and less widely practised today, declared that they neither were nor wished to be democratic. The historical movement, the point of view, was utterly different from the one which we want to analyse.

Finally, the fascist regimes have for the present or perhaps for ever, less significance in Europe than the communist ones. These regimes need a nationalist exaltation, which has vanished from all the countries in Europe. It presupposes a grandiose, ambitious, foreign policy. Circumstances do not favour this.

To end this lecture, I should like to say something about the fundamental differences and the formal similarities (if they are not formal differences and fundamental similarities) between the communist and the fascist regimes.

The Nazi regime, like the communist one, brought with it a single party which had a monopoly of political activity. This monopolistic party was armed with a revolutionary ideology, by which I mean simply the will to transform radically the existing society. This monopolistic party in Germany had an idolized leader; in Russia the leader has not always been idolized and when he has been he ceased to be after his death.

The second similarity concerns a combination of ideology and terror. Regimes of this kind use terror in different degrees against their opponents in the name of an idea. The ideological enemy is held to be more guilty than the common criminal. These regimes are the complete opposite of a system such as the French one in which inevitably at every hour of the day one rubs shoulders with 'traitors', without attaching any importance to the fact. In monopolistic party regimes, the demands of orthodoxy make it dangerous to disagree with those in power. Certain institutions, for example, the herding of opponents, heretics and criminals into camps have been seen in the regimes of monopolistic parties of the right as well as of the left.

The differences on the other hand appear at once and are just as striking.

Voters and members are not recruited from the same social classes. The members of the Communist Party in Russia or in Germany before 1939 or in France today are not recruited exclusively from the working class, but one of their main sources of recruitment is the working class. Parties of the fascist type mobilized the masses, but in general did not recruit their troops mainly from the working class.

The ruling classes have a basically different attitude towards the fascist and the communist parties. In Italy, before Mussolini seized power, part of the Italian ruling class, above all industrial and financial circles, was favourably inclined towards the fascist party; in Germany, Hitler was subsidized by the great industrialists. Let us leave aside the controversial question as to whether the capitalists *organized* the fascist movement. Let us merely recognize that there is a difference in the attitude of the former ruling class towards such movements which present some similarities but whose ends are utterly different. The fascist parties gave hope to the privileged classes who were uneasy about the 'despoiling laws' of the constitutional-pluralistic regimes or about the revolutionary claims which they tolerated.

The attraction of fascism has greatly lessened since the end of the last war. Historically, it would seem that one of the necessary conditions of these tyrannical non-communist movements is the sympathetic support of an important part of the former ruling classes.

Finally, the third difference which appears clearly is the ideological one and therefore of difference in goals. To say that both these two types of movements or of regimes entail a monopolistic party is a clear, but not very enlightening statement. The vital question is: towards what do these movements tend? They have all set their sights on absolute power, on the party in power being given the right to act unimpeded by obstacles and without tolerating opposition – this again is evident, but the monopoly of power is a means, not an end. Objectives, ideologies, practices are different things.

Which are more important, the similarities or the differences between monopolistic party regimes? The reply depends upon the existing institutions and then on future ones. The communist regime does not wish to be judged by what it is but by what it will be; communism is defined less by its actual practice than, in its own eyes at least, by its self-image and by the goals which it claims that it will reach. As such one cannot study communism by omitting to study its goals.

In studying constitutional-pluralistic regimes it is not so necessary to contrast ideologies and reality. In the measure in which these regimes have too flattering an idea of themselves, one simply has to read their opponents to dispel any vain illusions. My study of it cannot pass as 'poetry'; it rather reduces these institutions to prose. The regimes reveal themselves warts and all, to the observer; they show themselves as they are. To some, the regime which I have described is not true democracy. Many of my critics would reply to me by conjuring up what democracy should be; to take only one example, there should be unity between the citizens despite the divisions between the parties. But these notions of democracy, which can be contrasted with actual practices, remain provisional, abstract and theoretical. The reality is well known – it is the party game, in which there is something perhaps not actually sordid but of necessity shoddy. It is therefore necessary to show that the party system as it actually functions is the reality, without betraying the ideals by which it is inspired. It embodies the institutional interpretation of self-government, of government by debate and consensus.

In the case of the communist regime, the reality is uncomfortably visible and ideology dogs our footsteps. I will take merely the simplest and most striking example of this. The Soviet Union has a constitution (there have been three since 1917) but the last, that of 1936 was proclaimed during the great purge, when several million opponents, real or imaginary, were imprisoned. This solemn constitution of 1936 guaranteed, on paper, the right of *habeas corpus* in conditions as impeccable as those in Great Britain. If, according to Marx, one must distinguish between what men are and what they believe themselves to be, this distinction holds good especially for regimes which claim to be ideological. They try to preserve their self-image, even when it has lost any link with reality.

CHAPTER THIRTEEN

CONSTITUTIONAL FICTIONS AND SOVIET REALITY

So much does the Communist regime call upon ideology and claim that it conforms to it, that it has often been called an ideocracy. It is always necessary to contrast ideology and reality, a distinction which is often difficult to draw. But it is particularly relevant in the case of a regime which is more directly based on ideology than any other.

To believe in a false idea is sometimes enough to make it true. To the extent to which the citizens do not believe in the existence of classes these cease to exist since they are defined by the consciousness of opposition between the groups which make up a collectivity.

Let us go back to the beginning, that is to the revolution. The Soviet regime was born of the revolution, that is of violence; the Bolshevik Party seized power in November 1917. In January 1918 the first and last free elections in the western meaning of the term which Russia has ever known were held. The freely elected constituent assembly was dissolved after a few days because it contained a large majority hostile to the Bolshevik Party.

It is clear that from the first the Soviet regime was unconstitutional. This, of course, as I have already said, is true of most regimes. But more often than not a regime which has established itself by force tends to become constitutional or in other words it promulgates a constitution, according to which those who govern will be appointed and authority will be exercised. The Soviet regime resembled all the other regimes in this respect and promulgated a constitution or to be more accurate it promulgated three, the first dating from 1918, the second from 1924 and the third which is still in force today from 1936. These three constitutions present many similarities and some differences.

In the first constitution which was approved by the Fifth Congress of the Soviets on 10 July 1918, the language used smacked still of the revolution; it spoke of establishing a dictatorship of the proletariat and a strong and centralized government; representatives of the exploiting classes lost both their right to vote and their right to hold public office. Business men, priests, monks, the great landowners were all said to belong to the exploiting classes. The fundamental rights in 1918 were reserved for the workers. A discrimination was established between the peasants and the workers. The peasants, less favourably disposed to the regime, had only the right to one deputy for every 120,000 voters in the Soviet and even these deputies were elected in two degrees; in contrast, in the towns there was one deputy for 25,000 voters, who was elected by direct vote.

According to the constitution the Soviet regime was a constitutional-pluralistic regime. It proclaimed that sovereignty appertained to the supreme congress of the Soviets elected by universal suffrage. In the intervals between sessions, there sat a central executive committee of 200 members, chosen by the congress of the Soviet and this central executive committee in its turn chose a council of peoples' commissars, or in other words a council of ministers.

The communist party was not mentioned. On paper the regime could be compared to those in the West, with a representative assembly, which elected a permanent committee. The latter, in turn, appointed those who exercised executive power. It is impossible to imagine anything more in conformity with western ideas. But the constitution played no part because real power was in the hands of the communist party.

In 1924 a new constitution was promulgated, very similar to the first. In 1918 the regime was not yet firmly established throughout the provinces which were part of the tsarist empire. Between 1918 and 1924, the revolution had won all these lands or if you prefer it, the bolsheviks had reconstituted the unity of the tsarist state.

The ideological declaration at the beginning of the constitution gave as the aim of the USSR to unite all the workers of the world in a world-wide soviet republic. A second part proclaimed that the principal republics would unite freely in the unity of a federal state; on paper these republics continued to enjoy the right to secede. The electoral difference between the countryside and the towns was maintained – that is in the countryside one representative for 120,000 voters and in the towns one for 25,000 voters. For the rest, there was no fundamental change: there was an elected assembly, but this time with two Chambers, one directly elected by the whole population and a second which represented the nationalities, the Council of the Nationalities. It was laid down that all the decrees and regulations issued by the executive power had to be approved by both chambers and that all the laws were to be promulgated in the name of the executive council which on paper once again was an elected body. Besides, the constitution provided also a juridical framework. No more mention was made of the Communist Party than had been in 1918. The constitution was a typical Western one, without any mention of the Communist Party which is, according to the communists themselves the decisive factor in communist practice.

The constitution of 1936, which is still in force today, with some minor modifications is an extremely interesting document. It contains sixteen chapters. First of all it deals with the social set-up of the country: the property laws, then the organization of the state, the higher organs of state power of the Soviet Union, then of the federal republics. The constitution outlines the administration at the federal state level, the federal republic level and lastly at the lower level. It lays down at the same time the judicial set-up, the fundamental rights and duties of the citizens and the electoral system. At the end the two final chapters decide upon the flag and capital of the Soviet Union and lastly the procedure for constitutional revision.

The document has a wider scope than a western constitutional document, for it anticipates the principles not only of the state but of society and it lays down in detail the administrative organization at all levels, from the federal state to districts. Fundamentally the regime appears to be identical to the two previous ones, but with some innovations. Class enemies are no longer mentioned, there is no longer discrimination between the towns and the countryside and officially all traces of this historical opposition have disappeared. The supreme power belongs to the two elected chambers: these chambers, which make up the Supreme Soviet, elect the council of ministers (this is no longer a council of people's commissars). The list of ministers is laid down in the constitution. This list has been amended several times, which has meant that the constitution has had to be revised each time. Soviet deputies have the right to put questions: when a deputy puts a question to a minister, the latter must reply within three days.

We are all aware, and so are the citizens of the Soviet Union, that this is not true. These constitutional documents are fictions. The deputies are freely elected, but there is no free candidature. As the list of candidates is a single list, the choice lies between voting for or not voting at all, and for extremely pertinent reasons 99 per cent of the citizens prefer to vote for. These elections are very different in style from western ones, with foreseeable and foreseen results, in which there is very little doubt about the actual percentages.

As for the sessions of the assemblies, they are all to a great extent prearranged, foreseen, at any rate by those in power, if not by the citizens. The speeches of the deputies are for the most part approved by the ministers. Sometimes they put forward criticisms, but a critical speech is delivered also according to a scenario arranged in advance at least along the broad lines.

The sessions of the chambers are short. They consist of representation, of ceremonies, of acclamation by which the governed publicly proclaim their agreement with the governors.

The governed enjoy, in theory and on paper, all the fundamental rights, freedom of speech, freedom of the press, free assembly. Individuals are sacred and dwelling places inviolable, all the demands of *habeas corpus*, all the demands of formal liberty, are guaranteed. But there exist two limits to the concrete exercise of these rights. The first is to be found in the document itself: these rights must be exercised 'in conformity with the interests of the workers' and the heart of the matter is to decide what these interests are. The second check is that, in some periods at least in the Soviet regime, the ministry of the interior and the police are not subject to the laws or to the constitutional regulations.

What was new in relation to the previous constitutions was that for the first time the Communist Party was twice mentioned in the constitution of the Soviet Union. Article 141 indicates that candidates for election should be chosen by a certain number of groups, among which the Communist Party figures discreetly with great modesty on the same level as the trade unions. On the other hand, in article 126 it is laid down that the most active citizens of the Soviet Union have formed in a Communist Party which is the vanguard of the workers.

What do these constitutional fictions mean? Why elections of 99 ... per cent? Why draw up in so much detail constitutions which do not correspond to the actual functioning of power?

The first answer which is often heard contains a part of the truth: it is a façade for the benefit of foreigners. Because Westerners consider constitutional regulations important, they must be shown that they have no reason to feel superior even in this respect. We must not forget that the 1936 constitution was contemporaneous with the Nazi threat and with the Popular Front. One of the reasons for the 1936 constitution was possibly to convince world public opinion that the Soviet regime was close in spirit to western constitutional practice and opposed to fascist tyranny or nazism. The regime want foreigners to see the distinction between the party and the state. Without this juridical distinction, relations between the Soviet Union and other states would be compromised. The party does not wish to give up its doctrine of world revolution, and therefore the Soviet state in theory cut itself off from the party which is inspired by ideological ambitions of expansion.

They want also to seize the opportunity to create or to reveal the unanimity of the people themselves. The leaders are in no doubt that they will win from those they govern the approval which they want, but the ceremonies of approbation do help to strengthen the allegiance of the citizens to the regime. The state management of enthusiastic applause and of apparent unanimity is part of a psychological technique of uniting people and rulers; this unity, even if it is fictitious, tends to become stronger if it is given expression.

But all this being said, one fundamental question remains: to what extent do those in power, doctrinaires or citizens, believe in the value of these constitutional fictions? To what extent do they believe that they will one day become a reality? The fascist or nazi regimes proclaimed their hostility to democratic principles but the communist regime proclaims its faith in them even although it does not apply them. We must try to understand why this is so.

Once again let us go back to the beginning. The Bolshevik Party seceded from the Russian Social Democratic Party, of which it represented the extremist and minority faction; it took power by force of arms, but it does not consider that it held power by virtue of being a tyrannical minority – it considers that it holds power by virtue of being the representative of the proletariat. How do the bolsheviks, in the light of Marxist doctrine, see their own power?

What is Marxist doctrine? It is essentially an interpretation of society, according to which above all the economic infrastructure determines the whole; the development of modern societies runs from capitalism to socialism. But Marxist doctrine contains practically nothing precise about what a socialist economic regime should be nor about what part political power should play in socialism.

From the economic point of view, the bolsheviks have only a few guiding ideas: the public ownership of the means of production and planning. They did in fact establish immediately the public ownership of the means of production; they have tried to plan the economy and they have gropingly, through trial and error, set up a regime of economic planning which can be justified in Marxist terms, because Marx never said how the economy should be organized.

From the political point of view, the situation is more complicated because the doctrine of Marxism on this point can be reduced to the following proposition: the state is the means of domination and of exploitation used by one class at the expense of another class. As for the future, the Marxist future was anarchic in tendency (once the class enemies had been destroyed, there would be no more state) or to some extent influenced by Saint Simon. Engels often used the expression: 'The administration of things will take the place of government by men'. Marx used an expression which is found in two documents, the dictatorship of the proletariat, conceived for the transitional period of the building of socialism. But what should the dictatorship of the proletariat be? The notion can be interpreted in two completely different ways. Either the dictatorship of the proletariat should resemble the Paris Commune in 1871; Marx once wrote: if you want to know what the dictatorship of the proletariat is, look at the Paris Commune; but according to other documents the dictatorship of the proletariat should be essentially absolute, terroristic, centralized power, on the Jacobin model.

The bolsheviks at once found an ideological solution; the proletariat is expressed in the Bolshevik Party and the latter being possessed of absolute power, is the realization of dictatorship of the proletariat. Ideologically the solution is satisfactory and justifies the monopoly of the party. The party possesses and should possess supreme power, because it is the expression of the proletariat and the dictatorship of the proletariat marks the intermediary phase between capitalism and socialism.

This justification of power thanks to the Marxist formulation of the dictatorship of the proletariat already brings with it certain consequences. The first is to ban other socialist parties. When the bolsheviks took power, at least one other party, the Menshevik, was based on Marxism. Since, by definition, the Bolshevik Party was the proletariat the Mensheviks, who were not in agreement with the Bolsheviks, could only be traitors. Thus, the first conclusion, drawn by Zinoviev, 'When the Bolsheviks are in power the place of the Mensheviks is in prison' is a perfectly logical one. If the Communist Party alone represents the proletariat those who also claim to represent it can only be traitors to the truth, thus traitors to the proletariat and should be eliminated. In other words, ideological doctrine gave birth to and founded *a monopoly of interpretation.*

But the formulation contained other difficulties: if the state is an instrument in the service of one class against another class, it should logically disappear when classes disappear. If the proletariat is defined as the exploited class, when once the proletariat has come to power, by definition it is no longer the proletariat. The proletariat can no longer be the proletariat in the Marxist sense of the word, once it is in power.

On the other hand, a class is defined by the ownership of the means of production. When there is no longer private ownership of the means of production, by definition there are no more classes. But if there are no more classes because there is no more private ownership of the means of production, what use is the dictatorship of the proletariat? The proletariat no longer exists because it is no longer exploited; there are no class enemies; why therefore must there be a dictatorship?

These are the problems which ideologically were and are put forward within the framework of the regime set up by the bolshevik party.

The answer given by the Soviets to these difficulties was as follows: the Soviet state is a state of workers and peasants. It contains distinct but not antagonistic classes. As for the Communist Party, it groups together the most active citizens and it plays a role comparable to that of a schoolmaster. It is thought of as an ideology of the Communist Party, the vanguard of the workers and peasants, the schoolmaster of the whole Soviet people.

In spite of this, one difficulty remains with regard to the original doctrine. If the state's only guiding principle is the exploitation of one class by another, why, when there are no more antagonistic classes, does the state still exist and why does the state tend to become stronger and stronger?

Stalin, a short while before his death, answered this question. He said: Before the state disappears it must strengthen itself. This is a satisfactory answer from the dialectical point of view; the state will come to perfection before exploding and disappearing. A state makes itself increasingly strong because it is surrounded by capitalist states. An ever more powerful state is needed because socialism is not worldwide. But then by the same token, the result is that the doctrine according to which the state is *only* the means by which one class exploits another is false; the state is necessary as long as mankind is not united. As long as there is no universal state, states must lead and represent each collectivity with regard to other collectivities.

The second formulation which Stalin discovered is startling: the class struggle is intensified in proportion to the building of socialism. The formulation is startling because it is utterly illogical. The classes have been defined by reference to the means of production; as long as there are class enemies a class must own the means of production. In the Soviet society, private ownership of the means of production no longer exists: the only property which is not publicly owned (with the exception of the individual plots of land) is that of the kolkhozes, under cooperative ownership. Now even in the days of Stalinist madness it could not be said that the class struggle was a struggle of Soviet society against the cooperative ownership of the kolkhozes. For the class struggle to intensify, there must be classes, therefore the classes are not linked to the ownership of the means of production. The hypothesis can clearly be made that the enemies are the survivors of the former classes, but these were made up of great landowners, bankers, business men and entrepreneurs. When these classes, which were only a minority, lost their property and wealth, they could no longer hold on to their power. One wonders how, thirty years after the revolution, the ex-bankers who are no longer bankers because there are no more private banks could still represent an enemy against which the Soviet state must pit itself.

The intensification of the class struggle in proportion to the building of socialism can only mean two things: either it means the struggle against the survivors of the former class, which is absurd, or it means the struggle against the classes created within the framework of a society with collective ownership and this is equally absurd because in the marxist system there cannot be classes when the ownership of the means of production is collective.

One detects, here and there, echoes of other doctrines and other ideologies. The Russians, leaders as well as governed, are human whenever they escape from their ritual formulation. They know that these formulations have no concrete meaning and they resort to many semiclandestine formulations to justify practice. One is that what matters is to create a basically new society, a new man, the socialist man. The maintenance of the absolute power of the party is not rendered necessary by the survival of the former privileged classes nor even by external threats but by the demands of education. The authoritarian school master is indispensable if a society is to be forged which conforms to the socialist ideal, mankind conforming to the values of socialism.

These difficulties, in which ideology is entangled derive from the errors of doctrine from which the bolsheviks started.

From the economic point of view, which I studied in my course two years ago, the Soviets have done valuable work, but this has nothing to do with the initial idea of what socialism should be according to Marx. Socialism, accord to Marx, should succeed capitalism, in reaping the benefits and distributing to the masses the goods, which are created by the development of productive forces. The Soviets discovered a method of economic construction and of industrialization which has its advantages and disadvantages, but which bears no relation to the idea which Marx had of the advance of the role of socialism.

In political matters, the gap between what the bolsheviks wanted to do and what they have done is still greater. They started with the idea of a temporary dictatorship leading in the end to anarchy. What have they accomplished? They discovered a system which has its advantages and disadvantages, a modern technique of absolute power, adapted to the masses and to the means of propaganda, they created a state which cannot be paralysed by disagreements between the citizens and the parties.

They have even refuted, without meaning to, their own doctrine. According to this, socialism can only arrive after the development of productive forces and as the heir of capitalism. They have shown admirably that the type of state which they call socialist can be established at any stage of economic development, provided that a Marxist-Leninist party takes power. A revolution of this kind is more or less likely according to economic circumstances but it is possible anywhere. They created a state, based on a single party, which reserves for itself the monopoly of ideological interpretation and of political activity – that is a type of state unknown to the pre-1917 Marxists and which the bolsheviks themselves never foresaw. The usual formulation: Men make history but they do not know that they are making history certainly applies to the disciples of Marx himself. What the bolsheviks have done for good as well as for ill, differs greatly from the idea with which they began of what they should do or wanted to do.

Hence one can understand the duality between the constitutional fictions and the reality. For the time being, the bolsheviks have not succeeded completely in reconciling their doctrine which remains, in purpose and aims, democratic with the practice of a one-party state, born of circumstances. It would be false to believe that the constitutional fictions are without significance, simply booby traps or 'Potemkin villages'; as long as the democratic constitution is proclaimed, there is a chance that the regime will evolve in that direction. In proclaiming this constitution, the regime itself proclaims one possible outcome.

In the meantime, the regime accentuates the contradiction between doctrine and practice. The gap between official ideology and institutions is wider than in any other regime and becomes more so as the semi-official ideologies, such as that of the role of the party in industrial construction draws nearer to reality.

Let us now look at the party. We find at first the same phenomenon: the party has a constitution, but this does not play any great part in its real life. The duality of the constitution and of its practice is found again within the party in the duality of statutes and in practice which is very far removed from the latter.

The Nineteenth Congress was the congress in which Stalin, the General Secretary of the Party, was deified. All those who spoke sang one after another the praises of the man of iron and lauded his genius to the skies. Then came the Twentieth Congress and the new General Secretary made his famous speech which became known in the west. The same man who at the Nineteenth Congress had sung Stalin's praises revealed the ghastly horrors which had taken place during Stalin's reign. Besides, he did not even then give a true version of what had happened. Khrushchev's speech to the Twentieth Congress is not the whole truth. It contains passages which we think are true because we know the facts and other passages which we believe are false because they do not agree with the direct experience of witnesses (for example Stalin's role during the war). In both congresses, all the speeches followed the same line, and were received with the same applause. The same men spoke, the same men applauded and equally enthusiastic applause greeted quite different statements.

Three questions spring to mind about the reality of the party.

The first is similar to the one I asked about elections: does the general staff of the party designate those who go to the congress to applaud the speeches or are the delegates elected by the members? Or again, to put the same question in abstract terms: who designates those who go to applaud the rulers?

Second question: Who takes decisions? Or again, who takes what decisions? At what level? One man alone or several men? Which men take the decisions?

Third question: What is the degree of unity of the party? To what extent are there factions? To what extent are the factions tolerated? What fate is reserved for heretics.

It goes without saying, in theory and ideologically, that the party is always united, monolithic, in the same way as the always united Soviet people knows no divisions. If divisions do exist, it is because of traitors who take the place of what in the west are called dissidents or heretics.

The answers to these three questions vary according to the historical phases of the Russian Bolshevik Party. By a process of simplification, five phases can be distinguished.

The first which unfolded before the seizure of power is that of a revolutionary party, for most of the time clandestine.

It was Lenin who in 1903 in his famous book *What is to be done?* invented the theory of this type of party; the workers left to themselves would not be revolutionary, they would adapt themselves to capitalist society, they would confine themselves to asserting their rights within the framework of the trade unions or of a democratic party. The party, indispensable to the fulfilment of the historic mission of the proletariat, must be a party of professional revolutionaries. It was a small party, obedient to the authority of the party leaders, ruled according to the doctrine of democratic centralism; the discipline was strict, discussion was free before decisions were taken, but once taken everyone had to obey them.

At this period, the party leaders, the clandestine leadership in tsarist Russia or the top leaders outside Russia had a dominant influence. The elective principle was better applied in the election of delegates to the congress but because of the situation the manipulation of delegations was easy. I call manipulation the art by which the top leaders of the party or of the secretariat of the party itself chose those who were to be delegates of sections and who at party congresses were to choose the supreme organ, that is the central committee.

This practice is not unknown in the West. Manipulative processes are not unknown in the French Socialist Party; in principle, delegates to party congress are elected by the active members, but the secretaries or the secretariat of its federations have many ways of bringing weight to bear upon delegates. The secretary general has a great influence on the federations; he is not free to carry out a policy to which the members are opposed *en masse* but one cannot say either that the members are supreme in decisions on party policy. There is a reciprocal or dialectical relation between the feelings of the members and the possibilities of action of the party leaders, the central committee or the Politburo.

This then was the first phase; a party of professional revolutionaries, governed by democratic centralism; the delegates to the congress are elected, but the elections were to some extent controlled by the general staff. Lenin, a past master of the art of handling party congresses, was able most of the time to impose his own will.

The second phase, after the seizure of power and during Lenin's lifetime, after the victory in the civil war, brought stability to the regime and to the party. Practice resembled in certain respects the practice of the revolutionary period, but openly and with far more lively discussions.

This was not a matter of the despotism of one man or even of the Politburo. Each party congress was the scene of passionate debates between the factions; Lenin was often in the minority, either in the Politburo or in the central committee; if in the end his opinion nearly always prevailed, it was because his comrades had almost complete confidence in him; experience proved that he was almost always right.

This was also the period of the bureaucratic organization of the party. It became larger, it played a more and more important role in the government of the Russian state; the secretary of the party began to apply the technique which was to be perfected in the subsequent phase, and by which the designation of the secretaries takes the place of their election; from then on, when the secretary of the party came to designate the secretaries of the sections or federations and indirectly to designate the representatives of the party to the congresses, the real authority passed from the mass members into the hands of a small number of leaders in the central committee in the Politburo or in the secretariat.

The third phase was that of Stalin's victory over his rivals and of the consolidation of a system in which the designation of the leaders of the party took the place of elections; the general secretaryship held by Stalin became the power centre from which the whole party was dominated. Stalin brought this about through semi-constitutional procedures. He always succeeded by playing the majority card. He gained a majority in the Politburo by allying himself with the left, that is with Zinoviev and Kamenev against Trotsky then in the subsequent phase by allying himself with the right, that is with Bukharin against Zinoviev and Kamenev who had been reconciled with Trotsky. At some moments when his majority was in danger in the Politburo, he assured himself of a majority in the central committee. Finally, each of Stalin's victories was sealed, if not actually achieved, at the party congress. Because of his control of nominations within the party, he obtained each time a majority over his rivals.

This formal allegiance of the majority has never disappeared from the official documents of the USSR. This lip service to principle does not guarantee but can act in favour of the return from the absolute power of a single person to the constitutional game. The constitutional game within the Party was distorted by the fact that those who were thought to give whole-hearted approval to the policy of the secretary general had been in fact designated by him. Stalin received the applause of those whom he had chosen to applaud him. These acclamations were no less ratified by the votes and the system, as it developed after Lenin's death, could be transformed from one day to the other.

During the fourth phase, that of Stalin's absolute power, the major decisions were taken by *one* man alone. This man was surrounded by colleagues with whom he argued in the Politburo, but he was able to impose his will and, even, after 1934 to terrorize them. Factions were ruthlessly eliminated, not only politically, but physically. Opponents, both real and virtual, within the party were treated as traitors; they were either solemnly tried, executed after having been sentenced and after having 'confessed' or purely and simply eliminated in the prisons.

In this system, the impulse clearly comes from above and the rest follows. But the rest is not necessarily hostile. When overt hostility entails the gravest risk the number of declared enemies inevitably diminishes, the percentage of heroes is not ever very high. It is also conceivable that the decisions taken by this man may have been in the interests of the masses. But since we are trying to discover where the power lay, we must state, without any hesitation, that power lay at the summit of the party hierarchy and that it was one man alone who held it. I have even more grounds for this statement, as his successors themselves make it today.

During the fifth phase, practice changed once more and reversed itself. We have gone from the proletariat to the party, from the party to the central committee, from the central committee to the Politburo and from the Politburo to the general-secretary. Now we reverse and there is no longer any question of one man holding all the reins. At the same time there unrolls a rivalry between the successors which resembles the rivalry between the successors in the years 1923–30.

It also resembles it in style. Between 1923 and 1930, there was no physical liquidation of opponents. Lenin had given to the comrades, along with other advice, the advice not to imitate the great revolutionaries of the French Revolution and not to kill one another. He had enjoined them not to step over what he called 'the threshold of blood'; for fourteen years this threshold of blood was not transgressed. Between 1917 and 1934 the struggle between the bolshevik leaders was violent but the vanquished were not put to death; Trotsky himself was sent first to Central Asia, then exiled, but he was never brought to trial or sentenced. It was from 1934, that is after the murder of Kirov and of the 'great purge', that opponents within the party were tried, sentenced and executed. Since the death of Stalin, it appears that his successors have once again decided not to transgress the threshold; opponents are eliminated, but they are eliminated politically and not physically. There are exceptions to this rule, the best known until now being that of Beria who was eliminated physically, probably for technical reasons. The head of the ministry of the interior or of the police in a regime of this kind, is clearly too dangerous a man for constitutional procedures to be applied to him. Apart from this case, the main opponents are today still alive and they have received secondary posts far enough away from Moscow.

These phenomena surprisingly to some observers are a return to the practices of the period 1923–30. Zinoviev, Kamenev, Bukharin and the others, were given minor posts after their defeat before being expelled from the party. Today, as yesterday, factions have no right to exist. But provisionally at least groups thought to be hostile, those who are called anti-party, are not treated as agents of international capitalism, they are treated as political opponents who are wrong, but they are not treated like traitors.

As for the decisions, they continue to be taken at the summit but they no longer seem to be taken by one man alone but by a group of men, by what is called collective leadership.

The struggle between the successors unfolds in a style characteristic of the bolshevik party of the second and third phase, that is with a mixture of majority lip-service to the clandestine secret cunning. Every time that a group is defeated, a majority appears against him, either a majority in the Politburo (as was the case the first time that Malenkov had to give up some of his offices) or a majority in the central committees as at the time of the last crisis when, it appears, Khruschev who was in a minority in the Politburo appealed to the central committee where he had a majority. One comes back to a certain lip-service to the majority which serves partly as a framework, partly as a regulator for the party struggle.

For the time being then, authority continues to be situated above rather than in the masses, but the number of those who influence decisions has broadened. The Soviet Union has emerged from the extreme, the fourth phase, during which the defeated in the struggle between the factions were immediately threatened with death.

CHAPTER FOURTEEN

IDEOLOGY AND TERROR

In the previous chapter I described the discrepancy which exists between constitutional fiction and reality in the Soviet state and in the communist party. If the formula of the dictatorship of the proletariat is used to justify the monopoly which the party jealously guards for itself, the formula of democratic centralism is used to justify and to camouflage the omnipotence of some individuals or even sometimes of a single person. The Soviet regime is therefore, to use again the term which I used when I spoke of constitutional-pluralistic regimes, essentially oligarchic, even when it is not actually tyrannical.

The oligarchic character of the Soviet regime goes some way towards explaining the obsessive communist denunciation of monopoly capitalism. Those who have lived under a Soviet-type regime find it hard to believe that the lack of organization in constitutional-pluralistic governments is not a façade behind which lurks the omnipotence of a few. This misconception has its counterpart: many democrats would like to find on the other side the equivalent of the diversities and conflicts which are the essence of constitutional-pluralistic governments. In other words, if I were not afraid of misusing dialectic, I should say that the reason why the communists consider constitutional-pluralistic regimes to be 'oligarchies of the trusts' is because they are trying to find in the West the features to which they are accustomed at home, while the supporters of constitutional-pluralistic forms of government believe that the same free play of forces and groups with which they are familiar must be taking place behind the oligarchy of the party.

By another contradiction, the Soviet-type regime lays claim to a doctrine which proclaims the paramountcy of economic forces. But the history of the communist party and of the Soviet regime is a striking example of the determining action of certain individuals on objective forces. According to this doctrine, the seizure of power by the Bolshevik party brought about the victory of the world proletariat. In reality, the transformation which that revolution wrought in the world is at once the confirmation and the consecration of the role of the few, a role which can sometimes be startling, in the history of human societies.

Constitutional-pluralistic regimes are an institutional interpretation of popular sovereignty. This sovereignty finds expression in elections which are themselves influenced by many different forces: the electors choose, more or less freely, their representatives, who go on to play the parliamentary game. The power of the communist oligarchy can be viewed as a different interpretation of the democratic idea. The sovereignty of the people or proletariat is delegated to a party, the vanguard of the proletariat or people. The two interpretations of popular sovereignty can be compared and contrasted. In the one case, the symbol of the interpretation is electoral competition; in the other, unanimous elections and acclamation which seal the pact between the real or mystical will of the masses and that of those who govern. The rivalry between the two kinds of regime is also a rivalry between two systems of institutional interpretation of the same ideological formula. Indeed, we all know that between the constitutional-pluralistic regimes and those with monopolistic parties, there lies an essential, and not merely a secondary, difference. This difference calls into question the whole way of life, method of government, the very character of the community.

In what does this essential difference lie?

The first reply which springs to mind is Marxist-inspired: the economic system will be completely different.

I do not propose to repeat here the analysis of the different economic systems which I have already undertaken.[1] The methods of production are similar; the organization of factories at a particular technical level cannot change with the regime. A certain measure of legal autonomy must of necessity grow up. In the span of a single year Soviet tribunals have dealt with some 330,000 cases between enterprises.

[1] *18 Lectures on Industrial Society.*

One foreign state, Israel, has even sued a Soviet oil company which, on government orders, stopped delivery at the time of the Sinai invasion. The Soviet state wanted to uphold the principle that tribunals in the Soviet Union enforce the laws, although these laws are applied to relations between enterprises which theoretically are all equally state property.

But a fundamental difference clearly remains: many of the decisions, taken by each individual enterprise, are simply the application of the administrative orders of the Planning Office. Others are taken by the directors of the enterprise, or are contractual. Soviet law necessitates a distinction between the results of an administrative decision and those of a decision taken by an enterprise acting on its own initiative.

Politically, what seems to me to be decisive is that in Western-type systems, one finds a plurality of organization, independent of the state; in the Soviet regime, enterprises or trusts do enjoy a certain measure of administrative or legal autonomy, but each organized group is of necessity linked to the state and consequently is subordinated to its ideology.

When I analysed class relations,[1] I showed that the soviet-type society brings with it differences in daily routine, in the level of consumption, in the whole way of life of the various groups; Soviet society is no more homogeneous than is Western society, but no industrial or political organization can exist independently of the state in the Soviet Union. Every organization – professional, industrial, political – is the expression of the state and of the party and is therefore imbued with official ideology.

Indeed, the state is as inseparable from the party as is the party from its ideology. Ideology, in turn, cannot be separated from a certain view of history and this view reveals not only the evolution of society towards a final form, but also a struggle to the death between the classes, between good and evil. The state, which absorbs all organizations, professional and political, is essentially in a transitional condition. The historical movement which carries both society and the state along together has two characteristics which at first sight seem to be contradictory: in theory it is ruled by historical determinism and in practice it is the result of decisions taken by a small group, sometimes by one person alone.

How does this relation between the doctrine of historical

[1] *La lutte des classes.*

determinism and the exceptional role of individual wills actually work? Marxist doctrine presupposes the paramountcy of economic forces, outlines the pattern of history, according to which history moves inexorably from capitalist to socialist regimes in accordance with the development of the productive forces and the sharpening of contradictions within the capitalist society.

This was the view of history held by the Second International and particularly by the German social democrats who dominated it. It was so deterministic that some of them were tempted to allow objective dialectic to do its work and to take refuge in waiting impatiently, but passively, for the revolution which would inevitably result from the sharpening of these contradictions. I remember hearing a German social democrat as late as 1932 saying: 'We social democrats can afford to wait, because we are the representatives of a class, we are a homogeneous party; the dialectic of history is on our side.' A few weeks later, Hitler was in power and, in spite of the dialectic of history, the speaker found himself in a concentration camp.

The Third International broke with this objective view of historical development. Lenin and the bolsheviks are distinguished by their refusal to accept passively historical determinism, that is by their voluntarism. When Lenin had to choose between the letter of the doctrine and the action suggested by circumstances, he never hesitated to sacrifice doctrine or at least to adjust it to the needs of the moment and to find a justification for an action which he had previously in principle condemned. Before 1917, Lenin violently opposed those who believed in the possibility of a socialist revolution in Russia, a country in which no capitalist development had taken place. In 1917 he seized power in Russia. Having started from the idea of the mission of the proletariat, the mission of the proletariat became the mission of the party, the party being the embodiment of the proletariat. Everything the party does in the Soviet Union is the expression of the mission of the proletariat and of the law of history. Yet the actions of the party in the Soviet Union are to a great extent arbitrary. Its doctrine has never defined exactly what form the state transitional between capitalism and socialism should take. Some of the ideas in *Das Kapital* have influenced its economic development, but the war-communism, the NEP, the five-year plans were bolshevik reactions to unforeseen circumstances. These reactions were influenced more or less by Marxism and the interpretation accepted by the bolsheviks, but were not determined by a theory or by the laws of history. This is the root of the fundamental contradiction: doctrine invokes historical determinism, but in practice decision is left in the hands of a group of people, or of one person alone. One of the expressions of this voluntarism is to be found in the transformation of Marxist ideology itself.

Marxist doctrine lends itself to many interpretations. Soviet Marxism includes many elements of which Marx never dreamed. According to circumstances, its doctrine expands or contracts.

It expands when it proclaims an orthodox attitude in painting, music, the humanities, history and biology. The ideological decrees on painting or music are completely unrelated to anything that Marx and Engels wrote about painting or music. Marx and Engels expressed various opinions, but in their personal capacity rather than as prophets of socialism. They stated that there is a relation between the social environment and art (a statement with which everyone, whether Marxist or not, agrees) but they never defined what kind of music or painting should exist in a socialist state. As a result of various circumstances into which I have no time to go at the moment abstract music was condemned as bourgeois and reactionary. As for abstract painting, it was for a long time considered to be the expression of bourgeois decadence. The German national socialists condemned it with equal severity.

In the realm of the social sciences, orthodoxy has a deeper significance. The Soviet state is based on an interpretation of history and of society and we sociologists can take a certain pride in the fact that sociology in our day serves as a religion to one third of mankind. But this pride means subservience in a regime in which sociology is part of the official state ideology. But here again we have some elbow-room, contracting or expanding according to circumstances.

In the nineteenth century tsarist Russia made various territorial conquests. Official doctrine could have given them one of two different interpretations: either tsarist Russia's conquest of Central Asia was the expression of tsarist imperialism and as such to be viewed with the same disapproval as western imperialism; this was the formula adopted during the early years of the regime; or, the territorial conquests in Central Asia by tsarist troops, although a form of imperialism, was also significant for the future, because the tsarist troops brought with them a higher civilization and because the great Russian people was destined to be the agent of the redemptive revolution. Everything which paved the way for a people to be included in the socialist state was in accordance with the progressive law of history. Between the two formulae – condemnation of tsarist imperialism or approval of this kind of progress – there are many intermediary variations to be found. Official interpretations have swung between two extremes: the individual's sole duty was to make sure that he was putting forward the right interpretation and was neither in advance of nor lagging behind his time.

The most advanced form of expansion is the application of orthodoxy to the natural sciences. More often than not for practical reasons this is not done; the spirit of orthodoxy does not lend itself easily to the development of scientific discipline. But the natural sciences are too useful to the state and to its power for anyone to run the risk of curbing their growth. One startling phenomenon which took place during the last phase of Stalinism was the condemnation of Mendelism because it was thought to run contrary to socialist truth. Some subtle commentators have discovered the reason behind this condemnation: the cogency of the doctrine of the homogeneous society grows in the measure in which the importance of the innate differences between people is underplayed. In Stalin's time socialist truth found fault with genetics for denying the heredity of acquired characteristics and for sanctioning a relative stability in the hereditary data.

Doctrine can be more constricted or more comprehensive without anything in the general premises of Marxism being changed. The general principles of the historical evolution from capitalism to socialism or the role of the party can be upheld while the significance of past events can be completely reinterpreted. But one of the consequences of the form taken by the doctrine is that, in place of determinism or of objective forces, there creeps into the view of history the action of individuals. The sacrosanct history of Soviet doctrine is becoming less and less that of the development of the forces of production and more and more that of the history of the party itself. The sacrosanct history of events which led to the revolution is that of the bolshevik party, of conflicts within the party, as well as that of the satellite parties.

I once met a Frenchman who had been a prisoner-of-war in

North Korea for several years and had undergone the ordeal of re-education. What had struck him was the importance given in Soviet education to the history of the communist parties, even to the history of the conflict between factions within the different parties. He realized the weight which must be given to the role of some obscure militants in the Roumanian or Bulgarian communist parties who, at various times between 1917 and 1945, had taken the correct or the wrong line.

The margin of discussion and of interpretation varies in the Soviet Union also according to circumstances. One of the main questions is to know to what extent some practice of the regime is or is not sanctioned by doctrine.

Let us take two examples. In Stalin's time, the percentage of 25 per cent of capital accumulation was considered an integral part of official doctrine; this percentage is still valid, although doubt was cast on it some years ago when Malenkov was Prime Minister. Another hallowed institution was that of the tractor-stations. Up to the present, the tractors have been the property of the tractor-stations, which put the machines at the disposal of the kolkhozes in return for payment. Several times the question has come up as to whether the tractors should not be sold to the kolkhozes. In his last book, Stalin declared that the sale of tractors to the kolkhozes would be counter-revolutionary and would represent a retrograde step in the development of the socialist economy. Khrushchev decreed that the tractor-stations had lost their use and that from now on the tractors would be the property of the kolkhozes, which would be free to buy them. A formula which at one minute was thought to be a doctrinal truth ceased to be part of dogma and became simply a question of expediency.

Here one is inclined to reverse the idea of relations between the party and ideology which I have submitted to you up to now and to say that after all ideology is perhaps merely an instrument of government. The temptation is to apply marxist methods of interpretation to the soviet regime. What did Marx tell us? That the bourgeoisie made use of high-sounding phrases in order to conceal their ignoble exploitation of the people. Using the Marxist method against the Soviet regime, we could say that the party or the few who lead it use this or that doctrinal formula according to the needs of the moment in order to remain in power and to create a society in which they hold the leading positions.

Marxist ideology is an instrument of government in the same way that democratic ideology is an instrument of government in constitutional-pluralistic regimes. But it would not be true to believe that doctrine is merely an instrument of power and that the Soviet leaders do not believe their own doctrine. The bolsheviks are not pure opportunists who make use of any idea which comes to hand in order to safeguard and extend their own power. The blend of doctrinal fanaticism and exceptional flexibility in tactics and practice is one of their characteristics.

A single party, enjoying the monopoly of political activity, dominates the state and imposes its own ideology on all the other organizations. Through the state, which acts as an intermediary, it has a monopoly of the means of coercion, and of the information and propaganda media. Ideology is neither the sole end nor the exclusive means; there is a perpetual interaction or indeed dialectic: sometimes it is used as a means to an end, at others force is used to change society so that it will conform to ideology.

One of the most striking results of the ideological regime is the use of terror. To understand certain aspects of the monopolistic party, the phenomenon of terror must be taken into account; this is a phenomenon which has for long appalled the rest of the world and has attracted and repelled foreigners in equal measure.

There are three formal categories of terror to be observed in the Soviet regime.

There is legal and codified terror. Soviet law specifies actions which would not necessarily be considered criminal in a constitutional-pluralistic regime. It is more concerned to make sure that the guilty do not escape punishment than that the innocent should not be unjustly sentenced. Thus, it tends to treat as criminal the planning of criminal acts, even if they have never even begun to be perpetrated. The formula of counter-revolutionary action is vague enough to lend itself to many different interpretations. The phrase 'an act which is a danger to society' can be very widely interpreted by the courts. And finally the well-known principle of analogy is used. This goes as follows: if an act is not actually criminal in law, because no article exists which applies to it exactly, one can proceed by analogy and condemn it because it bears a remote resemblance to an act which is in fact criminal according to the law.

Yet even this legal repression is not the essential aspect of the phenomenon of terror. Since 1934, the soviet criminal code has contained articles (which may possibly have been abrogated by now) which give the secret police or the Ministry of the Interior (which are the same thing) the right to arrest anyone who is a danger to society or who is engaged in counter-revolutionary action, to condemn him to years in a concentration camp, sometimes without allowing him to appear in court and in any case without the right to defend himself or to appeal.

The administrative tribunals represented a second formal aspect of terror, more to be feared than the first. The way the criminal code was applied reduced such guarantees as citizens of the West enjoy. Another legal text, published in 1937, provided for summary judgment in the case of counter-revolutionary activity: the case had to be dealt with in a few days, without any opportunity for defence or appeal. But even these laws were nothing as compared with the Stalinist terror.

The third aspect, not to be confused with the two I have just mentioned, was the deportation of whole populations. In order not to be accused of bias, I shall quote some lines about the transfer of populations from one of Khrushchev's reports:

> From the end of 1943, when the Soviet forces had succeeded in establishing a break-through on all fronts, the decision was taken and put into effect that the Karatchay people were to be deported from their land; at the same time, the end of December 1943, a similar fate overtook the entire population of the Kalmuk Autonomous Republic; in March 1944, all the Checken and Ingushakay peoples were deported and the Autonomous Checkeno-Ingushskaya Republic was liquidated; in April 1944, all the Balkar people were deported to regions far distant from the Autonomous Kabardino-Balkarskaya Republic and the Republic itself was renamed the Autonomous Kabardinskaya Republic. The Ukrainians only escaped the same fate because of their vast numbers – it was impossible to find enough land to which they could all be deported. Otherwise it would certainly have been done.[1]

There are more than forty million Ukrainians.

This is an extraordinary text taken from an authentic speech which confirms what was already known from external sources—that the transfer of populations on a vast scale had already taken place. This transfer was carried out in those parts of Poland which

[1] Taken from a quotation given by A. Rossi in his book *Autopsie du stalinisme*, Paris 1957, p. 119.

were occupied by the Russian armies in 1939–40. The number of those deported is at present put at one and a half million.

Over and above this formal classification, it might be useful I think to make a concrete or material classification of three kinds of terror.

I shall call the first form normal. This repeats the experience of the French revolution; it is terror used by a party or faction against parties or factions hostile to them. This is a form of civil war. During revolutionary periods, the group in power is constantly worried about the length of time it will be able to hold on to power and sees enemies everywhere. They are not always wrong to do so for, by definition, their grasp on power is new and their adversaries – those who hope for a turn of the wheel – must be many.

This first kind of terror appeared during the civil war, that is from about 1917 to 1921. This was the moment in which the militants and leaders of the rival socialist parties, social-revolutionaries and mensheviks, were eliminated and imprisoned. It was also the moment when the representatives of the former privileged classes defended themselves against the victorious bolsheviks. Every great revolution undergoes this. The terror of Cromwell, Robespierre, Lenin; history repeats itself.

The second was that unleashed in about 1929–30, at the beginning of the collectivization of agriculture which was aimed at eliminating the class enemies, essentially the kulaks. Here again it was a form of terror which, regardless of its legitimacy, offers a rational explanation. Once the collectivization of agriculture had been decided upon, the kulaks became the implacable enemies of the Soviet state; the Russian peasants slaughtered at least half their livestock. When, therefore, hundreds of thousands of kulaks were deported, real, and not imagined enemies of the state were being fought. It can rightly be held that other methods would have been preferable. Khrushchev suggested in a speech that the collectivization of agriculture could have been achieved at less cost. But this involves retrospective and economic considerations: once the final goal of collectivization had been accepted, the use of terror could be rationally explained, if not excused.

The third kind of terror, the kind which Khrushchev condemned, is the turning of terror hitherto used against political adversaries or class enemies against opponents or dissidents, real or potential, from within the communist party itself. I shall quote once more, in order to give some idea of the vast scope of the terror which engulfed so many militants:

> What was the composition of the XVIIth congress of the communist party? We know that 80 per cent of the voters at the congress had joined the party during the underground years of before the revolution and during the civil war, that is, before 1921; from the point of view of social origin, the delegates to the congress were mainly workers (60 per cent of the voters). Thus, it is inconceivable that a congress so constituted could have elected a central committee in which the majority would turn out to be enemies of the people. The only reason why 70 per cent of the candidates elected at the XVIIth congress were denounced as enemies of the party and of the people was that honourable communists were slandered, that they were falsely accused and that revolutionary legality was violated. The same fate was reserved, not only for the members of the central committee, but also for the majority of the delegates to the XVIIth congress. Of the 1,966 delegates, who had either the right to vote or who had consultative votes, 1,108, that is more than half, were arrested for counter-revolutionary crimes.[1]

70 per cent of the members of the central committee, between 50 and 60 per cent of all the delegates to the congress of the communist party! Here we come to the third, the most astounding and, if I may say so, the most abnormal aspect of the terror. It is that from 1917 to 1936 revolutionary terror, instead of gradually abating, redoubled in force in proportion to the stability of the regime. Terror was aggravated at the time of the second Russian revolution, that of the collectivization of agriculture; after 1934, it increased still more, once most of the old members of the communist party had been eliminated. It led to two institutions which have played a considerable part in arguments either in favour of or against the Soviet regime; on the one hand, the concentration camps and on the other the notorious Moscow trials. I shall leave on one side the concentration camps and speak briefly about the Moscow trials because they represent the culmination, the apex of ideological terror, which is one of the essential aspects of this extraordinary regime.

The defendants accused themselves of crimes which we are now told they had never committed and which no one in his right mind could ever have believed them to have committed. From this springs a series of questions, which have often been confused, but

[1] A. Rossi, *op. cit.*, p. 82.

which should be kept distinct. First, the *logic of the confessions*; then, that of the *psychology of the accused*. Finally, there is the question of the *function of the trials and purges* in this kind of regime.

The logic of the confessions. The answer is simple: one must simply draw the final conclusions of the statement that 'Who is not for me is against me' and add that the central committee of the Politbureau of the communist party *is* the communist party, which *is* the proletariat, which *is* the meaning of history. Consequently, whoever is not for the central committee of the communist party is an enemy of the sacred mission of the proletariat, and is therefore guilty of the most heinous crime and subject to the direst penalties. In every revolutionary period, the revolutionaries have tended to confuse their opponents with criminals and traitors. No great effort of the imagination is needed to recognize this.

The system of confessions is approximately as follows: anyone who does not wholeheartedly agree with the central committee or with the secretary of the communist party is behaving like an enemy of communism. But we have decided not to take account of intentions and simply to judge actions. Anyone who is in opposition is undermining the central committee, thus undermining the proletariat. He is behaving like an enemy, thus like a traitor, and since we do not take intentions into account, we consider him *objectively* as a traitor. In order to make it clear to the masses that there is no difference between *behaving like a traitor* and *being a traitor*, it is enough to imagine that Zinoviev, Kamenev, Bukharin or Trotsky were connected with the Gestapo. Here we reach the conclusion. The starting point was the political significance of a course of action, but as the actions which should have symbolized this course had never taken place, they had to be invented in order to validate the meaning attributed to the attitude of the opponents.

Khrushchev said almost exactly what I have just said: 'Stalin was the originator of the idea of the "enemy of the people". This phrase made possible the use of the most cruel repressive measures against anyone who in any way did not agree wholeheartedly with Stalin.'

Some more subtle formulae in this chain of identification have been suggested by Maurice Merleau-Ponty in his book *Humanisme et terreur*, which develops the logic of the confessions in semi-Hegelian, semi-existentialist language. This logic has never seemed to me to present any difficulty, once one has taken the paranoic step of accepting that there is no difference between an opponent who behaves like a traitor, whose conduct was like that of a traitor in the eyes of the men in power and an actual traitor.

The second question is that of the psychology of the accused. There are three possible answers and in spite of the rivers of ink which have been spilled, there are in the end only three answers.

The first, which appeals most to idealists, is that of devotion to the party. The party member has a guilty conscience, either because he was worsted in the factional struggle, or because he agrees with his vanquisher. Feeling that his life is drawing to its end, he strives to find a final purpose for the few days still left to him. In order to strengthen the party at a moment when it is threatened by external agression, he decides to proclaim solemnly that the central committee or the Politbureau was right and that he was wrong.

This interpretation had often been compared, in its devotion to the party, to the attitude of the Japanese kamikazes. The kamikazes were the pilots who were given a single mission from which no return was possible, because it meant crashing their aircraft on the deck of an enemy battleship. In the same way, the militants who accused themselves before the whole world were basically the supreme servants of the cause. They abased themselves in order to glorify their vanquisher, who embodied the party and the proletariat.

The second, less grandiose, theory is that of a secret pact between the police and the accused, by which the accused would be spared if they lent themselves to the ritual of the confessions. According to reliable information, the accused really were executed; most of them were aware of the fate which had befallen their predecessors. Perhaps they were anxious to save not their own but the lives of their families. Possibly such pacts were made.

A third theory, perhaps the simplest, is that of torture. I am going to quote once more from Khrushchev, because his words seem to me among the most reasonable ever written on the subject.

When Stalin said that someone should be arrested, it was taken for granted that he was an enemy of the people and Beria's clique, which was responsible for the organs of state security, outdid themselves in proving the guilt of the accused and the authenticity of the documents which they themselves had forged. What proofs were offered? The confessions of the detained which the prosecutors took seriously. And how can one confess to crimes which one has not committed? In one way only – after the application of methods of physical pressure, of torture leading to a state of unconsciousness, of mental disorder, of the loss of human dignity. It was in this way that the confessions were obtained.[1]

The third theory certainly contains the greatest amount of truth, without excluding entirely the two previous ones.

The psychology of the accused was strange. The prosecutors knew that the confessions were false, they could not believe in confessions which they pretended to take seriously. Those who confessed knew that their judges did not believe them. The man who had staged all the trials could not be unaware of the fact that he himself had given the order that this surrealist world be created. No one was entirely duped, but few were brave enough to say 'Nonsense' or 'Lies! Lies! Lies!' And what is even more surprising is that this world of macabre fiction was not utterly base and vile. In a strange way it had its attraction or, at any rate, it was fascinating because everything had a meaning, nothing was fortuitous. The deep forces of history mingled with the class struggle and the conspiracies of individuals. Hegel's dialectic led to a nightmare of police action and everyone asked himself what were the reasons for this tragic façade. No one dared to say as Khrushchev said: 'The General Secretary of the Russian Communist Party was the victim of persecution mania and he ended by seeing in Marshal Voroshilov an agent of the British Intelligence Service.'

[1] A. Rossi, op. cit., p. 10.

CHAPTER FIFTEEN

ON TOTALITARIANISM

The preceding chapter ended with an analysis of one of the most puzzling features of the Soviet regime; the combination, in certain periods, of ideological frenzy and terroristic police methods. The perfect examples of this are the period 1934–8 and 1949–52.

We know today, and it is Khrushchev who has told us, that in the year before his death Stalin prepared a great purge which would perhaps have been comparable to that of the years 1936–7. It would be unjust to judge the whole of the Soviet regime and its work by the phenomenon of terroristic police methods but it does seem to me to be relevant.

Khrushchev's secret report is a striking example of Montesquieu's theory on despotism according to which the mainstay of despotism is fear – insidious fear which gradually takes hold of the whole community, with the exception of one individual. Khrushchev himself, at one moment asked the question: why did we do nothing? And he replied frankly and naïvely: it was impossible for us to do anything. When we were summoned by the supreme Master we never knew whether he wanted to consult us on an important decision or to throw us into the dungeons of the Lubianka prison. Fear was widespread in a regime born of the most noble aspirations of mankind.

This terror which in a revolutionary period might have been expected, appeared some twenty years after the seizure of power; it struck not only at real or potential adversaries of the regime but at those who were loyal to it. In fact, the terror wrapped itself up in ritual confessions which were in themselves extraordinary because they besmirched the regime. Again, if the confession of

Lenin's old comrades or the accusations hurled against the generals who commanded the Red Army had been taken at their face value the world would have been forced to conclude that the regime had been or still was governed by men who conspired against it and who betrayed it to a foreign power. If the confessions were to be believed the indictment of the regime was terrible. If one did not believe them, how was one to judge a regime which forced men to confess to crimes which they had not committed? One could only wonder what the truth was? Where was ideology? In what did the leaders, the supreme leader and the intermediary ones and the masses believe? One man and one man alone decided the fate of all the others, covered them with glory or condemned them to ignominy, transformed servants of the regime into faithful servitors or traitors. But precisely because this man disposed of the power of life and death, he himself could not believe in the sur-reality which he wanted to impose on all the others and they themselves could scarcely believe in it. It was a strange world which lent meaning to each event but the whole of which was absurd.

One is tempted here to reject ideology as purely and simply a framework and to draw the conclusion that there is only one reality – despotism, in the end even the despotism of a single man, the rest being camouflage which deceives no one.

I myself believe that it would be wrong even at this extreme point to overlook ideology. The fact is that these pathological forms of despotism are inconceivable except in an ideological frenzy, even if this frenzy inspires the majority with more scepticism than faith.

Of what does the totalitarian phenomenon consist? This phenomenon, as all social phenomena, lends itself to many definitions according to the aspect which the observer has in mind. It seems to me that the five main elements are:

1. The totalitarian phenomenon occurs in a regime which gives to one party the monopoly of political activity.
2. The monopolistic party is animated or armed with an ideology on which it confers absolute authority and which consequently becomes the official truth of the state.
3. To impose this official truth, the state reserves for itself in turn a double monopoly, the monopoly of the means of coercion and those of the means of persuasion. The means of

communication, radio, television, press, are directed and commanded by the state and its representatives.

4. Most economic and professional activities are subject to the state and become, in a way, part of the state itself. As the state is inseparable from its ideology, most economic and professional activities are coloured by the official truth.

5. As all activity is state activity and subject to ideology an error in economic or professional activity is by the same token an ideological fault. Thus at the very root there is a politization, an ideological transfiguration of all the possible crimes of individuals and in the end police and ideological terrorism.

It can be seen that in the definition of totalitarianism either the monopoly of the party or the state control of economic life or the ideological terror can be considered essential. The phenomenon is complete when all these elements are united and fully achieved.

The five elements which I have just listed were linked in the thirties, in the period 1934–8; they were once again linked in the forties between 1948 and 1952. It is easy to understand why it was possible to link them thus. In the case of the Soviet regime, the monopoly of the party and of ideology is the essence itself of bolshevism and of its revolutionary will. The centralization of the armed forces, of the means of coercion and of persuasion is linked to the idea of the monopoly of one Party within the state. The state control of economic activities is the expression of the communist doctrine. The links between the elements which I have listed are easily intelligible. As for the final result, the ideological terror, it is to be understood precisely through the other elements, the party's monopoly of ideology, of the means of coercion, and the state control of individual activities.

It would not be fair to confuse *intelligibility* and *necessity* in the combination. One must understand that these different elements are combined, but the fact that they are in a number of cases combined does not prove that they should always be and that every regime of a monopolistic party ought to end in the extreme kind of terror. In reality three fundamental questions about totalitarianism come to mind:

1. To what extent is this a question of a unique historical phenomenon or of the repetition of already known historical phenomena?

2. To what extent is Soviet totalitarianism comparable with that of other regimes in particular with that of national socialism?
3. To what extent must the regime of the single party or of state planning lead to totalitarianism?

Let us first take the last question.

In the twentieth century there are authoritarian regimes which are not one-party regimes and there are one-party regimes which do not become totalitarian, which do not develop an official ideology and which do not shape all their acvitities through ideology. There exist one-party regimes in which the state does not absorb the society and in which ideology does not take this insane expansion which can be seen in the Soviet regime. What is true is that every one-party regime in industrial societies brings with the *risk* of totalitarianism. The rulers must address themselves to the ruled and justify their authority. They do not claim to have traditional authority; they have not the indisputable right to be in power; they are obliged to explain why and in whose name they rule. Now every leader in a one-party system is forced to cut short the discussion at a certain point and I should say at the very point at which it becomes interesting. Many questions are freely debated except that of why one does not have the right to join some party other than the unique one? The inevitable result of this is the temptation with which the leaders of the one-party state are faced in order to justify their monopoly. In order to do this, any ideology suffices (men have never been fastidious about the quality of ideologies) but it must be an insidious ideology which can be elaborated, and can become increasingly insidious.

It is true that in Fascist Italy, which was a one-party system, there was neither ideological proliferation nor was the totalitarian phenomenon comparable to the great Soviet purge or to the excesses of the last years of the Hitler regime. In both cases, which we call totalitarian, the essential phenomenon, the original cause, appears to me to be the revolutionary party itself. The regimes did not become totalitarian through a kind of gradual impulse, but through an original intention – the will to transform fundamentally the existing order by means of an ideology. The features common to revolutionary parties which have ended up as totalitarian are the extent of ambition, the radicalism of attitude and the extremism of the methods used.

Do these similarities allow the two totalitarianisms to draw near to one another and enable us to see two species of the same kind? Two contradictory arguments have been developed, one denying, the other confirming the close kinship of the two regimes. Both seem to me to be unsatisfactory or at least unconvincing.

The first argument puts forward the clear difference between the membership of the communist and nazi parties. This cannot be denied. In Germany, the membership of the two parties was very different; many workers voted for the Nazi Party, but until the end most of the industrial workers voted either for the Social Democratic or for the Communist Parties.

However there is one reservation. In Germany, in the years which preceded Hitler's seizure of power, it was noticeable that people frequently moved from one party to the other. If the social origin of the members is different, the psychological temperament is not always so. There exists a common attitude which does not contradict the difference in social origin.

But this is not the main point. Let us admit that the grass roots are different. What is important is to know whether, starting from different social classes, similar phenomena cannot arise. To say that from a social point of view the grass roots of the parties are different does not answer the question. Those who argue the kinship of the two regimes maintain that in spite of the different social origins of the members, these two parties, once they are in power, have many features in common in the way in which they exercise power.

According to the second argument, Nazism and capitalism share a profound community of interest, Nazism being simply a regime forged by the capitalists or the cartels to maintain their own power.

The argument is false, with a basis of truth. In pre-Hitlerite Germany, it is true that many capitalists, industrialists and bankers subsidized the Nazi Party; they thought that they would be able to manipulate it and they saw in it a means to defend themselves against a socialist or communist revolution. But when the regime became totalitarian, it was in no way controlled or led by the monopolists.

Industrialists, bankers, representatives of former ruling classes were for the most part in opposition during the last phase of Hitler's regime; after 1944, they were the victims of a purge, different in nature from the Soviet purges, but sufficient to demonstrate that the policy of the Nazi Party in power was not the expression of the will of the capitalist class.

According to the third argument, communists and fascists are locked in a life and death struggle. Once again the argument is a true one. But it is not the first time that these brothers fight. The question is still clear cut; to what extent are totalitarian phenomena common to these two kinds of party once they have seized power?

In spite of their relentless struggle, the parties are sometimes akin. Von Ribbentrop, arriving in Moscow in 1939, spoke of the meeting of the two revolutions and Stalin himself returned the courtesy by raising his glass to Hitler, so beloved by the German people. This proves nothing except that both can swiftly switch from one language to the other.

The fourth argument in the same order of ideas as the three others is that of the radical incompatibility of the ideologies. I do not cast doubt on the validity of the argument, but once again it does not settle the question. It is true that, according to communist ideology, fascism is the incarnation of all that is evil in history and of all that is base in human nature. It is true that according to fascist ideology, communism is an evil in itself, the absolute enemy. But when, on the one hand, ideology is universal and humanitarian and on the other nationalistic, racial and anything but humane, this does not prove that men in the name of opposing ideas do not resort to similar practices. To invoke the contrast in ideas when analysing similarity or differences in practice is to beg the question. Those who argue their kinship want to show that ideologies or noble aspirations weigh very lightly in the scales of history and that men obey impulses which do not depend on ideology. But this is to say that there can be no close kinship, since the ideologies are opposed from every point of view; it is to assume that the problem which we are discussing, whether ideologies decide practices, is answered.

I would add, I think with truth, that most arguments in favour of the kinship of the two totalitarianisms do not convince me either, for reasons which are not the same, but are in the same line of reasoning as those for which I rejected the foregoing arguments.

Certain similar totalitarian features are to be found in particular periods of the history of the Soviet regime and in particular periods of the history of the Nazi regime. One-party, official ideology, absolute power of the head of the state, all-pervasive police, ideology which more and more encroaches on all activities, police terror, all this was to be seen in Nazi Germany as well as in Soviet Russia. The extreme form of Nazi terror took place during the war, some years after the siezure of power, just as the extreme terror in the Soviet Union did not follow immediately the seizure of power, but took place twenty years later.

The second argument which is put forward in support of the kinship of the two totalitarianisms is that which I have already outlined, according to which power alone counts and ideas have no significance, only efficacity. Now, just as I refuse to accept the argument of the incompatibility of ideologies as decisive, so I reject the argument according to which the beliefs of the communists in universal and humanitarian values are irrelevant.

The book which has founded most firmly the thesis of the kinship of the two totalitariansisms is *Origins of Totalitarianism* by Hannah Arendt, who compares Soviet Russia between 1934 and 1937 and Nazi Germany between 1941 and 1945. But it would be unfair to confuse the comparison between these two periods, these two terrors, with a comparison of the regimes as wholes.

Differences and likenesses between these two totalitarianisms are undeniable. The similarities are far too striking to be treated simply as accidents. On the other hand, the differences in inspiration, ideas, goals are too marked for one to admit without reservation the essential kinship of the two regimes. The accentuation of the kinship or of the contrast depends on many considerations. We will never arrive at a completely positive answer because the national socialist regime did not have the time to develop, as did the Soviet regime. The latter already has a history of its own; it has passed through various phases; we can understand the meaning of the successive phases. In contrast, the Nazi regime only knew six years of peace. After 1939 it was engaged in a military operation which shaped its ultimate future.

In order to measure the relative importance of the kinship and of the opposition we must not be content simply with comparative sociological analysis: the two other ways of understanding, history and ideology must be taken into account.

Historically the Soviet regime, as we know, was the outcome of a revolutionary will, inspired by a humanitarian ideal. Its goal was to create the most humane regime that history had ever known, the first regime in which all men could be treated as human beings, in which classes would have disappeared or in which the homogeneity of society would allow of mutural respect between people. But the movement towards an absolute goal did not hesitate to use any means, because, according to its doctrine, only by force could this completely good society be created and the proletariat was engaged with capitalism in a merciless war.

The difference phases in the Soviet regime sprang from a combination between a sublime goal and a ruthless technique. This first and well-known phase was the civil war and the political terror which accompanied it. Then came the second phase in which the terror abated and at the same time private enterprise made a slight comeback; this was the phase of the NEP. But a third phase began in 1929 – a new revolution in the true meaning of the word, which is a fundamental transformation of the social structures, but it was a revolution carried out by the State from above. The regime, ten years after it had conquered, set in motion a second revolution which, in one sense, according to the testimony of the leaders themselves, was more violent and more terrible than the first. This second revolution, the collectivization of agriculture, brought with it, according to Khrushchev, new terrors which the General Secretary of the Party did not condemn; he confined himself to saying that perhaps it should have been possible to carry it out at a smaller cost, but just as he tolerated the use of terror against the enemies of the party, so did he tolerate its use against the land owners, against the peasants and the kulaks who refused to accept collectivization.

What still surprises us is the subsequent phase. Why, after 1936, did we see the unleashing of the great purge, of a new phase of terror, although the agrarian revolution had been carried to a triumphant conclusion and the regime was no longer in danger? Why was there a purge, when the battle was already won? It is not only western interpreters who ask this question, but Khrushchev himself. According to him, the personality cult began during the terror of the years 1934–8; terror used against the members of the party, first to put to death the adversaries whom Stalin had already vanquished – which Khrushchev thought was a futile undertaking – then to strike at the most faithful Stalinists. Why was terrorism directed even against members of the communist party who had not deviated in any way from the party line?

For the time being Khrushchev gives only one answer, one interpretation – the cult of personality. This explains nothing. As a very distinguished Marxist, Togliatti, the late General Secretary of the Italian communist party has said, to explain it by the personality cult is not a Marxist explanation. To explain such important phenomena by *one* person is the kind of explanation that Marxist doctrine, by definition does not allow.

It is possible to understand, not the great purge itself or the terrorism directed against the members of the party, but the *possibility of these phenomena* by starting with the technique of communist action. When a party gives itself the right to use force against all its enemies in a country in which to start with it is in a minority, it condemns itself to perpetual violence.

In theory, the party is democratic, but the meaning of democratic centralism is to give back the essentials of power to the party's leaders. The leadership can manipulate elections, ensure the designation of the elections by the elected; it is conceivable also that under this system, instead of an oligarchy, one man alone can become the master of the whole party. Khrushchev agrees with western sociologists on this point; at a given moment, democratic centralism degenerated into the absolute power of a single man. It is clear to me that this phenomenon is understandable because Trotsky foresaw it in an astonishing way. When in 1903 Lenin first developed the theory of democratic centralism in his booklet *What is to be done?* Trotsky objected that he was putting the party in the place of the proletariat, and then the central committee in the place of the party, finally the general secretary of the party in the place of the central committee and that the end would be the absolute power of one person in the name of the proletariat. Trotsky himself never fully realized how true his prophecy had been.

In other words, the phenomenon of the personality cult was made possible not only by the singularities of one man, but also by the technique of organization and of action of the party as it had been since the beginning of the movement.

How did it change from the potential to the actual? Why were there purges? What ends did they serve and what were the reasons for them?

There are many explanations for the great purge. They are all to be found in an excellent little book *Russian purge and the extraction of confession*[1] by a Swiss doctor and a Russian historian who shared the same cell during the great purge in 1936–7 and who discussed the reasons for their misfortune. These two men, who have since left Soviet Russia, recount how the favourite subject of conversation among the prisoners from 1936 to 1938 was the purge itself. From the conversations they constructed seventeen theories. I will spare you the list, but will indicate the the main aims which were attributed to the purge in Soviet Russia in the only place in which there was complete freedom of speech – the prisons.

According to the first interpretation, the main cause was the struggle within the party. The party, once in power, continued to lead an existence comparable to that of all other parties, with groups, factions, rivalry, and opposition. The faction which finally won wished to seal its victory by eliminating the defeated factions.

The second interpretation stresses the will to orthodoxy which inspires the power-holders. The men who rule in an ideocratic regime want to eliminate, not only the actual enemies of the party and of the regime, but any potential ones as well. All those who are likely, in certain circumstances, to rebel against the regime, become enemies and are treated as such. Those who have survived from the past, those who keep in touch with the outside world, as for example the Jews, those who were, at any time, hostile to the faction which defeated them, are in the end treated as actual enemies. The purge is a technique of social prophylaxia; it is designed to eliminate in advance anyone who in unforeseen circumstances could go over to the opposition. This technique carried to extremes leads to strange phenomena but at least it has an intelligible purpose.

According to another interpretation, the recruitment of workers for the labour camps was an important function of the purges.

According to yet another, Soviet society is both bureaucratic and revolutionary; it has a single hierarchy which is also the state hierarchy. But the state's aim is to transform perpetually the modalities of the organization. Everything tends to influence Soviet society towards stability in bureaucratic forms; its whole ideology prevents Soviet society from accepting any form whatsoever

[1] F. Beck and W. Bodin, *Russian purge and the extraction of confession*, New York, 1959.

as definitive. The purges are a way of maintaining revolutionary dynamism in a society which is drawn towards bureaucratic crystallization.

All this being said, and many other hypotheses could be added, the fact remains that the purge, as it was carried out between 1936 and 1938, was completely irrational, or if you prefer unreasonable. According to Soviet witnesses themselves, it affected the army and the administration. The number of officers who were put in prison or executed was between 20,000 and 30,000. Marshal Rokosovsky, who was minister of defence in Poland, was imprisoned during the purge and many of the great Soviet leaders, among them Marshal Tukhatchevsky, were executed. A purge on such a scale is not in the highest interests of the party for the simple reason that the party needs the regime to work and the army to be strong.

It also seems to me inevitable that we must add to these interpretations that of the intervention, not of the personality cult, but of a particular personality. To pass from the potential to the actual, from the comprehensible reasons for the purge to the excesses of the great purge, something quite unique was needed – Stalin himself.

Regardless of what theory of history is adopted, sooner or later individuals must be taken into account. It is possible that without Napoleon Bonaparte another general would have been crowned, but it is unlikely that if the general who was crowned had been someone else and not Napoleon events would have been the same. This holds good for the Soviet Union too. One can see how the regime could degenerate into the phenomena which I have studied but, without Stalin, the extreme forms of ideological madness, of police terror and of the rite of confession would possibly not have appeared. I do not swear to this nor can anyone do so, but what does seem true to me in the interpretation which the Russians themselves give of these phenomena is that, over and above what can be explained by the party, its ambitions, its technique and the function of the purge in a bureaucratic regime, an unexpected factor intervened: one individual and the part he played, thanks to his absolute power.

In the beginning, historically, Nazism was created by a will which was different from the communist one; it was created by the will to remake the moral unity of Germany and, more especially, to enlarge the territory of the Germans, which meant to wage war and to conquer. There is nothing new in this; it is a repetition of the ambitions and illusions of Julius Caesar.

After the seizure of power, the nazification of German life was a gradual process; the great terror only appeared in the last two years of the war. It is tempting to say that the war itself explains the terrorist phenomena, but the facts do not bear out this explanation. The terrorist phenomenon of which the nazi regime is an example is the extermination of six million Jews during the war between 1941 and 1944. This was ordered by one man, with advice from one or two others; the undertaking itself was as unreasonable in relation to the aims of the war as was the great purge in relation to the goals of the Soviet regime. While Germany was fighting on two fronts, its leaders decided to divert transport and important material resources so that millions of human beings should be put to death, one after the other.

This terrorist phenomenon is unprecedented in modern history and almost unprecedented in history itself. Not that there were not great massacres in other ages. But, in modern history, no head of state has ever decided in cold blood to set in motion the industrial extermination of six millions of his fellow men. He sacrificed resources which would have been useful to him in the conduct of the war in order to satisfy his hatred to the full, in order that, no matter what the outcome, those whom he hated would not survive.

The aim of the Nazi Party was to remake the racial map of Europe and to eliminate certain peoples, whom it thought were inferior and to ensure the victory of those whom it claimed were superior. The Nazis produced an even more ghastly terror than any which could have touched Soviet citizens and, above all, its aim was different. The aim of Soviet terror is to create a society which conforms completely to an ideal, while in the Nazi case, the aim was pure and simple extermination.

This is why, passing from history to ideology, it can be taken as a starting point that between these two phenomena the difference is essential, no matter what similarities there may be. The difference is essential because of the idea which inspires the two undertakings; in one case the final outcome is the labour camp and in the other it is the gas chamber. In one case, it is the will to construct a new regime and perhaps a new man, regardless of means; in the other the truly daemonic will to destruction of a pseudo-race.

To sum up the meaning of these two undertakings, I think that these are the formulae which I would suggest: for the Soviet undertaking, I would recall the well-worn formula: he who would create an angel creates a beast; for that of the Nazi undertaking: man should not try to resemble a beast of prey because, when he does so, he is only too successful.

CHAPTER SIXTEEN

THE THEORIES OF THE
SOVIET SYSTEM

In the previous chapter I put three questions about the totalitarian phenomenon. The first was about the nature of the links between the different elements which constitute totalitarianism. The second was that of the kinship or opposition between the different kinds of totalitarianism.

This leaves the third question, that of the originality of totalitarianism when compared with historical precedents. I am going to answer it by summing up the theories of the Soviet system which have been developed. Since the communist system stems from Marxism, I shall first analyse the Marxist theories of the Soviet system.

Let us start with the Marxist theory of the Soviet regime, formulated by the Soviet leaders themselves, the Soviet Union's own interpretation of itself. We are all familiar with this theory by and large; the revolution was a proletarian one, the party was its interpreter and the vanguard of the proletariat; the Soviet regime is building communism according to the ideas of Marx; it is still in the socialist phase, in which the income of each one is proportionate to the work done, but on the horizon of history appears the communist phase in which each will receive according to his need.

This self-interpretation takes no account of the one major fact which needs to be reinterpreted, the fact that the so-called proletarian revolution took place in a country in which the proletariat was in a minority and in which capitalist development was still in its first phase. Everyone acknowledges this, including the Russians. This itself does not run counter to reasonable

Marxism; it is understandable how in a country in which capitalist development had not reached its full height, a revolution in the name of the proletariat could be successful. Lenin, Trotsky and Stalin all explained this fact, which nevertheless had various consequences. Today, the historical scheme of classic Marxism according to which historical evolution unfolds from the feudal system to capitalism and from capitalism to socialism can no longer be held to be either self-evident or even probable. One conclusion at least must be drawn from the Soviet experiment and this is that history can bypass the phase of capitalism. The main task of the Soviet regime has been the growth of the economy, the building of heavy industry, which were tasks which Marx allocated to capitalism. A scientific theory should at least show that the regime which has been established in the Soviet Union and which is responsible for the development of the productive forces heralds the one which will be established in the countries of the West as the heir of capitalism. In other words, it is possible to preserve, if need be within the framework of a supple form of Marxism, the proletarian character of a revolution in a country in which the proletariat is in the minority, but not to assert that the institutional forms adopted by the proletarian revolution in order to build a heavy industry will reappear once the phase of building characteristic of the Soviet experience has been left behind. Thus, when the leaders of the Soviet Union present their regime as the same as socialism as conceived by Marx – as the regime which must succeed western capitalism, they contradict Marxism itself.

The second weakness of the self-interpretation of the Soviet regime is that it does not fit the theory of the political regime which exists in the Soviet Union. To say that power is exercised by the proletariat is clearly nonsense. Power is never exercised by millions of workers in factories; it is clearly exercised by a minority of flesh-and-blood individuals who are members of the Communist Party and who are the party élite. It is possible that the party leaders govern in the interests of the proletarian and peasant masses, but the regime is not one in which the proletariat itself is in power, except in a mythological way comparable to the one in which, through the mediation of Louis XIV, God himself reigned in France in 1700. The substitution for men who exercise power by the supreme, transcendent and immanent power, in the name of which power is exercised, is mythological.

Failing this theory of the state, the self-interpretation swings backwards and forwards between various formulations. According to one, there is no plurality of parties and ideas because the society is classless. According to another, as socialism is built, so the society ceases to be homogeneous and the monopoly of the party and of propaganda is a form of spoliation.[1]

The third fundamental weakness of this self-interpretation is that it does not conform to the Marxist explanation of totalitarian phenomena admitted by the General Secretary of the party himself. Khrushchev has revealed in detail, adding some imaginative details, what happened during the last phase of Stalin's reign. He denounced the police terror which was turned against party members during the personality cult.

It is difficult to reconcile phenomena such as the great purge or the police terror, both brought about by one man, with the Marxist philosophy of history, which does not eliminate the part played by individuals, but does not allow that such important phenomena, as the police terror of the thirties, can be due to one man alone.

A final weakness in this self-interpretation lies in the vagueness of the interpreters themselves. It is never clear what the doctrinaires think of as transitory and what they hold to be definitive. Is the single party a phenomenon restricted to the period of the building of socialism? Or is Soviet democracy defined by the monopoly of the single party? Is the official ideology tied to the needs of socialist construction? Or is the ideological monopoly explained by the absolute truth of the doctrine? It is easy to understand why this should be so. We have seen the transformation of a political party which, in 1916, numbered some thousands of members whose leaders were in exile, from a conspiratorial sect to a state which is master of the greatest empire in the world. The doctrine of this party has become the official creed of 40 per cent of mankind. All this took place in the space of forty years. Since the spread of Islam there has probably never been such a rapid and impressive half-spiritual, half-political conquest.

How can the theoreticians of this crusade, so different from their dreams, not have doubts about the final direction their adventure will take?

The second Marxist interpretation is the social democratic and particularly the Menshevik one.

[1] A second formulation, fashionable in 1965, is that of the whole people.

At the time of the 1917 revolution, between the collapse of tsarism in February and the Communist Party's seizure of power in November, the Mensheviks and Bolsheviks debated the following question: is it possible to bring about a socialist revolution before the development of capitalism? The Bolsheviks replied unhesitatingly that it was and it must be admitted that they have proved their point by their success. The Mensheviks were possibly the better Marxists or at any rate they took Marxism more seriously. With the support of texts they showed that a socialist revolution was impossible in a country which had not passed through capitalism. Lenin, some years before the war, stated that a socialist revolution was inconceivable in a country which had not gone through the development of capitalism. Trotsky, too, thought that the capitalist phase was not indispensable. The Mensheviks then affirmed that a socialist revolution was impossible and added: if by ill chance the workers' parties tried to take power and bring about a socialist revolution, they would doom themselves to half a century of despotism.

The man who formulated this criticism with the greatest force was at that time the great doctrinaire of Marxism, the high priest of the Second International, the German socialist, Karl Kautsky. After the Bolshevik seizure of power, he stated that the establishment of an absolute power by a minority party in the name of the proletariat was the negation of socialist hopes; socialism without democracy was not socialism. Kautsky wrote at the time words which have since become famous: 'this is not the dictatorship of the proletariat but the dictatorship of the party over the proletariat'. This was the argument to which Lenin replied in his little book on *The Renegade Kautsky*.

The opposition between the Mensheviks and the Bolsheviks at the beginning of the century seemed unimportant; Bolsheviks and Mensheviks were simply two factions inside the Russian Social Democratic Party. In fact, the rivalry between them became irreconcilable and it is easy to see why this happened. The two conceptions, half a century later, each gave rise to a particular type of regime and the two types are opposed on the essential point. The Bolsheviks carried out the revolution; they took power, they built a one-party regime which the Mensheviks denounced as contrary to democracy. As for the Mensheviks or the social democrats, they never brought about a revolution, but they did carry through reforms, greater or smaller according to the country, within the framework of what the communists call capitalism.

We are thus, I think, historically confronted with an alternative; either we envisage the seizure of power by violent methods and bring about a type of regime which is not necessarily the same as the present Russian regime as far as we can see, but which, to say the least, bans formal and parliamentary liberties; or we reject violence and agree to play the game of multiple parties within the framework of a parliamentary regime and, if the communists are to be believed, never emerge from capitalism. In one case, there survives the more or less socialist democracy which I analysed in the first part of this book, the multi-party regime; in the other, after a revolution springing from Marxism and from the proletariat, a one-party regime is established.

Is there a third alternative? As always, we dream of a third alternative, a revolution which will be economically as radical as that of the communists, while it is politically as liberal as the British Labour party. Historically, the European social democrats discovered two, and not three, paths. Why is the third path only a figment of the imagination? If we stick to the game of multi-parties, important reforms can be carried through, but not the wholesale nationalization of the means of production and complete economic planning, which implies a break with habits, ways of life, contempt for the legitimate interests of individuals and groups. Today, between the Bolsheviks and the Mensheviks there is a gulf; the first represent an authoritarian, if not totalitarian, type of regime and the others, even while they base themselves more or less on Marxist doctrine, are integrated into what are called constitutional-pluralistic regimes.

The third Marxist theory about the Soviet revolution, that of Trotsky, springs both from Soviet self-interpretation and from social democratic criticisms: it borrows from both theories, without confusing them. Trotsky began by justifying the seizure of power of 1917, and by asserting the proletarian character of the communist revolution. He maintained that a revolution could be proletarian before its phase of capitalist maturity. Trotsky came round slowly to the conception of democratic centralism, to the dictatorship of the Bolshevik Party, but once there, that is in 1917, he approved unreservedly of the methods which had been used.

In contrast to the orthodox position, he criticized what he called bureaucratic degeneration. But, anxious to explain his own defeat, Trotsky was too good a Marxist to imitate Khrushchev and to adopt a theory of the cult of personality. The reasons for Stalin's victory had to be compatible with some kind of Marxism. The theory which he put forward was that after the victorious revolution, the working class was exhausted and a bureaucracy had to be created to administer the planned economy. This bureaucracy modelled itself on Stalin rather than on Trotsky because Stalin was the kind of leader they wanted. Trotsky, with his theory of permanent revolution, disquieted those who had been put in power through a kind of Thermidor.

Trotsky's explanation combined two schemes, the Marxist scheme for a bureaucracy which was necessary to administer the planned economy, the scheme of a revolution which, after its violent and terroristic phase, died down into Stalinism, rather in the way that Thermidor survived the crisis of Jacobinism.

In spite of this criticism of Stalinism and of the bureaucracy, Trotsky maintained, at least until 1939, that the Soviet regime was socialist because it was based on public ownership and on a planned economy. The Soviet state, he declared, is a socialist and proletarian state which at present contains phenomena of bureaucratic degeneration. In the struggle between bourgeois democracy and the Soviet regime, Trotsky chose the latter as being nearer to the socialist ideal. Towards the end of his life, however, Trotsky had doubts about the Marxist scheme itself; and he did not exclude the fact that the Marxist hypothesis might be false. The Marxist hypothesis is that a revolution, made by the proletariat – a regime based on public ownership of the means of production and on a planned economy – liberates mankind. He mentioned the dangers in a system based on public ownership and on planning, without democracy, without the liberation of men. If the proletariat is not aware of its own destiny, if internationalism does not carry the day against nationalist crystallization in the Soviet Union, then, it must be admitted, that the Marxist hypothesis itself is contradicted by events.

Two weaknesses, at least, are apparent in Trotsky's theory. The first is the use of the notion of Thermidor. Trotsky thought that the Stalinist regime was the equivalent, after the frenetic phase of the revolution of 1917, of the French Thermidor after

Jacobinism. But the comparison is not valid. A second revolution took place after 1929–30, at the time of the collectivization of agriculture and the building of heavy industry. To call the phase which ran between 1929 and 1939 Thermidor seems to me nonsensical. After Thermidor, a widespread appetite for enjoyment was unleashed, while, on the contrary, in the phase 1929–39, extreme austerity was imposed in order to build a heavy industry.

One answer can be that the revolutionaries, the party members, wanted security and affluence. But the great purge and the terrorism disappointed these hopes. The Soviet phase which corresponds to the Jacobin terror is not only the phase 1917–21, but also that of 1934–8.

Trotsky never explained clearly how a regime based on public ownership of the means of production, a planned economy and a single party could be at once democratic and liberal. He was shocked by the bureaucratic domination which he saw in Soviet Russia. The privileges which the men in power arrogated to themselves were to him contrary to the essence of socialism. To the socialist ideal, naturally. But, in such a regime, the entire upper class is composed of state representatives, that is of bureaucrats. Why should a class which holds all the power, both political and economic, not allocate to itself material or moral advantages? Never in history has an all-powerful class refused to profit from its privileges.

A system of planned economy can be good or bad, better or worse, than the capitalist system; the question is open to debate. There is no reason, apart from ideological considerations, why, under the system, the leaders of the economy, who are all state officials, should not allocate to themselves benefits comparable to those which the directors of private enterprises in the West enjoy; to use jargon, to 'exploit the masses'.

I shall go on now to other interpretations of Marxism, which are more directly anticommunist than the Menshevik interpretation.

The most interesting of the heterodox interpretations of Marxism is that of the American sociologist Karl Wittfogel, who recently published an important book, *Oriental Despotism*. His theory, roughly, is as follows:

Marx himself in his preface to the *Contribution to the critique of political economy* listed the different methods of production.

Apart from the old methods of production, feudal and capitalist, he put forward another which he called *Asiatic*. This method was held, not only by Marx but also by Lenin, to be essentially different from any that could be observed in western societies.

In this method of production, the state absorbs, so to say, the society or at least is more powerful than the society because the administrators of the collective work are bureaucrats. Agriculture needs a regular flow of water from the rivers. This is why, in Egypt or in China, an economic and social system was established in which the state, if it was not the owner of the means of production, was at any rate the organizer of the community's work. The privileged are those who in one way or another are attached to the state or represent it.

Lenin, before the revolution of 1917, was aware of the danger that socialism, instead of bringing about the complete liberation of mankind of which he dreamed, would bring mankind to what he called the Asiatic method of production. The suppression of the private ownership of the means of production and of the market economy would lead to the absorption of society by the state and the transformation of those who administer the collective undertaking into state officials. Asiatic methods of production do not include classes in the western sense of the word, but a bureaucratic and state-controlled hierarchy.

Political power is absolute, one might almost say sacramental. The sovereign proclaims the faith, at the same time relying upon the strength of the bureaucracy. A British ambassador, in the last century, refused to prostrate himself before the emperor of China. Etiquette at the court of the emperor required him to do something which to a westerner was an intolerable humiliation; it symbolized the distance between the sacred leader and his subjects.

The theory of oriental despotism and of the hydraulic society can be said to be Marxist. The infrastructure is created by the need to regularize the waters and to centralize the administrative functions. Russian society, according to this conception, was half-Asiatic before the revolution; Lenin himself was inclined to admit this.

In this hypothesis, a unique scheme of historical development must be abandoned. Classic Marxist theory presents a process which runs from feudalism to capitalism and socialism, eventually leaping over the capitalist stage. If the truth of the Asiatic method of production is admitted, two types of society, fundamentally different, and two kinds of development must be recognized.

The great empires of Asia or of the Middle East, founded on this method of production, were exceptionally stable. Such a social structure is both simple and solid. The State absorbs all the managerial functions of society, eliminating the centres of independent forces. When the state is the incumbent, and the state alone, society is both homogeneous and hierarchical. Social groups are separated by their way of life and standard of living, but no group holds power by itself because they are all integrated in the state structure.

Some of the characteristics of these bureaucratic empires are to be found in a Soviet-type society; the state, the sole administrator of the collective undertaking, the state bureaucracy, a single privileged class, and without the antagonisms of the class struggle in the western meaning of the term. In last year's course[1] I showed that the class struggle, in the western meaning of the expression, demands not only a plurality of social groups on the horizontal plane, but the ability of these groups to organize themselves and to make demands. In a Soviet-type society, the ways of life and the levels of income differ according to the group, but no group can be autonomous or can oppose other groups on the same plane, as they are all part of a single hierarchy. This method of social organization is neither a transitory nor a surprising phenomenon but is the inevitable result of the suppression of all private ownership, of all free movement of the market. These two radical transformations mean that the director of an enterprise must be a state official and that the individual only has a share in power or wealth if he is part of the privileged state class.

I shall sum up very briefly the two main questions which this theory puts forward.

The Asiatic despotisms which we saw in the past were linked to societies which were economically static. Can the same phenomena be produced and can they endure in an industrially progressive society?

Ideological fanaticism and police terror are revolutionary rather than bureaucratic phenomena. Can some of the characteristic features of the Soviet regime which I have analysed in the previous

[1] *La lutte des classes.*

213

chapters be explained by taking the Asiatic society as a precedent? Here we come to a last theory of Marxism or rather of neo-Marxism.

This is put forward by Isaac Deutscher who is by inspiration a Trotskyist. Trotsky is his hero and Mr Deutscher thinks, like his hero, that a revolution of the communist type answered to Russia's historical needs. Then in Marxist terms he justifies industrialization; this was necessary in the Russia of 1930, which was surrounded by enemies and threatened by attack. The regime had to speed up as much as possible the building of heavy industry to counter the external dangers as well as at the same time to answer to the needs of a modern society.

This is why Stalin was the man who was needed. Deutscher, like Trotsky, does not use accidental reasons to explain the defeat of his hero. He wrote somewhere that, from every point of view, Trotsky was superior to Stalin, a better speaker, more intelligent, a better Marxist, a better general. If we compare the merits of the two men, Trotsky carries the day. Stalin, nevertheless, was the victor because history needed a Stalin and not a Trotsky.

This interpretation does not convince me. Stalin did have advantages and perhaps they were decisive: a higher position, because he was general secretary of the party, and a superior use of tactics. He knew better how to manipulate the Communist Party than Trotsky was able to do. The men who succeed in a bureaucratic party or state are not necessarily the best doctrinaires or the most intelligent, but those who have the support of the members or leaders of the party. Perhaps it is not necessary to invoke historical laws to explain why in the end the party chose Stalin rather than Trotsky.

Be that as it may, the neo-Marxist interpretation presents what took place in Soviet Russia as the result of the historical situation and, above all, of the phase of industrialization through which Russia was passing. But instead of saying as orthodox communists do 'we have built socialism' – which is contrary to Marxism since socialism can only appear after the development of productive forces – the neo-Marxists say Russia has constructed a great industry, which is something that the west has already done, but in order to succeed quickly Russia was forced to use terrible methods. Stalin, in order to drag Russia out of barbarism, had to use barbarous methods. An old spring of barbarism came once more to the surface in the tragic circumstances of industrialization. As the productive forces developed, the socialist hopes of Marx had more chance of being realized. Or again, more directly, the democratization of the Soviet regime became more probable as the progress of the productive forces became greater.

This neo-Marxist theory explains the despotic or tyrannical character of the Soviet regime, on the one hand through the exigencies of industrialization and on the other through the influence of the Russian cultural atmosphere. At the same time, it encourages socialist hope by relating the realization of democracy to the moment when the productive forces will have been sufficiently developed for the standard of living to be raised.

This theory does little to explain the contemporary phenomena of the first five-year plan and of the collectivization of agriculture; it does not explain the great purge, the ideological and police terror, when once the first five-year plan had succeeded and when logically, according to this interpretation, Russia should have entered upon a period of stabilization.

Furthermore, it completely ignores the link between the technique of action applied by the Communist Party from the very beginning and the characteristic phenomena of the regime. The technique of action was the seizure of power by a party and the democratic centralism within that party. One can see a clear link between the communist technique of violence and the establishment of a one-party state.

Deutscher explains the great purge, the trials, the confessions by the old Russian traditions; he ignores an important aspect of the regime, the link between the will to ideological orthodoxy and the perpetuation of terror. In fact, the link between economic progress and democracy does not seem to me to have been proved. The Soviet regime will probably be less ruthless towards dissenters and dissent once it has attained a higher level of production. It is rash to affirm that economic progress in itself is enough to promote a politically democratic regime. This is a simplistic explanation, according to which a given economic evolution is enough to create automatically a certain type of political regime.

What conclusions can be drawn from this résumé of the various theories?

Any theory about the Soviet regime is bound to be a complex one; its different aspects cannot be explained by a single scheme or a single cause. The Bolsheviks had the advantage of having discovered a technique of industrialization, hitherto unknown, and of which they were only vaguely conscious beforehand. This technique was set in motion by a political system which is a combination of the absolute power of one or several men and a vast bureaucracy which controls all the functions of the technical economic administrative and ideological direction of society.

This bureaucratic absolutism is reminiscent of the absolutist bureaucracies of the past. Many of the Asiatic empires had similar institutions. But the Soviet regime contains also survivals from its revolutionary origins. What gives it its contradictory and fascinating character is that bureaucratic absolutism does not exclude the revolutionary will. It is still inspired by a will of expansion; of ideology and of power and retains an ideological monopoly; it forces orthodoxy on all its citizens.

The despotisms of the past were based on religious faith; the Soviet despotism is based on an ideology, western in origin, which claims to be rational and which is brought to bear on the reality itself. From this springs the originality of the synthesis: to the usual features of bureaucratic despotisms is added the will to change of the revolutionary party and an ideology of rationalist inspiration which in itself is a criticism of reality.

Lastly, the modern industrial society has given to the Soviet regime means of action such as no despotism in the past disposed of, the monopoly of the means of persuasion and of new techniques of psychological action.

Asiatic despotism did not demand the creation of a new man and the expectation of the end of prehistory.

CHAPTER SEVENTEEN

THE FUTURE OF THE
SOVIET REGIME

Marxist or neo-Marxist interpretations are not the only ones possible. The Soviet regime can also be explained through the history of the Bolsheviks or of Russia itself.

The Bolshevik Party at the beginning of the century was composed of a small group of professional revolutionaries. Today, it has become master of a huge empire, but the men who have lived through this extraordinary experience still retain an outlook going back to their youth. One example of this is their obsession with the police. Why is a great personality who has been disgraced described as an agent of a foreign Intelligence Service or of the Gestapo? Perhaps the answer is that one of the five members of the clandestine central committee before the 1917 revolution was in fact an agent of the OKRANA, that is of the Russian police; after the seizure of power he was unmasked and executed. Lenin had several times vouched for him. This episode explains why an opponent must be an outcast and a tool of the police, the enemy. The historical world which the trials in Moscow presented to us is still today, some forty years later, the sort of world which a conspiratorial party is liable to imagine.

A great deal has been written about the present regime and the Russian traditions. The tsarist empire was historically a bureaucratic hierarchy. The links between Church and state are traditional in Russia where there has always been an ambivalent attitude towards the west, just as the communists have today, in that they want to overtake the United States and yet continually hurl insults at the west. This twofold attitude, at once pro-western and slavophil, to use the classic expression, prolongs the great debate of

the last century. Here are some theses which are often heard.
The communist regime is original in three ways:

1. It is able to use police techniques and persuasion such as no despotic regime in the past possessed. The population, more closely knit than in former societies and increasingly urbanized, is also more indoctrinated.

2. It is based on a strange combination between an authoritarian bureaucracy and the will to build socialism. The administration of an economy by a bureaucracy is not new but the bureaucratic administration of an economy in order to develop rapidly the means of production is a new phenomenon.

3. This bureaucratic absolutism is subject to one party, which is in a sense a revolutionary one; hence the conjunction, once again novel, of an authoritarian bureaucracy and revolutionary phenomena. The communist party, which can be compared to the Jacobins, is established in a bureaucratic state which appears to be stabilized.

These new features of the soviet regime give us a starting point for a few remarks about the outlook for the future. I have described the possible corruption of a constitutional-pluralistic regime; now I must evoke also the possible corruption of a monopolistic party system. But the corruption of such a regime would be the *desovietization* of the regime. Corruption in an objective sense means to abandon some of the practices which are characteristic of the regime.

The simplest way, it seems to me, to put the problem is to contrast two versions of Marxism, the optimistic and the pessimistic version. The optimistic version is that held by Isaac Deutscher who links the less reputable aspects of the Soviet regime to the phase of economic growth. He explains the ideological orthodoxy, the use of terror, the trials, the excesses of the single party, by the need to build industry. Once this phase has been achieved, all that we in the west dislike about the soviet regime will tend to disappear, because these pathological traits could be set down either to Stalin's personality (and Stalin is dead) or to the demands of industrialization which are gradually decreasing.

The pessimistic version is the one which takes up again the idea of the Asiatic method of production, and explains the Soviet regime by the total bureaucratization of existence and affirms that the phenomena which the optimists think of as pathological are inseparable from a regime of bureaucratic absolutism, of a single-party and of ideological orthodoxy.

Between the optimistic and the pessimistic versions, all sorts of intermediary versions are possible. The search for an intermediate version prompts us to ask the following question: What features are there in the Soviet regime which should be attributed to the needs of industrialization? What are those which are explained by the permanent structure of a Soviet regime?

Let us start by recalling the main changes which have taken place since 1953.

1. From the point of view of terrorism and of individual liberties, there have been great changes. There are no more great purges like that of 1936; there are no more spectacular trials, with forced confessions, there has been a widespread amnesty, the concentration camps have begun to disappear, the harshness of the laws and of the judicial practice has been attenuated. The principle of the analogy, a principle according to which to a crime not specifically laid down in the code of law, could be added, by analogy, the definition of a crime, laid down in the code, has been officially abandoned. The special police commission which had the right to judge *in camera* and to send to concentration camps all those who were suspected of counter-revolutionary activities has, we are told, been officially suppressed. The articles of the code which laid down that, in the case of counter-revolutionary activities, the trial could be concluded in twenty-four hours, without any defence for the accused have also been suppressed.

The threat or the constraint which weighed upon the Soviet citizen has been relaxed; relations between Russians and foreigners have become possible; in the intellectual sphere, we have seen a thaw, there has been more debate; orthodoxy in the writing of history or of art is neither so dogmatic nor imperative. The style of the regime is different from what it was before 1953.

These genuine and substantial changes do not as yet constitute a revolution.

The style of the destalinization has often remained Stalinist. Khrushchev, after the elimination of Beria, could not refrain from branding him as a traitor and a foreign agent, just as Beria called anyone whom he wanted to eliminate a foreign agent. Many of the facts recounted in his famous speech by the (present) General Secretary of the Communist Party had no more truth than the facts put forward in previous official speeches. Stalin was not the ogre described by Khrushchev; he was not incapable of understanding and of directing military operations. To reduce someone who was idolized a few years ago to a subhuman level is to create a new mythology.

2. The police no longer play the same role; above all, they no longer carry out their activities at the expense of party-members, as they did a few years ago. They remain on the alert and act according to the government's decisions. For the time being the police apparatus is nearly only a peace-keeping force, but not quite.

3. There are no more great purges in the spectacular style of 1936, but a kind of purge goes on all the time. This is apparent if we compare the members of the Central Committee from one session to another. What the Italian sociologist Pareto called the circulation of the élite is always rapid; outstanding personalities disappear after a time. They are no longer executed. The fact that those who hold high offices are frequently replaced suggests the continuance of struggles among factions or personalities.

4. Lastly, and this is the essential point, the theory of the monopoly of the party, of the guiding role of the party in the economy, in the state and in intellectual life has been left intact. The scope which is given to this theory in practice varies and can vary, without any of the essential features of the regime being transformed. The regime of ideological orthodoxy and of political monopoly of the party is still with us. Some of the bizarre features or the oddities and excesses which could be imputed to the former Secretary General in his old age have disappeared.

From a political point of view we know that there has been a striking change. It is not a single leader who has appeared – journalists are already saying that Khrushchev has beaten Stalin's record and won complete victory in less time than it took his predecessor – but I do not think that this is so. Khrushchev is at the moment the most powerful man in the Soviet Union, but his power bears no resemblance to that of Stalin after 1934. The present Secretary General is not idolized in the way that Stalin was. There are no signs that he terrorizes his colleagues. But what was special about the last phase of Stalin's regime, according to Khrushchev himself, was the perpetual fear in which his oldest colleagues lived. None of the observers at present in Russia feels that this is true today; there are no signs that the members of the

Politburo, the Presidium or the members of the central committee live in dread of the Secretary General and fear that each time they visit him they will not come out again as free men. The party continues to play its leading role, but its structure is not the same as the one we observed during the Stalinist phase. The central committee seems to have regained some importance; it appears that Khrushchev was outvoted in the Presidium in 1957 and he carried the day and defeated the 'anti-party group' by rallying the central committee.

At the same time, relations with the peoples' democracies are less hidebound than they were previously. Here again, there has been no essential change, the Soviet Union's domination of the East European countries is maintained, but a certain free play is left to the national governments, in implementing common directives.

In the economic sphere, changes can also be seen. The present leaders lay more stress on the standard of living; they try to produce more consumer goods; above all, they are less rigid in their technique. They do not hesitate, in order to bring about an increase in agricultural production, to resort to the machinery of prices, to use the incentives employed in all countries with a western economy and which are normal once doctrinal eccentricities have been thrown off.

One example of this easing is the suppression of the tractor-stations. The example shows us an institution, which had nothing to do with Marxist or Leninist doctrine, which was possibly raised to the level of a doctrine only to fall later to the level of a method. Stalin stated that the tractor-stations were an integral part of socialist doctrine; he stated repeatedly that to suppress the tractor-stations and to sell the tractors to the kolkhozes would be to regress. Khrushchev thought that the tractor-stations had ceased to be useful. The kolkhozes are richer, thanks to the rise in price of agricultural produce, they are buying the tractor-stations; probably the Kremlin thought that they would be kept in better shape if they were the property of the kolkhozes; perhaps, too, it was hoped to get rid of a purchasing power which threatened to provoke inflation.

From the economic, as well as from the political point of view, these changes have not affected what seemed to me, two years ago, to be the essentials of the economic system. The primacy of heavy industry is more strongly affirmed than ever; more than ever, the priority of aims is set and, in case of need, the other aims are sacrificed: more than ever, there is planning by decree, leaving, it must be admitted, more room for free play, more flexibility in the enterprises, by allowing more adaptation to circumstances.

The conclusion which I want to draw can be summed up in the following formulation: hitherto, there have been changes *in* the regime, but there have been no fundamental changes *of* the regime itself. The latter, like all political and economic systems, is composed of various versions; reforms, provided that they do not impinge on fundamentals, are not excluded. Still, today, the foundations are untouched, but, within the framework of the system, there have been changes. What changes must there be before we can say that the essential structure of the regime itself has been modified?

It seems to me that the basic features are:

1. The domination of the single party and the maintenance of ideological orthodoxy of which the party is the sole interpreter;
2. Centralized planning, directed by a bureaucracy;
3. The existence of a bureaucratic hierarchy which constitutes a principle of discrimination within the society itself.

There are not, there cannot be and there should not be autonomous forces outside the state. A western society is, in its essence, a class society in which groups are distinguishable, oppose each other and compete. A Soviet-type society is composed of separate groups, all enclosed within a bureaucratic hierarchy, within a state hierarchy. This structure is intact, five years after Stalin's death, and for the moment there is no sign that his heirs want to touch it.

What are the more distant prospects of corruption or of change in the Soviet regime? Here I shall use relatively abstract schemes. What are these schemes which support the optimistic theory of the transformation of the regime itself?

We already know about the first; I mentioned it in the previous chapter; it is the scheme which I called neo-Marxist and which explains the harshness of the Soviet regime by recourse of the economic phase which ran between 1917 and 1940 as well as in recent years. This neo-Marxist scheme shows first, that the standard of living is rising and will go on rising; and secondly, that the standard of education of the people is continuously rising. These two facts are true. The theory of pauperization in the Soviet regime is quite as false as the theory of poverty in the capitalist system. No system of industrial economy, no matter how incompetent the government may be, can prevent the translation of an increase in productivity into a rise in the standard of living. The translation may be rapid or less rapid, but it takes place in all industrial societies.

The rise in the standard of living and in the level of education is in itself *favourable* to a liberalization of the Soviet regime. An urban population of workers and of employees who have been given a technical training cannot be governed by the same process as a peasant mass.

The moment that we leave behind these obvious truths, we come up against a difficulty. The neo-Marxist scheme implies a direct link between the standard of living, the level of education and democratic or liberal institutions. This direct link has not been proved and we unfortunately saw a tragic example which contradicts it, that of Germany under Hitler. The Germans had a high technical level, a high cultural level, but they still accepted a monopolistic party regime and an extraordinarily crude ideology. The experience we have had of one-party regimes and democratic parties confirms that men, even educated ones, easily accept ideologies, some absurd, some less so. In the long run, anyone, no matter who he is, in some circumstances is ready to believe almost anything.

Even if we agree that the Russians have less and less faith in their ideology (which is possible), this does not mean that ideology will cease to play a part. In history, most of the official doctrines have been maintained as a way to govern, decades and sometimes even centuries after everyone, at least in educated circles, has ceased to believe them.

Finally, why should the only social and political system suited to an industrial society be a pluralistic regime of the western type? Can a regime of bureaucratic hierarchy, of authoritarian planning, be reconciled to a developed industrial society? It seems to me impossible to say in advance that a developed industrial society will necessarily produce a social and political system similar to the one we know in the west.

The second scheme of transformation, which the sociologists

who tend to be optimistic use, is that of the future of revolutions. Revolutions appear to have one feature in common: they do not last for ever. In the long run, no one really believes that the existence of mankind is going to be completely altered. The fervour wears out and with the passing of time what Max Weber called *die Veraltäglichung der Revolution* (which can be translated approximately as the return to daily life of the revolution) takes place. The Communist Party in the Soviet Union will undergo the fate which has overtaken all revolutions, the Puritan, the Jacobin and others which ended, in failure or success, by accepting that men are as they are. In the end they, too, became resigned to a stable order.

This argument stresses either the gradual disappearance of revolutionary faith, or the gradual stabilization of a privileged class. The Bolsheviks began by being a party of professional revolutionaries, completely dedicated to the task of subversion; today these professional revolutionaries in the countries of Eastern Europe have become a privileged class in the regime. Djilas denounced his former comrades because they had become bourgeois. But what to a revolutionary appears as corruption of the system, appears to a less optimistic sociologist as a necessary *embourgeoisement*, a return to normal practice.

This scheme which uses the gradual exhaustion of revolutionary fervour seems valid to me; it is probable that in the long run that revolutionaries or their sons will become bourgeois middle-class. It would seem that such a process is taking place on the other side of the iron curtain. It also seems to me possible that faith in Marxism is growing less with time. This is not to say that the Soviet citizens are ceasing completely to be Marxist, they retain the Marxist vocabulary, they accept many Marxist ideas, but Marxism itself has a decreasing influence on the thought of the leaders and of the people. The doctrine continues to be respected, but it no longer dictates action.

For the moment, this evolution does not appear to be very advanced and Khrushchev himself has told us that it will never take place.

But if such an evolution were to take place, the result would not necessarily be the overthrow of the regime as we know it. At most, some of the features such as ideological terror which are linked to the permanence of revolutionary fervour would disappear, but not the monopoly of the party, ideological orthodoxy or bureaucratic absolutism. The structural features of the regime could survive. The third scheme invoked by the sociologists who believe in the transformation of the regime is that of rationalization.

The American sociologist, Barrington Moore, who has written some very interesting books on the Soviet Union, sees in the Soviet regime a combination of three principles – traditional, rational and terroristic. As time goes by, normally the regime should become increasingly traditional and rational. Traditional, in the sense that customs would become rooted in the Russian soil; rational, in that society would try to produce as much as possible as cheaply as possible, it would become less concerned about ideology and, at the same time, less given to extreme measures.

Personally, I am inclined to argue that, in the long run, economic considerations will become predominant in the Soviet regime as in most other regimes. But there remains an insurmountable objection to the optimistic consequences which some see as a result of this prospect: it seems to me likely that the present leaders of the Soviet economy are less concerned with doctrine and more concerned with efficiency, and even today we can see some signs of this. But when we speak of the rationalization of the Soviet regime, we must ask a necessary, if startling, question. Are intellectual liberty and pluralistic parties rational phenomena? Are those who govern, and who are inspired by the desire to lead the economy and the society towards maximum production, while preserving at the same time their own privileges, obliged to give all the people the right to discuss their decisions? Will they tolerate a multiplicity of parties competing for power? The rationalization of the economic and political regime, the elimination of pathological excesses, such as the rigidity of the planned economy or the purges, are something which may come to pass; the advent of a regime, similar to those we know in the west, is quite another matter. Is it reasonable to want to have several parties and the right for each person to have a say in what does not concern him? To conclude that the rationalization of the regime will lead to democratization is to affirm something which is dubious, to say the least; it is tantamount to saying that a multi-party system is the only rational policy which can be imposed on an industrial economy.

What conclusion do I want to draw from this brief examination? I agree with one part of the optimist's argument about the totalitarian regime. I do think that the ways of life will draw nearer to each other on both sides of the iron curtain; they are already doing so. Even a brief visit is enough for one to see that many of the anxieties and considerations which concern us in the west are to be found in the same form on the other side of the iron curtain, because both are building an industrial society. I agree that economic administration will tend to become more rational and consequently the general standard of living will improve. I agree that ideological relaxation is more probable than the maintenance of the extreme forms of orthodoxy and of ideological terror. I think that the picture of the world of 1984 drawn by George Orwell applies rather to 1951–2 than to 1984. These extreme phenomena are contemporaneous with the first phases of industrialization, rather than with phases of economic ripeness. Lastly, I admit that there is a tendency towards the stabilization of a bureaucratic hierarchy. But when all this has been said, and I have come down rather on the optimistic side, I am still doubtful.

These transformations are in no way incompatible with the maintenance of two essential elements of the regime. First, the *monopoly of the party*; now, the monopoly of the party excludes or at least hinders both the constitutionality of the struggle for the exercise of power and ideological pluralism. In the second place, *bureaucratic absolutism*; as the whole privileged class has a feeling of solidarity, the creation of centres of independent forces becomes almost impossible. The maintenance of these two elements has far-reaching consequences. It is in the nature of the essence of such a regime to confine intellectual liberty within strict limits, because its ideological justification must not be questioned. It must be able, in case of need, to use violence or terror. Lastly, and this is perhaps the essential point, the man who carries most weight in the regime is a party man, an *apparatchik*. Most of the optimistic forecasts about the transformation of the Soviet regime are based on the idea that in the end the technicians and the managers will take precedence over the party men.

The victor in the struggle between the heirs seems above all to be a party man. At the present moment, we are witnessing not the restoration, but the confirmation of the decisive role of the party, and of the *apparat* in the leadership of Soviet society.

The privileged are not divided into factions which can be compared to western parties. It is ridiculous to imagine a party of technicians against a party of ideologists or a party of soldiers against a party of the police. Many technicians have joined the party. But what is true is that the different categories of managers which I have picked out represent specific preferences or habits, but not necessarily opposing doctrines. The party men take a growing part in the administration as well as in propaganda. They are the political personnel and this personnel on the whole determines the characteristics of the regime. After all, in the West we have professional politicians. In the United States they are men like Truman or Nixon; in Britain, Macmillan or Gaitskell. Why should we be surprised that the men of the apparatus in the Soviet Union continue to mould the regime, when we find it quite normal that professional politicians in western regimes should set their mark on the actual system? I know that in the West many people think that the professional politicians are merely puppets, whose strings are pulled by the oligarchs and the great concerns. This picture of the power of the oligarchs leads one to believe that there are men in the Soviet Union who are more powerful than the politicians.

Let us take the facts as we see them: politicians usually see the problems of government as a means of coming to power, in such a way as to insure the loyalty of the voters. Constitutional-pluralistic regimes succeed in maintaining these constitutional processes and in acting effectively according to the style of conflicts and of compromise characteristic of such regimes. In the Soviet Union, the equivalent of these professional politicians are the *apparatchiks*.

All industrial societies include managers of nationalized industries, owners or directors of factories. These men are the same, from country to country, because they are faced with the same kind of conditions. When it comes to the professional politicians, this is not so. Of course, some of the problems which face the politicians are universal; to remain in power, govern the country, surmount their own differences. But the problems are solved in different ways. Politicians may organize themselves within a one-party state with a particular style of competition within the party. The single party has great advantages. It is assured permanently of its own justification; it professes an ideology which preaches the legitimacy of the established authority and of the men who exercise it. It excludes the official recognition of conflicts. Homogeneity reigns in principle; it is easy to understand why politicians accustomed to a single party should want to preserve this particular structure. The foreseeable changes, linked to the growth of industry, to the rise in the standard of living and of education, do not imply the elimination of the single party and of ideological orthodoxy any more than they imply the disappearance of the bureaucratic hierarchy, common to the society and to the state.

Are the prospects of bourgeois stabilization good? Why should they not be? Of economic rationalization? Why not? Of elimination of terror? Probably. Abandonment of the pathological forms of terror? Possibly. Introduction of multiple parties and liberal institutions such as there are in the west? This is possible, but there is no demonstrable necessity or even probability that the evolution of industrial society brings with it the results which we wish.

Deutscher advances the argument that the working class, as its standard of living increases, will become more active, more politically dynamic. For my part, I think that the Soviet working class must become less and less dissatisfied; the conditions of existence improve, the pressure of authority dies down. Why, in a regime which is advancing, should the popular masses be more and more dissatisfied; why should they press for fundamental changes?

I have left on one side a hypothesis about which I should like to say a word to finish, that of revolution. We know of revolutions against pluralistic regimes; why should there not be revolution against regimes of the monopolistic party? Up to the present, in the east of Europe there have been two revolutions against regimes of the monopolistic party or rather pseudo-regimes of the monopolistic party. In Poland as well as in Hungary, the essential factor was missing: the national character of the regime itself. In Poland as well as in Hungary the regime could never have been established nor could it have lasted without the Soviet Union. Even today the Polish regime of Gomulka is a compromise between the sentiments of the people and geographical necessities. All Poles are in favour of Mr Gomulka, and it is often said in Warsaw, some support him because he is a communist and others support him despite the fact that he is a communist. In Hungary, the regime lacks the minimum of national support which is indispensable to every authoritarian regime of this kind.

In order that a revolution may take place in a regime of the monopolistic party, which is solidly entrenched as in the Soviet Union, a scission in the privileged minority must be made. As long as the political personnel and the bureaucracy as a whole remain united, it is difficult to see how the governed could have the opportunity to revolt. Not that anything indicates that they desire to do so. I do not say that if there were to be free elections they would vote for such a regime, but, by definition, a regime of this order is not established by means of free elections in the western meaning of the term and they do not put their fate to the test of elections. The Soviet regime rests on the conviction that those whom they govern should not be asked their opinion about the merits of the state. It has brought greatness, power, and economic progress to the Soviet Union, year after year. Either a strange optimism or a curious pessimism is needed to count on its being overthrown, just when the Russians take pride in being today the second country in the world and are sure that tomorrow they will be the first.

There remains the hypothesis that freedom is the strongest and most enduring desire of all mankind, but the word freedom is so equivocal that it calls for a further study.

CONCLUSION

CHAPTER EIGHTEEN

ON THE IMPERFECTION OF REGIMES

I have come now to the last two chapters. First of all, I shall unravel the meaning of the difference between the two kinds of regime, then I shall try to situate this difference in history; in other words, the analysis will be static and then dynamic.

The antithesis between the constitutional-pluralistic regime and the monopolistic regime can be explained in four different ways: antithesis between *competition* and *monopoly*; between the *constitution* and the *revolution*; between the *pluralism of social groups* and *bureaucratic absolutism* and, finally, between the *state with parties* and the *party-state* (this last antithesis can be translated by secular-state and ideological state).

The destruction between competition and monopoly is part of the vocabulary of political economy. It seems to me that it can be used elsewhere, but only with some reservations.

In the political order, as in the economic one, the problem is how privileges which are necessarily scarce are to be shared out. Not everyone can become a deputy or a minister. The competition for political benefits can be compared to the competition for wealth.

However, the comparison is not absolutely valid. In the strict meaning of the term, there is no free competition in politics. An economist would say that political competition is always oligopolistic. A few individuals or groups compete for benefits, of which the most important is to have a share in power. The best organized politics leads to oligopoly or duopoly, the rivalry of two parties. The more tightly competition is organized, the less democratic it is, in one sense: the ordinary citizen has less choice. In the case of a duopoly, he must opt for one of two parties.

The French system, which is least organized, is, in a way, a perfect democracy, for it gives the most people the widest range of choice. There are so many possible choices that no collective decisions emerge.

Political competition, no matter how many groups or parties there may be, takes on a different meaning according to the organization of the parties themselves. Once again, within the parties, there is competition, a duopoly or oligopoly, and the internal structure of the parties completes and often improves that aspect of the regime which is defined by relations between the parties. At one extreme, the party is embodied in an all-powerful individual and at the other there is wide open competition which is as free as possible.

The two following concepts, *constitution* and *revolution*, are borrowed, not from political economy, but from juridical terminology.

The notion of constitutionality has several meanings. The organization of competition for the exercise of power and the subjugation of this competition to precise rules is constitutional. Another, probably more important, form of constitutionality is the subordination of governmental decisions to these rules. In order to promulgate a law, those in power in a constitutional system need the intervention of other bodies. In an authoritarian system, a decision taken by the governors automatically becomes law. It can happen that any whim of an individual can become law. A striking example of this was the suppression on 30 June 1934 by Hitler of a plot or of a pseudo-plot; Hitler had the conspirators or pseudo-conspirators put to death. After this had been done, a law was passed according to which these summary executions were made legal. A retrospective constitutionality was conferred on summary executions, thus combining the arbitrariness of the deed with the comedy of law (retroactive).

The constitutional state in its relations with individuals is neither judge nor partisan; anyone who is arrested and illtreated has or should have the opportunity to appeal to impartial courts against officials who may have been guilty of an infringement of the law; or again, anyone whose interests have been damaged by an administrative decree can appeal to a juridical body, to ordinary or administrative courts. Bodies, independent of the government, empowered to deal with problems arising out of relations between the state and individuals, constitute a third form of constitutionality.

Revolution, on the other hand, seems to me to be the negation, in its essence, of legality. To be sure, this is a question of definition. A French politician spoke of 'revolution according to the law'. There was, in fact, no revolution but one can imagine changes brought about legally which were so important that, in a wide sense, they could be called revolutionary. It seems to me preferable to retain the authentic meaning of the notion of revolution – a break with legality. In this sense, monopolistic party regimes are essentially revolutionary from the beginning, because they seize power by force. They remain revolutionary, some for a longer and some for a shorter time. Those who govern do not allow themselves to be hamstrung by constitutionality or by the laws. In the Soviet Union, the party in power has promulgated a constitution, or rather three constitutions, but it has never felt tied by constitutional rules. Monopolistic party regimes, especially communist ones, tend to be regimes of permanent revolution. They boast that they are in a state of permanent revolution until they have attained their goals.

The following antithesis, that of the pluralism of social groups and of bureaucratic absolutism, is a repetition of the analysis which I made elsewhere[1] of the social structure of Soviet-type countries and of western-type countries. All societies are heterogeneous, with unequal standards of living. On one side, groups have the right to organize themselves and to become aware of themselves, and to oppose each other openly; on the other, individuals and groups are ranged in a unique hierarchy which in the end is a bureaucratic one.

A bureaucrat, in its sociological use, is not someone in a government office. He is the representative of an anonymous order. He does not act as a person, but as an individual defined by his function, with a set place in the hierarchy. Each one has a specific role and all must obey the rules. The great American companies have bureaucrats who are exactly the same as those in the collectivized Soviet enterprises. Our age has rightly been called the administrative age. The administrative officers are as characteristic of an industrial society as are the factories themselves. Regimes of the Soviet type are not unique in this.

What does authorize us to speak of bureaucratic absolutism is

[1] *La lutte des classes.*

that the labour organizers, engineers and managers are all part of one administration, instead of being spread among autonomous companies, each with its own bureaucracy. All the organizers of collective labour, in a regime of the monopolistic type, are part of a state hierarchy. The same men may pursue careers both in business enterprises and in the ministries. But this is not unknown in the West; in all the sectors of a nationalized economy the same men may serve as heads of business enterprises and as officials. The characteristic feature of monopolistic party regimes remains nevertheless this combination, with state-control of the bureaucracy carried to its limits. When this point is reached we find a privileged class composed of men who owe everything to the state – their work and their income – and who stand to lose everything if they are dismissed or purged. There is only one way to reach important positions and it is through the state bureaucracy, with all the servility that this entails.

The fourth antithesis is that of the *state with parties* and the *party-state*. In one case, there is a plurality of competing parties, each with its conception of the common good, and, in the other, the single party and its conception of the good which is obligatory for everyone. I have used another expression, meaning more or less the same thing, that of the secular state and the ideological state, which is a transposition, in the age of political struggle, of the opposition between a state tied to a faith and a state with no creed.

The distinction is not a simple one. Every community must have common values, without which it could not exist as a state. In the secular states, the idea of the state tends to be diminished by the constitution itself. The main idea of the constitutional-pluralistic regime is the soundness of the constitution; everyone must agree to settle their disputes according to constitutional rules. The renunciation of violence becomes, so to speak, the ideology of the non-ideological state. By the same token, it must be said that the non-party state, the state of parties, in order to tolerate the pluralism of parties and of doctrines is not devoid of doctrine, because the renunciation of violence is itself a philosophy. It implies confidence in debate, in the possibility of gradual change. Every political system is defined by a particular method of settling social conflicts and of renewing the teams in power. The constitutional-pluralistic regime inclines to a peaceful settlement of conflicts and a regular renewal of the teams.

What conclusion can be drawn from this comparative analysis? It cannot reasonably be said that one of the systems is good and the other bad, that one represents good and the other evil. Both are imperfect. But the imperfections are not of the same kind. Constitutional-pluralistic regimes are flawed in practice, the flaws in the monopolistic party regime are inherent.

Constitutional-pluralistic regimes are imperfect because they contain either too great a degree of oligarchy or of demagogy, and they almost always suffer because of difficulties in being effective.

They are imperfect because they contain too much oligarchy, when behind the give-and-take of the parties there is the omnipotence of a minority; they are imperfect because they contain too much demagogy; when in the party struggle the groups lose sight of collective needs and the sentiment of the common good. They are imperfect because of limited efficiency since, inevitably, a regime in which all the groups have the right to defend their interests can seldom take radical steps.

The imperfection of the monopolistic party regime is something different and it is fundamental. If we imagine a homogeneous society, without any conflicts of interest between groups, in a planned economy with public ownership, the monopoly of the party is no longer indispensable. But if public opinion is forbidden to express itself freely, if uniformity of thought is maintained, the society is no longer homogeneous. From the moment when society is no longer homogeneous, the group which imposes its will by force can carry out a task, which is in itself admirable, but it can no longer claim that it has established democracy. In the end it comes down to the question of how to have a perfect society; it contradicts itself when it puts forward the one-party regime as the realization of democracy.

A second argument is based on the Soviet constitution and the elections. If elections in themselves have no significance, if the constitutional forms are devoid of meaning, why does the Soviet regime preserve rites such as elections or convocation of an assembly? Elections are the tribute paid to the virtue of these processes. If one does not believe that power emanates from the governed, what good are elections? The fact that in the Soviet Union elections are held and that there is a parliament proves that the intention or hope of one day restoring these democratic processes has not disappeared. Repression or manipulation is justified by the circumstances; the society is not yet homogeneous enough. The day when it becomes so, things can be done differently. The result is that the single-party regime, because of the way it acts and the ideas which it professes, is only a transition, perhaps a prolonged and necessary one. It has no justification in itself. But it is often justified by various pragmatic considerations.

Sometimes it is impossible to eliminate oligarchies, without resorting to violence. It may be that the choice lies between a barren conservatism and violence. The resort to force is not an evil in itself. The constitutional-pluralistic regimes of the west which declare themselves to be irreconcilably hostile to the use of violence proclaim by the same token that they are hostile to their ancestors. In England and in France, they put a king to death. The English often wonder whether they were right to do so; the French think less about it; in both cases, a revolution overthrew the traditional authority. In the United States the revolution – the war of liberation – lies also at the root of the constitutional pluralistic regime. Historically, western systems are not against the use of violence, in all circumstances. But violence must be stabilized in constitutional rules. Violence which perpetrates itself condemns itself by the same token.

The monopoly of one party after the revolutionary phase can be useful to the construction of the state. Its justification oscillates between the formulae of the vanguard and of the teacher. The monopolistic party is the vanguard of the masses, it leads them to the conquest of the future, it selects the best, and the best form an élite which gives a framework to and teaches the others. The monopolistic party is, so to speak, the teacher, who knows the historical truth and shares it with the as yet untaught masses, just as the schoolmaster passes on acquired truths to children.

The real question is to know in what precise cases these justifications can be held to be valid but, on this point, there is no general doctrine, either philosophical or sociological. It is difficult to reach agreement, when it is a question of deciding in what circumstances the use of violence is justified. The victims find it difficult to concede the necessity. Or again, contemporaries find it more difficult to admit its legitimacy than the heirs. But these are obvious statements. The important idea is that there is no general theory which enables one to determine when the use of violence is historically justified. We can follow Kant and state, once and for all, that the use of force in itself is morally wrong, but on condition that we immediately add, as Kant did, that this morally wrong use of force was indispensable to create states and to raise mankind to reason.

Can a monopolistic party regime be justified intrinsically? As an ideal?

This justification can be borrowed from Spengler. Man, a beast of prey, is essentially violent and regimes which try to eliminate violence are thus decadent. The argument is subdivided into two statements: a metaphysical argument which states that violence is in itself, if not actually good, at least inherent in human nature; a historical argument, according to which constitutional egalitarian regimes are the harbingers of decadence.

Men do not live according to Spengler's pessimism, they do not think that they are beasts of prey nor do they wish to be. Spengler would probably reply that this denial only proves how hypocritical men are. This answer, which is not entirely without foundation, is still unconvincing. Men do not want only to be violent; the moral judgments which they make about good and evil decide to some extent how they behave. They cannot govern by means of such a philosophy. Spengler, had he been a politician, would have been forced to be a hypocrite, because mankind does not accept the goal which he set for it.

The doctrine of violence, in the age of thermonuclear bombs, would probably end in the self-destruction of mankind. This is a factual objection, but a strong one; men dedicated to war, with the technical means which are now available to them, would inevitably in the short or long run be condemned to death. Spengler's philosophy, which claims to be realistic, is invalidated by history itself.

Modern societies are rationalist and peaceful. Spengler's anthropological conception is ill-suited to the nature of industrial societies which are defined by economic activity that requires equality of opportunity or, at the least, some minimum of education for all. The socialist, egalitarian trend which was, to Spengler and perhaps also to Nietzsche, a sign of decadence is today not so much the result of human decision as it is a social necessity.

The provisional conclusion is that the imperfection of the two systems differs in its nature. Many objections to this conclusion can be made and I shall now discuss them.

The two main objections are:

1. Can a plural-party state fit the purposes of a modern society? When we see the mediocrity or the turpitude of the plural-party systems as they are reported daily, can we, in 1958, in France, say that these systems, as they are, conform to the essence of the societies in which we live?

2. Does not the monopolistic party regime, the one-party state, tend to create its own values, which differ profoundly from those of the multiparty state?

1. Is not the multi-party state in itself as imperfect, when compared to the ideal, as the one-party state?

I am thinking here of a study by Simone Weil on political parties. She advocated the banning of all parties in order to restore democracy to its pure state. Rousseau utterly condemned factions, party organization and parties of citizens within the Republic. True democracy could not, according to him, exist together with established rival groups. I have described the parties as one of the fundamental elements in constitutional-pluralistic regimes. I do not deny that they have faults. If I am ready to make a case for the parties, it is on condition that I do not have to belong to any of them – I am aware of their legitimacy in the abstract without being blind to their concrete faults. If one could imagine that men were different from what they are, then one could envisage a system of free elections and of debate without the citizens being subject to party machines which are always unpleasant and often deplorable. The parties secrete demagogy; they force their members to think in certain terms, and to defend certain interests. Every politician knows that he cannot at the same time be a party man and a scholar, which is another way of saying that one cannot be a party man and always tell the truth. Those who are as intransigent as was Simone Weil, who thought that every lapse of truth was an absolute evil, will utterly condemn the confused mixture of truth and falsehood which are called party struggles. Yet one must understand why the plurality of parties is essential to modern societies.

First of all, the organization of competition is essential. I have spoken of competition and of monopoly. Using a comparison with economics, I suggested that modern economic societies entailed organized competition in most realms. The political game of the constitutional-pluralistic regimes is the organization of competition, a competition and organization inevitable in our societies. Rivalry is inevitable because there are no more rulers by divine right or by tradition. Once there were no more hereditary rulers how could legitimate rulers emerge except through competition? If competition is not organized, it is given over to arbitrariness and violence.

In the second place the potential participation of all the citizens in politics is essential. Elections as they are now conducted are perhaps only a degenerate form of the universal participation of the citizens in the state, but they are a symbol which could become a reality.

Another essential factor in a multi-party system is the right to debate what should be done and what is the best constitution for the city. It seems to me, once again, fitting to our subject that all who want to should take part in the debate. I know the objection which Paul Valéry made; politics has long been the art of preventing men from having any say in their own concerns: it has become the art of asking them about matters of which they know nothing. This is a very brilliant simplification but, if men are not asked, they will always be ignorant. This kind of regime creates the hope that by dint of questioning them, they will one day become less ignorant.

The debate inside the parties touches on many interconnected themes. The allocation of collective resources, the organization of the economy, the structure of the political system, as well as the interests of the community in relation to others are debated.

The debate on the allocation of collective resources or publicly owned enterprises can be settled reasonably and publicly between the citizens. The debate on foreign policy is unfortunately more difficult.

Systems of this kind would be closer to their ideal if the method of choosing the rulers and the constitution were accepted by everyone. Conflicts about the system itself would be eliminated and reasonable debate between the groups would take place on the fair distribution of resources and on the best way to organize the economy.

Public discussion about the best ways to manage the economy is not only reasonable; it can contribute to efficiency. However, in troubled times, when the interests of one community are opposed to those of other communities, there is a risk that if every decision is debated openly all action will be paralysed.

These facts, and many others, are the result of imperfections, inherent in human nature and in present-day social realities; they do not seem to me to invalidate the propositions which I want to support. In the societies of our time, I do not see how the organization of competition or the potential participation of everyone in elections and debate can be eliminated without violating the principles on which our culture is based.

2. Let us pass on now to the second objection to the specific values of monopolistic party regimes.

The specific values which are most frequently invoked are on the one hand genuine liberty, as against formal liberty and, on the other, the creation of a new man who will be born from socialist construction.

The word 'liberty' is equivocal and has many meanings. Liberty in the vocabulary of Montesquieu means above all security, the guarantee that the citizens will be unmolested if they obey the law. Liberty also means the citizen's right to his own opinions about almost everything without the state dictating what he should think. To Rousseau liberty meant participation in public affairs, a role in the designation of those who govern; in such a way that the individual feels that he is only obeying himself when he obeys the state.

These three notions of liberty are classic in political philosophy; I shall add two more.

A man who has from his early youth the feeling that he is the prisoner of his condition, without any hope of escaping from it and of bettering himself, can feel that he is not free. In our time, liberty implies some social mobility.

Working people must have the feeling that they are treated fairly, are not being subjected to arbitrary authority, and are receiving rewards commensurate with their efforts.

The feeling of being free, which is different from the abstract notion, clearly depends on various circumstances.

I imagine that a Russian who has received a scholarship for secondary and then higher education, who has risen in the social scale, who today has a profession which brings him satisfaction, feels that he is free, although perhaps he does not enjoy complete security or the right to have his own opinions on Marxist philosophy. Opportunities for social advancement can give rise to a feeling of freedom when other kinds of liberty are lacking.

The feeling of being free is also determined by the idea that men have about what is just and what is unjust. When a worker thinks that private ownership is an evil in itself and that profits of big business derive from the exploitation of the workers, security, the right to read *l'Humanité* every morning and to criticize the government, are of little use to him. He is probably aware that an essential freedom is missing. The feeling of being free is not proportionate to the objective guarantees of freedom, in the first three meanings of the word.

I have added these two last meanings in order to acknowledge that there is some truth in the criticisms which are often levelled at constitutional-pluralistic regimes. They are criticized for affording freedoms which affect the more privileged classes, especially intellectuals, rather than the ordinary man in the streeet, for not giving to the masses the two ultimate forms of concrete freedom, which are the feeling of having a good position and a fair wage for their work and an opportunity to rise in the social scale.

Security, freedom of thought, a share in sovereignty are not enough. But the fact that constitutional-pluralistic regimes do not assure *all* the freedoms does not mean that the monopolistic-party regimes give another meaning to freedom. Neither do the latter always give the workers the feeling of freedom in work and of a fair return. I do not think that any theoretician of the Communist Party has held that the security of the citizen, freedom of thought and participation in politics are not valid forms of freedom. What they have said, and often rightly, is that other aspects of freedom are not always guaranteed by constitutional-pluralistic regimes.

The result of this argument is that there is not one meaning of freedom for monopolistic party regimes and another for constitutional-pluralistic ones. It is not true that these words have different meanings on either side of the iron curtain. It is true that all the freedoms have not until now been simultaneously assured to all the citizens. Each ideologist pleads his own cause, putting forward what his system gives to men and what the other system neglects. There is at once an intelligible and reasonable argument about the merits and demerits of the different regimes.

Is there a philosophical conception of freedom which would

justify the choice of a regime, in particular of a one-party regime? I do not think so. Philosophers explain often that the highest liberty is part of reason. Reasonably, the individual rises above the particularity and reaches a sort of universality. But this elevation of reason passes necessarily, as Kant and Auguste Comte have said, through the subjection to work and to the law, a subjection which is imposed equally by any regime.

I myself do not believe that any political system in industrial societies genuinely creates a new man. Industrial societies, being affluent societies, cannot but arouse in every man the feelings of self-interest and, as the moralists of the past would have said, of egoism. After a short period, the limitation of the income of members of the Communist Party was abandoned. Lenin imposed at first the rule that a member of the Communist Party, the aristocrat of the regime, should not receive a higher salary than a worker. As in so-called bourgeois regimes, a scale of salaries was re-established because it was found that inequality of reward was technically necessary if an industrial economy was to work. Can one at least say that a monopolistic party regime creates a new man because of the faith which it spreads? I am not sure that these kinds of regime can in the long run spread the materialistic faith and do away with religious belief. Can this new man, who must be as selfish as are men in bourgeois societies, be regenerated through loyalty to the doctrine of the state? Such allegiance, permanent and complete, is in the long run impossible. What makes the theory attractive and stirs up enthusiasm are the hopes which inspire the members. The moment such a doctrine becomes the justification for an established state, the discrepancy between the grandiose ambitions and reality does not require abandonment of the theory – it is still possible to hold that the regime is the best of all possible regimes – but it inevitably weakens and erodes faith. Man, as created by the communist regime, is not a single-minded being interwoven into a creed and a society; he is a dual man, who professes the general doctrine with varying degrees of conviction and knows what he must say, the world being as it is. He is a human being, a man of industrial societies with, in addition, a doctrine in which he believes with a mixture of fanaticism and scepticism.

This is why I do not think that the contrast between the two kinds of regime is a contrast between two fundamentally different ideas. We do not have to believe that the modern world is torn between ideologies and is doomed to an inexpiable conflict. It is possible to discriminate between the *visible* imperfections of constitutional-pluralistic regimes and the *essential* imperfection of monopolistic party regimes. But it is possible that in some cases the latter kind of regime can be preferable to the former. In other words, it is possible not to put all regimes on the same plane from the point of view of values, but that does not mean that science or philosophy can dictate what must be done at any particular moment. Politicians are right to say that there is no truth of action; this does not mean that the philosophers are wrong when they remind us that peaceful regimes, as such, are better than violent ones.

CHAPTER NINETEEN

ON HISTORICAL SCHEMES

As long as violence is not preferred to argument and war to peace, a constitutional-pluralistic regime is, in itself, better than a monopolistic party one. This theory presupposes, as I have tried to show, that the monopolistic party does not have a particular function, such as the bringing about of true freedom or the creation of a new man. I would like to end by looking at the historical schemes which *put the different kinds of regime into perspective.* I will mention four main schemes.

The first, the most fashionable today, is that of a unilateral evolution towards a particular regime. This scheme is one of progress, it being understood that, according to the Marxists, the final achievement is a regime of the Soviet type and according to western democrats a regime such as those we know in the west. The doctrinaires of the two opposed regimes both affirm that history is on the side of the regime which they prefer; according to the communists, the future will be communist; according to the west, sometimes even according to Marxists in the west like Isaac Deutscher, as the productive forces develop and capital accumulates, the political regimes will tend to draw nearer to the western model. It does not seem to me that either of these two hypotheses is demonstrable.

The monopolistic-party regime may sometimes be necessary, in some circumstances, for instance to set in motion primary industrialization; but no other universal function can be attributed to the monopolistic party regime. All the functions which it claims can be fulfilled by regimes of a different type.

The first function which is widely attributed to it is that of the initial development of the forces of production. As you know, the development of the forces of production was the task which Marx assigned to capitalism. Experience proves that the accumulation of capital or industrialization can be brought about without passing through capitalism.

The second function which is attributed to it is the elimination of classes and the creation of a homogeneous society. If it is agreed that classes only exist where there is private ownership of the means of production, if it is agreed that classes will cease to exist once private ownership has disappeared, it goes without saying that the suppression of private ownership is necessary to the elimination of classes, but this statement is strictly tautological; it derives from the definition itself. If the notion of class or of heterogeneity is taken in its ordinary sense, then the suppression of the private ownership of the means of production allows considerable discrepancies between the standard of living of the different groups to continue to exist. A society in which the standard of living and the ways of life and of thinking are homogeneous can be reached by the way of private property as well as by the way of monopolistic party regimes. The fundamental condition, if this goal is to be reached, is the development of the means of production; or again, the indispensable condition is an economy of affluence to which a system of the western type leads just as much as a system of the eastern type.

Lastly, according to a third justification, the proletariat, and only the proletariat, is historically able to create a classless society. This line of argument seems to me valueless for the simple reason that the proletariat does not play this role in the Soviet societies; it is the party, interpreter of the proletariat, which plays it. Consequently, it must be shown that the party has a universal function, and we are brought back to the demonstration which has not been proved of the necessity for a monopolistic party regime, if the end of history is to be reached.

Let us imagine that we have arrived at what is called the final state and the classless society. In a classless society and in an affluent economy will politics have any meaning? For politics to disappear, there must, in any case, be a universal state only and not a plurality of collectivities. Even in a single collectivity, a rivalry will probably persist, with for stake the privileges which only a few can enjoy at the same time; for example the leading role in the administration of public affairs. The struggle for leading positions, for power and fame will probably continue. Politics in a classless society will come to resemble more and more closely those in constitutional regimes rather than those in monopolistic regimes, since it seems to me that a peaceful policy is in itself preferable to a policy of violence, and more normal in times of tranquillity.

As for the other theory, according to which constitutionality will be the *heir* of the monopolistic party, it supposes very optimistically that *all* the industrial societies must have the same political superstructure and that only one kind of regime fits exactly in an industrial civilization. I do not think that this theory is sound. The political systems of industrial societies have features in common, the extension of the administrative sphere, the growth of the bureaucracy, but why should all industrial societies have to choose between the extreme bureaucratic centralism of the Soviet type and the extreme pluralism of autonomous forces of the western type?

Let us put aside these two versions of the scheme of unilateral evolution towards a single end and consider a second scheme, that which is found in Max Weber's sociology.

Every kind of economy, every phase in economic development favours to a greater or less degree a particular regime. A relation can be established between the phase of economic development and the likelihood of a particular regime.

We are all familiar with the circumstances which favour a monopolistic party regime, the periods of rapid accumulation or again of transition between the traditional society and the industrial one. Aristotle held that these phases of transition were favourable to tyranny. The classical form of tyranny, according to him, was the regime which came into being usually when a patriarchal society transformed itself into a commercial society. During periods of social upheaval, the tension between the groups was violent; it is difficult to have peaceful cooperation between the representatives of the different classes: it is more difficult still for the state to remain neutral and for the citizens to accept an anonymous and rational society. In such circumstances, the monopolistic regime has various functions; it takes the place of private businessmen and it has an ideological justification; it demands sacrifices and it heralds affluence (there is no better way to make sacrifice acceptable than to announce that the time is approaching when poverty will give way to absolute wealth); it creates a moral and social framework for a disarticulated society; it is an organ of temporary integration at a time when people are no longer able to live within the former structure or to accept the slow formalities of parliamentary processes.

Hitherto, no industrially developed country has of its own free will adopted a monopolistic party regime of the communist type. But it would be rash to draw any conclusions about the future from this fact. Two possibilities at least remain: such a regime, particularly in the modern world can come from abroad, by ideological infection, even if it does not conquer by force. Developed industrial societies threw up monopolistic party regimes; the Nazi regime was the heir of the Weimar republic. Constitutional systems are vulnerable at two moments and not at one. They are vulnerable in the first period of industrialization, and they are vulnerable in any period of crisis. Between the two wars, we passed through economic crises; since the Second World War we have gone through every kind of crisis. A constitutional-pluralistic regime, such as we have in France today, is not immune from accident.

The third scheme is that of the diversity of systems, a pure and simple diversity according to various circumstances.

Several countries have been governed, just after independence, by a regime which was largely constitutional but which was not pluralistic in the sense of the plurality of parties; a constitutional regime with a single party *de facto* but not *de jure*. Tunisia is an example of a country which is governed according to a constitution, but which has only one political party because before independence this party was the embodiment of the national will. A Tunisian who is following this course recently asked me if a regime with only one party in power must necessarily develop the pathological symptoms which I imputed to monopolistic party regimes. I replied that I thought that this was not necessarily so; a single party in control in the phase which follows immediately after the struggle for independence is nearly normal. After Attaturk's revolution, such a regime existed in Turkey.

There is a second category of countries to which I should like to allude, without any critical intention, those which have established neither constitutional pluralism nor ideological monopoly.

I mean Spain and Portugal, which are not very highly developed industrially, which are exceptions to the general course of political evolution in Europe, which are in no way monopolistic party regimes, neither fascist nor communist, which profess a Catholic philosophy and which tolerate the plurality of forces, but not of parties. To what extent can one combine the pluralism of family, regional and professional organizations with the denial of pluralism to the political parties? The answer is not easy; as the case of the present elections in Portugal shows. This is not a question of a monopolistic party regime for which even the opposition is forced to proclaim its support. Portugal allows a candidate from the opposition, who has no chance at all of winning, to stand. It is not a system of open competition, but neither is it a monopolistic party regime in which everyone is forced to swear loyalty to something in which he does not believe.

The third case is that of revolutionary movements and regimes which are neither ideological nor again movements with a nationalistic ideology. I am referring to the countries of the Middle East, Egypt in particular, which does not fit into the category of monopolistic party regimes. These countries do not have a constitutional-pluralistic regime; the state does not allow any organized opposition, it professes one idea and in this sense it is neither neutral nor secular in the manner of party states. But the conceptions put forward by the power-holders have not the character of an ideology systematically imposed on all; its essence is a will, a national goal – which excludes the constitutional rivalry of the parties, but which does not imply the gradual extension of terror and of ideological dogmatism. These countries seem to me to present a mixture of tradition and of revolution. They are in a phase of revolutionary change which must not be confused with the phase of transition of traditional societies to industrial societies which we have seen in the West. They are going through a double revolution: industrialization, but also the birth of a nation. The conjuncture of these two revolutions is typical and peculiar.

The fourth scheme is that which the classical authors have so often put forward, that of the cycle.

Let us start from constitutional-pluralism. This regime degenerates into anarchy out of which emerges, through a revolutionary process, a one-party regime, inspired by a dogmatic ideology. This party once in power, the fervour of the ideological belief is gradually eroded and the regime, while still remaining a one-party regime, comes to resemble more closely a bureaucratic autocracy, which becomes less and less dogmatic. This rationalized bureaucracy, this unique party, one day comes to the conclusion that the foundations of the society are stable enough to allow an ordered competition to develop between the parties and the wheel has more or less come full circle.

This cycle is possible. You will find it outlined in a note in *Philosophie politique* by Eric Weil. We have not yet seen the fully completed cycle. The Weimar republic did indeed degenerate into anarchy, if its last years can be called anarchy, then came the seizure of power by an ideological party and the establishment of a regime of one monopolistic party, armed with a doctrine, but the later phase, the bureaucratization and the rationalization of the one-party state did not reach its full term. As for Russia, the starting point was not constitutional-pluralism but a traditional autocratic regime, which was overthrown during a phase in which it was attempting constitutional change. The regime of the single ideological party of the Soviet Union is perhaps about to change itself into a rational bureaucracy, but for the moment there is no proof that it has abandoned its ideological dogmatism nor that it is inevitable that dogmatism should be abandoned.

Unfortunately, the liberalization of the regimes of the monopolistic party is not set down before hand in the book of history. Fortunately or unfortunately, the degeneration into anarchy of the constitutional-pluralistic regimes is not predestined either. The cycle is possible, but not inevitable.

The analysis of these four types of scheme leads to two essential ideas.

The various phases of economic growth favour this or that regime, but unless one reckons with the coming of absolute affluence it is not proved that industrial societies correspond only with one single type of political superstructure. It is possible to imagine broad industrial civilizations with different political systems.

At present, the economies and the nations are at such different stages that the variety of situations is reflected in an extreme variety of political institutions. Countries which are only now stepping on to the national stage can probably not afford to indulge in the competition between the parties which older countries find it difficult to maintain. Countries which are passing through the first phases of industrialization probably find it difficult to afford the luxury of constitutional-pluralistic regimes, that of competition between rival parties. No cycle that we can imagine seems to us either regular or inevitable.

To bring this chapter and this book to an end, I want to come back to my favourite authors, de Tocqueville and Marx, and then to complete the analysis of the French situation.

Let us go back first to Tocqueville and to Marx who gave me a starting point for this sociology of the industrial civilization. It is, I think, easy enough to see what each of them saw clearly and what each of them failed to see or underestimated.

Tocqueville recognized, with lucidity, the tendency of all modern societies towards democratization, the gradual disappearance of class distinctions, but he misinterpreted or perhaps even was unaware of the essence of the industrial civilization in that he saw it as only a modality of commercial societies. His thought was still deeply political. What struck him was the disappearance of the former social classes in France. The disappearance of the aristocracy meant the advent of a society in which economic activities took pride of place, and brought wealth and prestige. He never, at any time, clearly realized how original modern societies were; I mean original in their capacity to produce, thanks to which they could gradually decrease, not only differences in status in the old meaning of the words, but differences in income and ways of life.

Marx recognized very clearly what was specific to our societies. He had the merit of discerning that modern societies are quite different from those of the past, because of the prodigious development of the means of production. In the *Communist Manifesto* Marx wrote that, in a decade, ways of life and the means of production had been more profoundly altered than during all the centuries which had gone before. Oddly enough, Marx did not draw all the conclusions from this analysis of the industrial society because he was both a pamphleteer, a politician and a scholar. He wrote like a pamphleteer; he blamed what he did not like – capitalism – for all the aspects of contemporary society which he thought bad. He held capitalism responsible for what can be imputed to modern industry, to poverty, to the first phases of industrialization and he thought up a regime which suppressed everything which he hated in the societies of his time. Through an extreme simplification, he suggested that one had only to nationalize the means of production and to plan the economy for all the unpleasant or horrible features of the industrial society to disappear.

The process was effective from the point of view of propaganda but it is difficult to defend it from the point of view of scientific analysis. In more accurate terms, he overestimated the importance of the class struggle. As Marx believed that capitalism was unable to give the rewards of technical progress to all, he forecast apocalyptic upheavals and he hoped that from them would come the elimination simultaneously of class distinctions and the injustices of capitalist society.

The world today, objectively seen, clearly does not fit into any simple scheme. It is possible, at a pinch, to say that industrial societies can choose between a liberal or a tyrannical democracy. We thus go back to Tocqueville's alternative of the opposition between the two types of regime characteristic of our age.

One can also say that industrial societies can choose between two types of economic organization, the market economy and private ownership or the system of public ownership and of planned economy. But these two summary alternatives do not cover the variety of present phenomena. The only conclusion compatible with the facts is that, for the time being, nothing is clear-cut nor can it be so, because we are in a phase of uneven development, both economic and national.

In the developed countries, there is an ideological conflict, but this conflict is largely out of date, it is a legacy of the mythology of the nineteenth century. The societies which see each other as the greatest enemies, that is the Soviet and Western societies, differ less from one another in that they are developed industrially, than they both differ from societies which are only starting along the path of industrialization. It thus seems to me vain to prophesy about the future. In any case, the future of economic and political systems depends on factors which are too numerous for it to be possible to know what type of regime they will bring. To suppose even that one can lay down an ideal scheme for the development of industrial society and that one can foretell the victory of peaceful regimes is still to have said nothing. The regime which will win will perhaps be the one which in the inter-state struggle is the strongest. It has not been proved that the regime which is best adapted to the highest calling of mankind will be at the same time the one that possesses the best weapons for war, whether cold or hot.

Let us leave aside forecasts and confine ourselves to stating that alternatives do exist; that the world today is bound to diversity because of the inequalities of economic and social development; that, in this diversity, ideological conflicts are partly conflicts of myths and that these myths can for a long time withstand the facts.

Let us, to end, go back to the situation in France today.

When, a few months ago, I analysed the corruption of the French system, I stressed what, to me, was most important: a part of the French community refused to accept an eventual change in the Algerian policy.

For two years, an incessant campaign has been under way to convince French public opinion that the way the Republic functions is essentially responsible for the misfortunes of the country. The war in Algeria drags on because French governments are ineffectual and the state is weak. The regime, we are told, is on the verge of collapse, without prestige and weakened by glaring defects.

For nearly two centuries there has been no French regime which has been so rooted in the soil and conscience of France that it could withstand a national crisis. The doubts of French public opinion about the legitimacy of the regime have the inevitable result that each time the country has to solve a difficult problem, authority itself is called in question. France, especially for the last two years, has been going through a serious crisis and, as usual, it is deeply divided, as it has been so often, on what is good and what is bad, on what the community is doing and what it should do. Some of the French think that in Algeria France is fighting to preserve the last shreds of grandeur. They are the prisoners of what I call the Spanish complex, the conviction that with the loss of the empire, the future of France itself will be in jeopardy. Other Frenchmen hold that it is contrary to the destiny of France to forbid people whom they colonized yesterday to become independent. These Frenchmen, at the same time, hold that a passionate attachment to the colonies is an anachronism in the twentieth century; colonial domination could be a source of profit in the last century but it has become a burden in the twentieth. They do not have the Spanish complex and are convinced by the *Dutch example*. Both are fiercely convinced that they are right.

To this crisis of the national conscience there is added for the first time for some time, a crisis of conscience in the army. Since 18 Brumaire, the French army has been loyal to the regime. In spite of many *coups d'état* and revolutions, the army has never directly been responsible for a break with legality; it was not the army which made either the revolution of 1830 or that of 1848, nor even the *coup d'état* of Napoleon III. Napoleon III had to look for generals who were willing to support his undertaking. Throughout the history of the Third Republic, the army was loyal; the military leaders were never very enthusiastic about the republican regime (in this they resemble many other Frenchmen). But at no time did they rise up against the legal authority.

In recent years, the constitution has been safeguarded, but at the price of the submission of the governments in Paris to the will of the French minority in Algeria. All the politicians from the non-communist left to the extreme right are agreed on a policy which corresponds more or less to the wishes of the French in Algeria and which all the so-called national parties support, in spite of the doubts and uncertainties which many politicians feel and express in private.

For a year, a minority inside the parliamentary majority has hurled a double defiance at the majority. It defies them to govern without them; without their fifty or sixty members, the majority would be swallowed up by the communists. And, in a double defiance, it announces that any change in Algerian policy would provoke the French in Algeria to revolt – a revolt which the army would support.

The threat has been confirmed by events. Perhaps it has confirmed it to the point that we ask whether those who brandished the threat did not help to make it a reality. Let us leave this question to historians. It is a fact that the choice of a man who had made speeches and written articles which hinted that he intended to change this policy slightly was enough to unleash events which had been feared for two years.

These two questions which are fundamental for the future of the French constitutional-pluralistic regime evoke the conditions which are indispensable to the functioning of a constitutional regime. Is it possible, is it normal for a minority to impose its will on all?

Can constitutional legality survive? Will the change from this regime to another be legal? France, in the twentieth century, has mastered the art of legal *coups d'état* or if I may say so has mastered the art of being able to make *coups d'état* apparently legal. The present situation is characterized by an inextricable tangle of legality and illegality. It is further complicated by the existence of a unique personality, to whom is attributed, according to the moment and one's individual preferences, contradictory intentions. The Republic of Rome had an institution which answered to French needs, the dictatorship. The Roman dictatorship was the opposite of tyranny, all authority was given to one man, but in accordance with the law for a limited period. It is conceivable that the man whom I have in mind could for a limited period assume the office of Roman dictator. This candidate for the dictatorship, that is for legal omnipotence, does not want to prolong the existing system, but to change it; he must therefore be not only a dictator but, to use once again the classical ideas, also a legislator.

Until quite recently he was the hope both of some of the ultras and of many of those who say that they are liberals. Some days ago, he was cheered in Algeria by those who yesterday hated him and he is beginning to be feared by those who most wanted him to come to power. As he wraps himself in the mystery which is thought to be indispensable to men of action, no one knows, if he does come to the supreme office, who will be the dupe and who the victor. It is difficult to imagine that the representatives of opposing parties will all be satisfied the day on which their candidate will no longer have only to speak or to hold his peace, but to act.

Let us come back to generalities. In an industrial society, *coups d'état* and breaks with legality are often national catastrophes. When a civil government can no longer take decisions and impose its will on those who serve it, the unity of the country is endangered. Those who, no matter how sincere they may be, today oppose constitutional procedures represent rather an attachment to traditional values than the fulfilment of the French future. Probably the present crisis was inevitable. It was impossible to continue the former policy which was officially supported by everyone and questioned by everyone in private. Perhaps from the present evil, good will come.

All things considered, the events through which we are passing prove one incontrovertible truth: the constitutional-pluralistic regime which I think is the only one in France suitable to industrial civilization has not yet taken root firmly; the French, as deeply divided as they were a century ago, have only one shield against the threat of civil violence. The unique shield I called a few months ago the silken thread of legality; this thread has not yet snapped; God forbid that it should ever do so.

INDEX